THE PROSE FICTION OF VENIAMIN A. KAVERIN

by
Hongor Oulanoff

1976

SLAVICA PUBLISHERS, INC.

For a list of some of our other books, see the end of this book.
To obtain an up-to-date catalog, with price and ordering
information, write to:

Slavica Publishers, Inc.
P. O. Box 312
Cambridge, Mass. 02139

ISBN: 0-89357-032-X

q

Editor of Slavica Publishers: Charles E. Gribble,
The Ohio State University

Printed in the United States of America by
LithoCrafters, Inc., Ann Arbor, Michigan 48106

For Constance,
gratefully

CONTENTS

Part One
Patterns of Plot

Part Two
Representation

ACKNOWLEDGMENTS

I would like to thank two of my Ohio State University colleagues, Professor James P. Scanlan of the Department of Philosophy and Professor Leon I. Twarog of the Department of Slavic Languages and Literatures, for taking the time and trouble of giving me their valuable help. Both Professor Scanlan and Professor Twarog have carefully read the manuscript of this study and have offered excellent suggestions pertaining to its substance and form.

The College of Humanities of the Ohio State University awarded to me several Grants-in-Aid while I was working on this book. Moreover, the College has given a substantial financial support toward the production of the book. I gratefully acknowledge this generous help of the Ohio State University. In particular, I thank Professor Arthur E. Adams, Dean of the College of Humanities, for his support when it mattered.

Various technical problems and chores beset the production of a final manuscript. I thank Professor David F. Robinson, Chairman of our Slavic Department, for helping me solve such problems. Mrs. Rosa-Maria Cormanick, Assistant to Chairman of our Department, performed such chores, which I gratefully acknowledge.

In preparing Chapter One; Chapter Two, Section 3; Chapter Two, Section 4 and Chapter Four, Section 4, I expanded and reworked my previously published articles "Kaverin's Early Prose: *Masters and Apprentices*" (*Russian Literary Triquaterly*, Number 3, May 1972); "V. Kaverin's Novels of Development and Adventure" (*Canadian Slavic Studies*, II, No. 4, Winter 1968); and "Kaverin's *Xudožnik neizvesten*: Structure and Motivation" (*The Slavic and East European Journal*, Winter 1966, Vol. X, Number 4).

H.O.

The Dieter Cunz Hall of Languages
The Ohio State University
Columbus, Ohio
September 1976

ACKNOWLEDGMENTS

NOTE ON TRANSLITERATION

The transliteration system used in this study is the following:
a, b, v, g, d, e, ë, zh, z, i, j, k, l, m, n, o, p, r, s, t, u, f, x, c, ch, sh, shch, ", y, ', ě, è, ju, ja.

It is basically the transliteration system used in *The Slavic and East European Journal* (*vid*. SEEJ, Spring 1962, vol. VI, No. 1, p. 98).

In 1962, the profession had not faced yet the soaring production costs of scholarly books we face nowadays. To reduce these costs in any reasonable way becomes now in order. Even certain small changes of transliteration result in significant decreases of production costs. For this reason I use the transliteration signs *zh*, *ch*, *sh*, and *shch*. These signs create no confusion in the reading or understanding of the transliterated Russian text.

The names of authors generally known have not been transliterated.

INTRODUCTION

Veniamin Aleksandrovich Kaverin[1] (born April 19, 1902) made his appearance in Soviet Russian literature in 1921[2], and ever since has not ceased publishing works of narrative prose (tales, novels, fairy tales, war correspondence), plays, travelogues and critical studies. This represents more than half a century of creative and critical writing. These decades of literary activity have earned him the stature of a particularly distinguished and respected literary figure in Soviet letters.

Kaverin is, relatively speaking, not too much known in Western countries. Not too many studies have been devoted to this writer. It is with a view to contributing to our knowledge of Kaverin's works that this study has been undertaken.

In an average case, that is, when we study the biography of a Soviet writer exclusively through the material published by him or about him in official Soviet media, we usually embark on a rather not too rewarding biographical study. Not too rewarding in the sense that truly original and significant issues are almost invariably brought to ideologically standardized and predictable solutions. Or the autobiographer refrains from any independent inferences or generalizations and merely cultivates the anecdotal interest of the narrative. Somehow, the individual depth of perception and independence of insight seem to be missing in these autobiographies. From these autobiographical writings we usually do not learn too much about the deeper levels of the author's personality.

Kaverin's autobiographical writings are above the common run of Soviet autobiographies. However, I have chosen not to make any special effort of interpreting his autobiographical works. In the following pages I have translated the autobiographical essay that Kaverin wrote for his 1964 collection of works[3]. This essay is entitled "Ocherk raboty" (An outline of my work). As the very title indicates, Kaverin focuses his attention on his creative work rather than on his biography.

* * *

INTRODUCTION

An Outline of My Work

1

I was born in 1902 in the city of Pskov, into the family of a musician. In 1912 I started attending the Pskov gymnasium. Ju. N. Tynjanov, a friend of my elder brother and subsequently a well-known writer, was my first teacher of literature; he instilled in me a fervent love for Russian literature.

As a sixteen-year-old youth I arrived in Moscow, where in 1919 I graduated from secondary school. In those years I wrote verses, but, having met with severe criticism from well-known men of letters, I decided to give up my literary work. Scarcely half a year had gone by when I understood that it was too hasty a decision, but then I sincerely believed that from that time on I would devote myself to scholarly activity. In 1920 I transferred from the University of Moscow to the University of Petrograd and simultaneously enrolled in the Institute of Oriental Languages. I convinced myself that first I had to make a close study of literature from the theoretical side, and only then to try my strength. In reality things turned out differently. "The House of the Litterateurs" announced a competition for beginning writers, and I immediately began writing my first story "Odinnadcataja aksioma" (The eleventh axiom). My first book (1923) was entitled *Mastera i podmaster'ja* (Masters and apprentices). It was a collection of fantastic stories; in them, monks, devils, alchemists, students were active, and the author as well, who from time to time called his heroes together in order to find out from them what he should do next. It was, of course, a child's play, — Gorky nonetheless treated them with a seriousness and responsibility which struck me. It was very fortunate for me that in my youth I met this unusual man. Following the appearance of each of my new books I received a letter from him which contained exacting but kind criticism as well as advice; I should add, the advice was not only literary but also for everyday life. He taught me — and he did it with all the generosity of a great man. During the years of the blockade of Leningrad almost all my archives perished, but I carried Gorky's letters wrapped in a piece of tracing cloth in my map case throughout the entire war. Thus I succeeded in preserving them. Later in my book *Neizvestnyj drug* (Unknown friend) I told about our first meeting which impressed me very much.

My literary youth progressed happily. At the University I studied under strict teachers: from the academician V.N. Perec I learned medieval literature, from B.M. Eixenbaum the history of the 19th century, from Ju.N. Tynjanov the theory of literature. I attended the academician L.V. Shcherba's lectures about language. What did these outstanding men of our science teach us, students of philology of the twenties? First of all, they instilled in us the feeling that we must contribute something new to it. V.N. Perec taught us the art of discovering the new; repeatedly he said that a philologist can assert himself only by studying untouched areas not explored by others. He demanded of us an unconditional dedication to scholarship, and this rigorousness was stern and implacable and manifested itself in both the large and the small. Working on a routine paper, I came to a standstill, hampered by a Greek text.

— Oh, you don't know Greek? — Perec asked me reproachfully — Well then, you'll have to study it.

— But don't you know, my paper is scheduled for March.

— We'll postpone it. You will deliver your paper in May.

Fully sharing the rigorousness of the older generation, B.M. Eixenbaum, Ju. N. Tynjanov, and Viktor Shklovskij generously shared with us their doubts and hesitations, their pride in working in a great literature. They taught us this pride, this interrelationship of our own work — no matter how small it may be — with the work of Shaxmatov, Veselovskij, Potebnja. They demanded that we know not only the history but also the atmosphere of the development of our literary scholarship, and together with them we made fun of the pedantry of Pypin, lamented the superficiality of the talented Vengerov, and marvelled at the brilliant surmises of Buslaev and Vsevolod Miller.

Jurij Tynjanov in particular taught me a great deal; he was a profound scholar who did not tolerate the slightest idle talk in scholarship. His best articles were written in a terse language through which we had to "fight" our way at times. Without inconveniencing his disciples in any way, he learned along with us. Each of his lectures was based on a fine sense of history. In seminars it was enough for him to rearrange in his own way the material which the speaker had available in order to obtain an unexpected but always accurate picture.

Attendance of lectures was not obligatory in the beginning of the twenties. Of course, we did not cut the seminars that our favorite professors conducted. But if seminars were conducted by the the unpopular professors, that is, the untalented ones, — we did not attend the seminars. We spent much time in archives and libraries, working on our papers which we delivered frequently, irrespective of whether they were part of the course program. We were allowed to take examinations on the given subject not only during the term but also when the student was ready for his examinations. Of course, this free option was limited: one was not allowed to take second year examinations in the third year. But, to make up for it, we did not have to study all the subjects in the world — whether we would need them afterwards or not, — but only those which really answered our interest. At the age of twenty we were adults who had to choose their own way — in science and in life.

Were we inconvenienced by the absence of an external, limited, program of studies? No, we were not; it helped us. Disposing of my time as I pleased, I studied in two institutions of higher education simultaneously and graduated from both[4]. Many of my friends, now prominent scholars, made themselves known by their works long before graduating from the university.

We were closely connected with the literature of our time, and the numerous debates, discussions, and reports in literary and philosophical societies were for us just as much of a university and a school of responsible love for art which brought our generation an invaluable benefit.

2

It was Shklovskij who brought me to the "Serapions;" he introduced me not by name but by the title of my story — "The Eleventh Axiom," which had been sent to Gorky and about which the future "Serapion Brothers" had apparently known. They met every Saturday in the room of Mixail Slonimskij in the "House of the Arts." Subsequently Ol'ga Forsh nicknamed this house "the mad ship" and told of its inhabitants' life, full of surprises and inspiration. But the freshman student, who in the fall of 1920 walked with his head held high all over the still deserted Petrograd, did not find anything strange in this life. He had just arrived from Moscow, where almost every day he went to the famous "Stall of Pegasus." More than once he saw Mayakovsky, Esenin; he was present at the evening of bouts-rimés where Valerij Brjusov presided and the Moscovite poets recited verses improvised on given themes. He himself wrote verses, almost not doubting that none other than he would succeed in consummating the revolution in Russian poetry. Once he even went to see Andrej Belyj who showed him *Zapiski mechtatelja* (Notes of a dreamer)[5] which had just appeared, and talked with him in a way as if he, the boy who had hardly finished school, were one of these dreamers, the chosen ones of mankind and poetry.

Then Shklovskij left, and I began somewhat haughtily, as it befitted a metropolitan poet, to give heed to the rising debate. All were taking part in it. Fedin and Lunc were the main opponents; I felt that at once.

The debate revolved about the fundamental issue — about the main road of our literature.

With an all-absorbing passion in which it was difficult to tell conviction from literary taste and which nonetheless moved into the battle entire regiments of arguments (irrefutable arguments, as it seemed to me then), Lunc attacked Fedin who listened to him patiently without interrupting.

The famous thesis — first the "what," i.e., first the content and then the "how," i.e., form, lay at the foundation of Fedin's conception and he turned it skillfully from a weapon of defense into a weapon of offense: he contended that since so many immensely new things had entered into the life of Russia in those years, that since such thrilling material, still unknown to anyone, was forcing its way into literature, it was difficult to conceive the necessity of the previous close study of its laws on which Lunc insisted.

This was only the beginning of a long debate which dominated the evenings of the year 1921.

Another debate which remained in my memory touched upon the question of style. Anyone of us at that time faced the choice between two trends: the conversational and the so-called "ornamental." Ornamentalism was represented by strong writers who acted energetically and who did not want to let the youth out from under their influence at all. It is enough to say that Zamjatin conducted one of the workshops of the "House of the Arts." Remizov struck our imagination with the originality of his very attitude toward literature. Andrej Belyj was in the bloom of his talent, and it seemed that his pen was still able to raise high the refined prose of the symbolists. It may safely be said that ornamentalism exerted a noticeable influence on the early prose of Vsevolod Ivanov, and Nikitin. The other "brothers" bypassed this trend, leaning on the sweeping — from Leskov to Chekhov — classical tradition of Russian literature. As for me, among my first 16 stories which remained in manuscript form, one may find the imitations of Bunin and Belyj, Hoffmann and Edgar Allan Poe.

It is important to note that among the "Serapion Brothers" there were Ivanov, Zoshchenko, Fedin, Tixonov — men who had already had a chance to see and understand much, writers who regarded literature as the business of their lives. The Revolution broke up everyday life and customs, people came into literature not from studies but from the fronts of the Civil War; they were men of action, and not of contemplation.

I have already mentioned that we debated much about literature. It was difficult for me to agree with those who believed that we had spontaneously, simply to reflect that which was going on around us; I considered such writers to be naturalists, "writers of everyday life and customs" [bytoviki]. Vaguely sensing all the significance of the processes that were going on in the country in the beginning of the twenties, I did not know life yet and did not understand how I had to write about it.

My tale Konec xazy (The end of the gang) was my first excursion out of this circle of narrow literary representations; in it I attempted to depict the gangsters and robbers [naletchiki] of the years of the NEP, the thieves' world of Leningrad. Collecting material for The End of the Gang, I read the criminal chronicle, I attended trials at court, occasionally spent evenings in dives of which there were no small number at that time. I was preparing for the work precisely as my older comrades used to do, who more than once and correctly reproached me for my lack of knowledge of life; they reproached me for wishing to hide from it behind the walls of a student room piled up with books on the history of literature. I did not have any experience yet, I collected "material," trying to lay it out in a most complex pattern. I felt like conveying the peculiarities of the criminal world — and not only in its thieves' jargon. This last task was not difficult at all. The language of the thieves was reproduced with such a fullness that I had to append a dictionary of thieves' expressions ["blatnye" vyrazhenija].

The tale Devjat' desjatyx (The nine tenths)[6] brought me back to the libraries and archives. I was leafing through newspapers printed on the brittle yellow paper of the revolutionary years, reading the memoirs not only of John Reed but also of Denikin and Krasnov. However, it resembled the impassive work of a collector of facts least of all.

Here are a few lines from my autobiography pertaining to the year 1924: "...The verbal ornament is out date . . . Only in the complex concreteness of a plot built on the powerful general ideas of the present time can we look for a way out of the impasse in which Russian prose now happens to be," (Pisateli. Avtobiografii sovremennikov, "Sovremennye problemy," M., 1926[7]).

This was naive. Of course, there was not any "impasse." But it became difficult and uninteresting for me to write without carefully studying contemporary life.

In the winter of the year 1928, at Jurij Nikolaevich Tynjanov's I met an alert and witty man of letters who was in the bloom of his talent and deeply convinced that all the mysteries of literary craft were known to him. We talked about the genre of the novel, and the man of letters remarked that this genre had been above the strength even of Chekhov, so that there was nothing astonishing in the fact that contemporary literature did not succeed in it. I happened to have objections, and he, with an irony with which he had always been unusually good, expressed a doubt in my abilities for this complicated business. Infuriated, I said that the very next day I would set to writing a novel, — and that it would be a book about him. He ridiculed me, but wrongly. The very next day I set about writing the novel *Skandalist, ili vechera na Vasil'evskom ostrove* (The troublemaker, or evenings on the Vasil'evskij island).

Apparently, only youth is capable of such decisions and only in youth can one with such candidness follow, with a notebook, upon the heels of one's own future character. He made fun of me, cracked one joke after another, flashed witticisms which were sometimes extraordinarily well-taken and apt to be remembered for one's whole life, — I turned red but kept on taking notes. Probably, he was fully convinced that nothing would come of the novel; otherwise, perhaps, he would have been more cautious in this unusual duel.

I have remembered this story because the novel was my first attempt to turn to the experience of life proper, and my work on it compelled me for the first time to discern the vague outlines of realistic prose. A live hero "seen with an unarmed eye" cannot exist in the vacuum of the conventional literary world.

In the summer of the year 1930 I went to the Sal steppes to see the famous State grain farm "Gigant." There was nothing special about this trip. At that time a lot of people went to see the "Gigant" — the workers of the sovkhoz even complained that the delegations hindered their work. But for me, an indoor man immersed in books, this trip turned out to be a double discovery — a discovery of new people under new, still unprecedented circumstances, and a discovery of my own opportunity to write about these men. As a matter of fact, I did not have the occasion of ascertaining this just mentioned possibility at once. After ten years of work I, like a beginning litterateur, rushed to write down absolutely everything, having no idea of what I would be writing — a sketch, a novel, a play. Coming back, with a profound thoroughness (of which I had not considered myself capable) I wrote a book of travel stories *Prolog*.

An attack upon the stagnant world of rural life, a struggle for the consciousness of the peasant wonder-struck at what the men of the "Gigant" have accomplished — this is the theme of this book, little but so dear to me.

Each of us may have an account to settle with criticism — one a longer, and another a shorter. I had also been sharply criticized before *The Prologue*. But I would like to start my account precisely with this book. The transition which was described above was difficult for me. I doubted my strength, I was afraid that I did not have — or almost did not have — the writer's vision without which there was no use hoping for success in the new genre of the realist sketch story, unusual for me. Because of the inertia which still rules over certain critical minds even now, I was given a hostile reception. The book was disparaged without the slightest indulgence. One of the reviewers accused me of adhering to the philosophy of Comte [kontizm]. Why not of adhering to the philosophy of Kant [kantizm], which in equal measure had no bearing on my travel stories, — that has remained for me an unsolved riddle.

3

It is hard to convey the strange sensation experienced when the first chapters of the novel *Ispolnenie zhelanij* [Fulfillment of desires] were being written. As if for the first time in my life I took a pen in my hand — so awkwardly, unskillfully did line follow upon line, sentence upon sentence. It seemed to me that I had forgotten how to write, — a sad conjecture after 13 years of almost everyday work! I had to begin everything over again. But how to begin? Was it worth it?

I continued working, overcoming timidity, even terror which was seizing me, when after long hours of work I succeeded in writing out only a few sentences. And gradually it became clear to me that a decisive turn toward the real depiction of life had to entail a stylistic manner quite different from the previous. Until then I had been writing in a stylistically complex way, not only not striving for the simplicity and distinctness of language, but, I must confess, being shy about this simplicity if it unwittingly showed through. Now I started writing in the most ordinary conversational language, in the only possible manner that had been dictated by the transition to a depiction of reality which was quite new to me.

But it was not only a matter of that. My previous stylistic manner allowed me, as it were, to avoid the impressions and reflections, the knowledge of life that I actually possessed but that seemed to me simply boring for artistic literature. Now I understood that I mistakenly believed myself to be a man lacking experience and observation of life.

I knew the Leningrad University of the twenties, in which the old and the new had collided with extraordinary acuteness and strength. The Timirjazev-like[8] mutiny of some professors and the medieval stagnation of some others was clear to me. I understood the life of archives, numbed but guarding thousands of mysteries, and the reading of manuscripts was for me a fascinating and venturesome affair.

I had experience, but, in order to take advantage of it, I had to make (of course, for myself) a discovery in literature. Everything came in handy for *Fulfillment of Desires,* even the seminar in old Russian literature, even the enormous torn cloak which (a tribute to my enthusiasm for German Romantics) I wore when at one time I attended this seminar. With the key in my hands, very cheerful, I roamed all over my household and opened various secret drawers and chests keeping half-forgotten material for which until then I had seen no use. Subsequently, reading over Tolstoy's diaries, I understood that ruthless self-analysis was for Tolstoy nothing else but a school of self-knowledge — a psychological and technological school which determined much in his works of genius. Each of us strives to express himself in his books, and, working at *Fulfillment of Desires,* I succeeded for the first time deliberately to take advantage of my own, for the time being very slight, school of self-knowledge.

The novel was being written for a long time, over three years. The key that had opened my own youth for me, could not, regrettably, help me with another very important side of the business. I had to evaluate the recent past with the view of a historical novelist. Precisely of the historical novelist, although the action of the novel takes place at the end of the twenties, and it was written in the middle of the thirties. The enormous distance that the country traversed in this short time, turned contemporary material into historical material, and demanded another far more complex method of investigation. Not relying on my own memory, I leafed through newspapers and magazines, questioned my university comrades; in a word, I was building up (for the time being, still with a timid hand) the historical background, the scenery of the epoch. The affair was made a little easier by the fact that I was after all a historian of literature who learned from very strict and exacting teachers, so that I felt unconstrained in libraries. But the study of people, as it is known, is not the task of the history of literature.

I do not even speak of how much trouble the work on the plot of *Fulfillment of Desires* caused me. I always was and have remained a writer of pattern-plot[9] works and I have never understood why this powerful weapon is treated with disdain by many writers and critics who believe that pattern-plot and second-rate quality are close, if not identical notions. Because of my liking for sharp plot critics have castigated me all my life, and if it were not for Gorky who impressed upon me when I was still a youth that I ought to cherish this inclination of mine, probably I would, in the end, have started writing plotless boring works. The enormous importance of composition at which Tolstoy, Turgenev, Dostoyevsky had been toiling is not done justice in our prose.

4

In 1936 in a sanatorium near Leningrad where I was taking rest, the conversation turned to Ostrovskij's novel *Kak zakaljalas' stal'* [How the steel was tempered]. A respectable professor spoke coolly of the novel. The person with whom he was talking, a young scientist, fervently objected to him, and the agitation with which he was defending his favorite book amazed me: he turned pale, he was unable to refrain from sharp expressions.

This debate greatly excited my curiosity — at that time I was planning a novel devoted to the story of a Soviet young man.

We happened to be at the same table. My new acquaintance was gloomy, tired, and we did not immediately get into a conversation. But from day to day our relations were becoming closer and closer. He was a man in whom ardor was combined with straightforwardness, and persistence with astonishing definiteness of aim. He knew how to achieve success in any affair, even if it were a game of carom billiards in which we took a great interest at that time. A clear mind and a capacity for deep feeling could be seen in each of his judgments.

He told me the story of his life in six evenings — an extraordinary one, because it was full of extraordinary events, and at the same time resembling the lives of hundreds of Soviet people. I listened, then I started writing down notes, and the forty or fifty pages that were then written by me, formed the groundwork of the novel *Dva Kapitana* [Two captains].

Returning home, I started the work with ardor and completed it in three months with unaccustomed ease and speed. The manuscript was sent to one of the Moscow magazines and returned with a polite but quite definite refusal.

The failure was painful, stinging. I put the manuscript away and set about writing a book which I had planned long ago about the great Russian geometrician Lobachevsky.

...I did not write the novel about Lobachevsky although I spent over half a year reading printed and manuscript materials. It seemed to me that without a clear understanding of what the scientist's life had been devoted to, it was impossible to write about him, and I had never been good at mathematics. And after a long hesitation I returned to the first, unsuccessful draft of *Two Captains*.

Whether the time necessary to evaluate the written narrative with different eyes had gone by, or whether the study of Lobachevsky had helped — I do not know. But, reading the manuscript over, I immediately understood that the fundamental was missing in it — the main hero's views on his life, the ideal that he followed, the picture of Soviet society to which he owed his development. Between me and my hero there was an enormous difference in age, education, origin. I was searching for complex solutions when for him everything was simple. "Do you know what I would have become if there had been no revolution? A robber, " — I remembered these words with which my companion had ended his story. To see the world with the eyes of a youth shaken by the idea of justice — this task presented itself to me in all its importance. And I decided — for the first time in my life — to write a novel in the first person.

From the very first pages I promised myself not to give rein to my imagination. And indeed, even such unusual details as the muteness of the little Sanja were not invented by me. His mother and father, sister and friends were depicted exactly as they appeared before me for the first time in the story of the chance acquaintance who subsequently became my friend. But my imagination nonetheless came in handy. I learned very little about some of the heroes of my future book; for example, Korablev was depicted with only two or three features: a sharp, attentive look which invariably compelled the schoolboys to speak the truth, a moustache, a cane and the ability to sit over a book deep into the night. The author had to complete the rest of the picture.

In essence, the story that I had heard was very simple. It was the story of a boy who had had a hard childhood and who had been educated by Soviet society — by the people who became his own and who supported the dream that from his early years arose in his straightforward and just heart.

Almost all the circumstances of the life of this boy, then a youth and a grown man have been preserved in *Two Captains*. But his childhood was spent in the Middle Volga region, his school years in Tashkent — places which I know comparatively poorly. Therefore I transferred the place of action to my native town; I named it Ensk. Not without reason do my fellow townsmen easily discover the true name of the city in which Sanja Grigor'ev was born and grew up! My own school years (the last classes) were spent in Moscow, and it was easier for me to represent the Moscow school of the beginning of the twenties than the Tashkent school that I had never seen in my life.

When the first chapters in which the narrative deals with Sanja Grigor'ev's childhood in Ensk had been written, it became clear to me that in this small town something extraordinary — an incident, an event, an encounter — was to happen. The novel was written in the end of the thirties which brought the Soviet land enormous imagination-gripping victories in the Arctic, and I understood that the "extraordinary" I had been looking for, — was the light of the Arctic stars which accidentally fell in the small deserted town.

And, returning to the first page, I told the story of the drowned lettercarrier, and I cited the letter of the navigator Klimov which opened the second line of the novel. What was there, seemingly, in common between the story of a nine-year-old boy who was left an orphan, and the story of a captain who tried to sail through the North-East Passage in a single voyage? But there was something in common. Thus for the first time the idea of two captains flashed across my mind.

I should remark that the one who lent me valuable help in the study of aeronautics was senior lieutenant S. Ja. Klebanov; he died heroically in the year 1943. He was a talented aviator and a fine pure man. I was proud of his friendship. Working on the second volume, I came (among the materials of the Commission of the Study of the Patriotic War) across the opinions of S. Ja. Klebanov's brother officers, and I became convinced that my opinion of him was shared by them.

It is hard, and even impossible, to answer with exhaustive fullness the question of how this or that figure of the hero of a literary work is created, especially if the story is conducted in the first person. Apart from observations, my book included the historical material that became necessary for the character of Captain Tatarinov.

One should not, of course, look for this name in encyclopedic dictionaries. One should not try to prove, as a boy did in his geography class, that Tatarinov had discovered Severnaja Zemlja. For my "older captain" I took advantage of the story of two brave conquerors of the Extreme North. From one I took courageous and serene character, purity of thought, clarity of aim — all that reveals a man of great soul. This was Sedov. From the other — the factual history of his voyage. This was Brusilov. The drift of my "St. Maria" quite accurately duplicates the drift of Brusilov's "St. Anna." The diary of the navigator Klimov cited in my novel is fully based on the diary of the navigator of "St. Anna" Al'banov — one of the two participants of this tragic expedition who remained alive. However, only historical materials seemed to me insufficient. I knew that in Leningrad there lived the painter and writer Nikolaj Vasil'evich Pinegin, a friend of Sedov, one of those who after his death brought the schooner "St. Phocas" back to the Big Land. We met, and not only did Pinegin tell me many new things about Sedov, not only did he depict his cast of mind with extraordinary distinctness, but he also explained the tragedy of his life – the life of a great explorer and traveler who was not recognized and was slandered by the reactionary strata of the society of czarist Russia. By the way, in the course of one of our meetings Pinegin treated me to the canned food that he picked up at Cape Flora[10] in 1914, and, to my amazement, it turned out to be excellent. I mention this detail because it is characteristic of Pinegin and his "polar" house.

Subsequently, when the first volume had already been completed, Sedov's widow informed me of many curious things.

In the summer of 1941 I was working intensely on the second volume, in which I felt like making extensive use of the story of the search of the famous aviator Levanevskij. The plan had already been finally and carefully considered, the materials had been thoroughly studied, the first chapters had been written. The well-known polar scientist Vize had approved the content of the future "Arctic" chapters and had told me many new things about the work of search parties. But the war started, and for a long time I had to give up the thought of finishing the novel. I was writing reports from the front, war sketches, and tales.[11] However, probably I did not quite abandon the hope of returning to *Two Captains;* otherwise I would not have applied to the editor of *Izvestija* with a request to send me to the Northern front. And it was there, among the aviators and the submarines of the North Fleet that I understood in which direction I had to work on the second volume of the novel. It became clear to me that the moral make-up of the heroes of my book would be vague and unclear, if I did not tell of how they, together with the whole Soviet people, lived through the painful ordeal of the war and won.

From books, tales, and personal impressions I knew what the lives of those people represented in peaceful times, those people who, not sparing their strengths, were toiling selflessly at turning the Extreme North into a cheerful, hospitable region – who were opening its innumerable riches beyond the Polar Circle, building cities, harbors, mines, factories. Now, at the time of the war, I saw all that energy being flung to the defense of the native places, the first conquerors of the North becoming the defenders of their conquests.

One could object that the same thing happened in every little corner of our country. Of course so, but the rigorous surroundings of the Extreme North added a special character to this change.

The impressions of those years entered into my novel only in a rather small degree, and, when I leaf through my old notebooks, I feel like starting to write the book which I had planned long ago, dealing with the story of a Soviet sailor.[12]

5

At a literary evening in the dormitory of Moscow State University – it was shortly after the war – the conversation turned to the fact that we had absolutely no books dealing with the growth of creative awareness in science. "And in the meanwhile –

said one eager girl, who was very angry at Soviet literature because of that, — science has penetrated into the very depth of our life."

The girl was quite right. But she hardly imagined clearly the whole volume of work that one had to invest into a literary work dealing with men of science.

In essence, throughout all the thirty years of my work I have approached such a work from different sides. My first story, "The Eleventh Axiom," was sent to a competition of beginning writers under the motto" "Art must be built on the formulas of the exact sciences." I tried to tell the life of Lobachevsky. In *Fulfillment of Desires* the quest and the hopes of a young historian of literature are depicted. It has always seemed to me that the very principles of scientific work are instructive and important for the writer; not without reason has their study always been reflected with such fecundity in literature.

But how to approach this matter? What kind of scientific material to dwell upon? Should it have cognitive character or be part of the general historical background?

This and many other questions were solved by themselves when I focused my attention on microbiology. People of strong character led Russian microbiology, daring optimists ready for self-sacrifice who clearly visualized the place that this young science was to take among the other sciences of nature. Mechnikov, Zabolotnyj, and Gamaleja were such people. These high traditions have been preserved in our time too.

Working on *Two Captains*, I had surrounded myself with books on aviation and the history of the Arctic. Now their place was taken by books on microbiology, and this turned out to be much more complex. First of all, it was necessary to learn to read these books in a way different from the one in which the scientists themselves read them.

To reconstitute the train of thought of the scientist, to read behind the dry, short lines of a scholarly article what this man lived by, to understand the story and the meaning of the struggle against enemies (and sometimes even against friends), which is almost always present in scientific work, — this is the task without whose fulfillment there was no sense in even undertaking to write on such a theme. It is necessary to understand that which the scientist factors out [vybrasyvaet za skobki]: the psychology of his creation.

Another — and still greater — difficulty was the fact that at the basis of the novel I planned (I set about writing it soon after *Two Captains*) there lay the story of a woman told by herself.

The hero of *Two Captains* was near to me anyway, in spite of all the difference of age and education. In *Otkrytaja kniga* [Open Book] the story is told by a little girl, then by a young unmarried woman, then by a completely formed person — the voice of the narrator, her attitude toward those close to her, toward herself, toward her own pursuit keep changing from part to part. Stylistic peculiarities change, emphasizing the stages of her developing creative consciousness. Add to this the necessity of professional color — you know, the heroine follows a difficult path into the complex, rapidly developing field of science . . . In a word, I would not have

INTRODUCTION   13

started working on *Open Book,* if I had clearly imagined what unexpected riddles this side of the work concealed.

In my previous books, that which may only approximately be called historical background also cost me no small effort. The action of the trilogy *Open Book* goes on for thirty-five years. There is no need to speak of how important it was to convey this "movement in time" in characteristic features — and not only in characteristic ones but also in features tightly connected with the development of science. Memory easily deceives, and every fact of the past, even an insignificant one, requires painstaking verification. You cannot make a mistake even in trifles. Try to commit an inaccuracy, and twenty readers with an offensive indulgence will immediately point to it. In the second part of the novel I sent my heroes to an agricultural exhibition in a two-decker bus. My readers exposed the error! It was a two-decker trolley that went to the exhibition in the year 1940. In *Two Captains* I used the barely legible facsimile of the letter of Lieutenant Brusilov to his mother, and one meticulous schoolboy not only got to the source, but proved to me that two words of Brusilov's letter had been read incorrectly.

But the fact that I had to read books on microbiology and painstakingly study "historical background" was not the only reason why *Open Book* was being written so slowly and with such difficulty. For the space of almost ten years I had to struggle for this book mainly with some critics, who now blamed me for occupying myself too much with the theme of love, as if in the Soviet land people ceased falling in love, pining, reading and reciting verses, dreaming of love or even dying of it, and now tried to persuade me to part with my "not fully valuable" heroes and to start occupying myself with ones absolutely positive in all respects. It was very hard to step over the persistent striving to direct my novel along another path which did not interest me in the least and, in essence, was far from the task that stood in front of me. This does not concern the serious critical analyses of my novel, which helped me draw — it goes without saying, insofar as it was within my power and skill — the growth of the character of the Soviet man and woman in connection with the growth of their scientific consciousness.

The plot of my novel is the story of a discovery which exerted a profound influence on the development of medical science, and which started a new era in this science. But, working on the third part, I understood that the story of Tanja Vlasenkova had long before gone beyond the boundaries of this plot.

The novel is the result of many years of observations; in the character of the heroine I sought to combine the features inherent in many women working in our science. However, in the third part which relates the grievous calamities of the war and the ordeals that afflicted us during the postwar period, I was following in the trail of only one, quite definite biography. Whether it is typical or not — let the reader judge. Stalingrad, the scientific duel with the scientist from Oxford, and Andrej's arrest are not invented by me. The names are, of course, changed. Beginning from the third part, the book, as it were, started writing itself; there was nothing else left for me to do but watch that the main theme did not drown in details — painfully memorable, too numerous and, consequently, requiring selection.

Lev Tolstoy said that his heroes acted not as he ordered them but as they could not help acting. I believe that this law is one of the most important laws of realistic prose.

6

Each book has its own history, and my concise essay would have extended to infinity if I had started telling them one after the other. I will therefore dwell only on my work of the past ten years. The sad history of the tale *Unknown Friend* strangely contradicts the content of this most cheerful of my books. In the year 1957 I fell sick so severely that I was forbidden not only to read and write but also to speak. The latter prohibition, as a matter of fact, I did not need because I was unable to speak anyway. There was only one thing left for me: to recollect. This is exactly how I began to spend my time. I recalled my life year by year.

This occupation struck me in one respect: it became clear that I remembered that which seemed to have been forgotten long before and forever. It turned out that I remembered, for example, the arrangement of objects on the writing desk of my older brother or trifles which distinguished a usual winter school day of the year 1912 from a usual day of the year 1913.

In this way I started recollecting my childhood, picking out in it, already through the force of professional habit, that which might come in handy for a future book. I did not know yet what it would be — a story, a tale, or a novel. I began my recollections from the age of six, although I might have begun from two and a half.

Remembering myself under social, political, and personal circumstances, I tried to draw a pre-revolutionary school, a small provincial town, complex relations in the family of a regimental bandmaster, the 1914 war, the coming of the Revolution, the first revolutionary years in Pskov, then in Moscow and Leningrad. I told about my encounters with Gorky, and Mayakovsky, about my friendship of many years with Jurij Tynjanov. Gradually overcoming the illness, I was mentally writing separate pages, without observing chronological order. In this way this book was conceived and written in my mind.

7

I always felt like writing fairy tales. It is worth telling the history of one of them. It is named "Mnogo xoroshix ljudej i odin zavistnik," [Many good people and one envier].

In 1923 I sent Gorky my first book, *Masters and Apprentices*. "It seems to me, — he answered — that it is time for you to shift your attention from unknown regions and countries to the Russian, contemporary, rather fantastic everyday life." He prompts excellent themes, for example: about the devil who broke his leg, — you remember: "Here the devil himself will break his leg," — about a man who opened a shop and sells the trifles of the past in it, — this man may be an antiquarian whom

Satan hired in order to tempt people, to stir up in them a sterile yearning for yesterday ... "

The youth who received this letter could, of course, not have passed by a prompting so characteristic of Gorky. With all my energy I set about writing a fantastic tale for children. One of its heroes wore an iron belt so as not to "burst of envy," and another so easily hit his neighbor, that is, hit "not his brow but his eye," that one had immediately to call for emergency help.[13]

The tale was begun, but soon left unfinished. However, I did not forget about it. Among my old manuscripts I used to repeatedly come across a leaflet with the plan and the first jottings. The leaflet, turned yellow from time, reminded me of the fact that years had not deleted Gorky's idea and had not made it less interesting.

After the war I again got down to writing the tale, and again I did not bring it to an end. Another fifteen years went by and I completed it nevertheless. It is said that "an old debt stands at the threshold." Now, it was gone, leaving its place to others, more significant, but, to make up for it, not as old.

8

A plot, hastily narrated on a page of my war notebook, at first glance appeared to me incredible. Precisely for this reason I felt like turning it into a tale.

I began by going to see one of our best naval commanders and asking him whether I had not dreamed of this plot which I had written down from the words of a sailor in the year 1943.

— Perhaps, the narrator made up this story?

— No, — the admiral answered. — He told you the truth.

I got down to work immediately and very soon I came to feel that I was short of something — it was not enough to say short of material — I was short of the feeling of the material, of the air of literature. The action takes place in the Extreme North, and I have not been there for almost twenty years. Among the heroes there are sailors of the merchant marine and of the navy. I hardly knew the merchant marine sailors, but I used to know the navy sailors long ago, while working as a war correspondent with the North Fleet.

I put off the work I had just started and set off for Murmansk. I had to find a very old steamship of the merchant marine which in former times belonged to the Soloveckij monastery, — she was part of the "divine" flotilla consisting of three steamships: "Faith," "Hope," and "Love." Alas, arriving at Murmansk I found out that she had long before been sent to the scrap yard! It was suggested that I examine another ship no less old. A respectable captain, retiring on a pension, agilely climbed with me through all her cabins and holds. He had been on long voyages. First he told me the story of his life, then the story of the ship — it was hard to tell which of them was more interesting.

The action of the tale took place on a moving ship, and it was necessary to picture her voyage — first on the map, then in action. At midday we departed from

Murmansk for one of the naval bases on the shore of Kola Bay. I understood on that day that I had not noticed all the beauty of the Northern nature. This is understandable — at that time we had other things to worry about than beauty. At that time the nature of the Extreme North was weighed on the scales — first on the scales of the defense, and then — on the scales of the offensive.

It is hard to write on a fast moving launch, but I did not take my pencil off the notebook. The crew helped me. The helmsman invited me onto the bridge, where in the fresh wind it became even more difficult to take notes. The motor mechanic, without forgetting his duties, showed the light figures of clouds on a dark blue rolling sky.

On the launch there was a native northerner, an old sailor. In the end he also took interest in our occupation, discovering, to his astonishment, that he had lived forty years in front of a continuously unfolding miracle.

Here is what this miracle looked like when we were sailing toward the base: under the motionless clouds illuminated from beneath there was a hardened quiet conflagration, and in the depth of this conflagration, smudged as Van Gogh's canvases, other light clouds were impetuously scudding straight into the stone line of the hills. A small moon, with her back to the sun, was lost in the enormous, overturned oval of heaven. Everything seemed motionless in this oval, and everything was in continuous floating motion.

In Murmansk a new consultant was waiting for me, a new well-wisher of my future tale — an experienced sailor. But this time the talk went in another direction. I had to learn more about my heroes than I wanted to communicate to my reader. In order to distinctly visualize the man about whom you write, you need details which at times remain in rough drafts, in outlines. The rough draft of a character — this is a notion which takes a far larger place in the manuscript than in the book. It is precisely in these rough drafts that you have to look for the key to the life of the hero, the essence without which it is impossible to draw his image.

The last days in the Extreme North were devoted to Murmansk. In the years of the war sailors called that "free hunt." I roamed all over the city without any aim, writing down everything that could (or could not) come in handy. The Germans dumped on Murmansk almost more bombs than on Malta. The log-house town was burnt to ashes. On the site of the smoldering ruins a large capital of Zapoljar'e [the region beyond the Polar Circle] has risen. But I needed the old town, and I was not able to find it, no matter how much I looked for it. The famous district "Shanxaj" has disappeared without leaving trace; in it sailors who came from all latitudes on foreign ships used to spend time tumultuously. A contemporary stadium is built in the center of the city, on the site of a huge ravine. I succeeded in finding a few old wooden houses, which have turned black. I sketched them. And returning to Moscow, I began the tale "Sem' par nechistyx" (The seven pairs of the impure ones] in which I felt like telling about a tragic and instructive turning point of the first days of the Great Patriotic War.

9

I am often asked how I work. I am afraid that, if I had attempted to answer this question, I would have experienced the same thing as the centipede which, trying to explain how it walked, entangled itself and forgot how to walk. In my early years I used to painstakingly work out a plan — chapter by chapter. So it was with my novel about Lobachevsky: the plan was detailed, but the novel remained unwritten. Then I began to handle the plan with greater ease. I knew that it changed greatly once you started writing.

As a rule, I do not succeed in writing more than one printed sheet a month. I envy people who write fast, and I constantly try to find out their secret. One of my friends works like this: he quickly writes everything that comes into his head, and then retains one third of what he has written. I tried to write as he did, and threw out half of what I had written. It turned out to be still slower. A certain kind of experienced writer many times trims, polishes the written sentence and no longer reverts to it. I write differently: in front of me there are two sheets of paper. On one sheet I jot down the sentence, then, considering it, I carry it over to the other sheet. And this is my rough draft. On its margin I again make corrections.

Another and, perhaps, no less difficult task begins when you return to old books, hoping to make them more distinct and more harmonious. Twice — in the years 1935 and 1955 — I returned to the novel *Fulfillment of Desires*. With each new edition I tried to improve the novel *Open Book*. All this applies in full measure to the present collection. Preparing it for print, I could not have left without changes many pages which formerly had seemed to me fully finished. The experience of many years has not been in vain, and it would be a sin not to take advantage of it when I am preparing a new edition of books written by a young man or even by a not so young one. From among my early works only a very few have entered into this new edition — only those which have had substantial significance for my subsequent work.

. . . From time to time I put still another manuscript in front of me on my desk; many of its pages are deleted, individual chapters have not yet found their own places. It belongs to the number of those books that are being written all one's life. It is not a novel, not a tale — it is impressions, pictures of travel, pages from diaries, and echoes of literary life.

* * *

Since the death of Stalin (1953), Kaverin has been taking an active part in the cultural liberalization of Soviet life. In 1956 Kaverin became one of the editors of the famous two-volume anthology *Literaturnaja Moskva,* which was at the time one of the most forceful literary contributions to destalinization. Kaverin has actively been participating in the Soviet writers' effort to rehabilitate those of their fellow-writers whose names had become *non grata* in Stalin's lifetime. For example, in the mid-sixties he helped bring the name and the works of M. Bulgakov out of limbo[14] When Sinjavskij and Daniel' were sentenced to hard labor in February 1966, Kaverin, along with other 61 writers, signed a letter to the Presidium of the 23rd Congress of the Communist Party of the Soviet Union (March 29-April 8, 1966).[15] In this letter the 62 men and women in question begged the authorities to let Sinjavskij and Daniel' go for the sake of not obstructing the development of Soviet culture. The sixty-two would take the responsibility for the good behavior of the two condemned men[16]. Along with late Tvardovskij, Kaverin has been one of the staunchest supporters of Solzhenitsyn. The letter that Kaverin wrote to K. Fedin in defense of Solzhenitsyn (January 1968) has become well known internationally.[17] It is an outstanding document testifying to Kaverin's courage, decency and good judgement. The letter records the fact that Fedin, in his capacity of the First Secretary of the Governing Body of the Union of the Writers of the USSR, is responsible for *Cancer Ward* not having been published in the Soviet Union: Fedin was the one who had the plates of the novel destroyed. Kaverin describes Fedin and his action in these words: "The writer who throws the noose around the neck of another writer — this is the figure that will remain in the history of literature [. . .]."

This courageous activity of Kaverin attracted an angry response from the powers that be. In May 1968, along with some other writers, Kaverin received a warning from the Secretariat of the Union of Soviet Writers because of his "political irresponsibility," i.e., because of his public disapproval of the reprisals that the authorities made against those who dared openly to condemn Soviet political oppression, e.g., Ginzburg and Galanskov.[18]

In 1969, when the authorities tried to commit the perfectly sound Zhores Medvedev to a psychiatric clinic as a measure of political intimidation, Kaverin sent a protest telegram for which he was again seriously criticized at a high level.[19]

This is undoubtedly only a fragmentary picture of Kaverin's contribution to humanizing the system inherited from Stalin. It is not the purpose of this study to describe in detail this aspect of Kaverin's distinguished career, although to make the picture complete is certainly worth the effort. This study, however, centers on Kaverin's art of narrative fiction. As for Kaverin's public attitudes of a social thinker, one of the best tributes to it comes from the *samizdat* religious writer Krasnov-Levitin:

"Neo-humanism unites people of different beliefs, concepts, parties. Everywhere neo-humanism rises against injustice, oppression, against any form of oppression, be it of class, race, or state origin. Neo-humanism is the movement of Martin Luther King . . . the movement of Gandhi, . . . the movement of the European intelligentsia for peace, for the right of men to freedom, equality, fraternity . . . In our Russia the bearers of neo-humanism are such people as the just deceased Konstantin Paustovski, Veniamin Kaverin, Evgeni Evtushenko, Alexandr Solzhenitsyn, Academician Sakharov, and all those representatives of the intelligentsia who are known as "signers" — people who have been signing multiple petitions in the defense of the persecuted and the oppressed. [. . .] "[20]

This neo-humanism is also reflected in Kaverin's prose fiction.

It has not been my primary purpose in this study to undertake a general descriptive survey of Kaverin's literary works. I have not tried to discuss the whole literary output of Kaverin in a consistently chronological order.

While reading and studying the works of Kaverin I came to be interest in certain clusters of problems which seem particularly to characterize Kaverin's prose and which, hopefully, are particularly interesting to discuss.

The first chapter deals with the earliest creative attempts of Kaverin. His fantastic tales must have reflected the very early literary awareness of the author. It appears from his autobiographical essay [*vid*. p. 2 of this study] that Kaverin, from the 1964 vantage, attaches hardly any importance whatsoever to these juvenile tales of the early twenties. These experimental tales may, however, have some historical importance or implication in terms of a potentiality which did not happen to reach the stage of actualization, one which remained unfulfilled. In the second chapter I discuss the problem of the plot (*sjuzhet* in Russian) as it affects the narrative prose of Kaverin. This problem has a special significance in Kaverin's attitude toward literary representation. It also holds a special place in the literary philosophy of the "Serapion Brothers" and the literary following that they commanded. The third chapter is devoted to the discussion of a problem of literary representation which seems to be one of the focal points of Soviet literature. Namely, the representation of the "New Soviet Man." Kaverin handles this problem of representation and ideology in a way which prevails in this regard in Soviet literature. However, he subjects it to a treatment sufficiently idiomatic for the characterization of the "New Man" to develop a somewhat unconventional complexion. The fourth chapter examines one particular but vital outlook of Soviet reality that Kaverin conveys in his later works. In what respect were the years of Stalinism tragic for Russia? Kaverin dramatizes this tremendous question as it affected Russian science and Soviet people's moral attitudes.

The chapters in this study are arranged in what one might call a selective logical sequence. What justifies this sequence is the concept of the dynamics of literary structure as an integration of progressively more comprehensive strata of signification, from "pure sounds" and sound effects to syntactic structures, and from the latter to the representation of characters and their interactions, and to further possible levels of signification. Each succeeding stratum absorbs the elements of the preceding, whereas the reverse is not true. Experimental "abstract" plots develop into solid "life-like" plots. Kaverin's artistic perception of the "New Soviet Man" can materialize only within a specific setting supplied by plot. And the tragic experience of the decades of Stalinism results from the interaction of certain types of characters. A different sequence would be less desirable in terms of the intelligibility of the literary phenomenon.

Other links in this sequence might be no less significant, and therefore, as legitimate subjects of study. In this regard, it is the intellectual interest of the investigator that ultimately decides which specific significant points will come under discussion.

PART ONE

PATTERNS OF PLOT

CHAPTER ONE

EXPERIMENTATION IN A ROMANTIC KEY

The early narrative prose of Kaverin was to a great extent a product of literary experimentation. In it the young writer learnt the fundamentals of literary craft and tried to develop his own distinctive literary manner. In an autobiography Kaverin tells how he came to write his very first prose work:

A sixteen-year-old youth, I arrived at Moscow[1], where in the year 1919 I completed secondary school. In those years I wrote verse, but, having met with a stern evaluation of my experiments on the part of well-known litterateurs, I decided to give up my literary occupations and to devote myself to scholarly activity. In the year 1920 I transferred from the University of Moscow to the University of Petrograd, simultaneously enrolling in the Institute of Oriental Languages. However, a competition for beginning writers again prompted in me the idea of trying my strength in literature. Here is how it came about.
... Preparing for my examination in logic, for the first time I read an outline of the non-Euclidean geometry of Lobachevsky and I was struck by the daring of a mind that had imagined that parallel lines meet in space, and on the grounds of this strange idea built a new teaching, as accurate as the teaching of Euclid.
Professor L. examined me for forty minutes. Tired but cheerful, I was returning home and in Bassejnaja street I caught sight of a poster that had guessed my most secret thoughts. "The House of the Litterateurs" was inviting all who wished, to take part in a competition of beginning writers. There were five prizes set: the first − five thousand rubles, the second − four thousand, and three third prizes − three thousand rubles each.
From the "House of the Litterateurs" to the Grecheskij Avenue in which I lived, it was not far − ten minutes' walk. I think it is no exaggeration to say that these ten minutes have determined the main features of my life. Arriving home, I decided to give up verse forever, to turn to prose and to take part in the competition.
Finally, − this was the most important − I had time to think over my first story "The Eleventh Axiom." As is known, Lobachevsky disagreed precisely with the eleventh axiom of Euclid. Thus, the idea that formed the foundation of my first story had a direct relation to my examination in logic − I was then a student in my first year at the University of Petrograd.
Lobachevsky had parallel lines meet in space. What then prevents me from having two parallel plots meet − not only in space but also in time? It is only necessary that

independently of the place and the time of action there be an inner logical link between the heroes.

Coming home, I took a ruler and on a sheet of paper I drew a line dividing the page lengthwise into two equal columns. In the left column I started writing the story of a monk who loses faith, hacks icons to pieces and escapes from his monastery. In the right column — the story of a student who loses his own and another's money at cards. The action of the first story occurred in the Middle Ages. The action of the second — on the eve of the Revolution. At the end of the third page — it was a very short story — the two "parallel" stories came to meet. The student and the monk met on the bank of the Neva. They had nothing to talk about, and, trying to depict all the depth of his heroes' fall, the author turned to describing the gloomy picture of the autumnal Petrograd.

This story I wrote during three days and under the significant motto: "Art must be built on the formulas of exact sciences" — I mailed it in for the competition[2].

This first work of Kaverin as he describes it in his autobiography, testifies to his spontaneous interest in plot "engineering," in the energetic movement of the plot, and, especially, its reversals. It also betrays a certain intellectualism of the author and his attraction toward representing intellectual and scientific quests. The "experimental" period comes to its end by 1928, when his first major work, *Skandalist*, makes its appearance.

Two recurrent features mark Kaverin's narrative prose of the period. First, his works playfully defy the possible and the plausible. With considerable reservation, we might describe them as "fantastic." This vein Kaverin derives from German Romanticism, namely, its last, powerful, wave, E.T.A. Hoffmann. Second, Kaverin's early narrative prose tends toward the genre of the novel of adventure.

An author represents his experience and observations of reality in his own poetic language. At the same time, his poetic discourse occupies a certain place in the literary tradition. Neither can it escape the pressure of this tradition. Thus, at the point of maturity, literary performance flows from the confluence of poetic self-expression and literary tradition. Anton Chekhov, in the early, potboiling, period of his literary career, by virtue of his function of a petty newspaper chronicler, had to observe life, to note "fragments of Moscovite life." Hence, a great deal of data is taken "directly from life" and little from literary tradition. The reverse is true in the case of Kaverin's early works. The latter bear the mark of emphatic "literariness." At this initial stage, Kaverin draws all his material from literary tradition, and little "from life." At the university, he was a student in philology and literature. This professional background may partially explain this view from behind "the walls of a student's room, piled up with books on the history of literature"[3].

In this chapter I would like to discuss Kaverin's first collection of stories *Mastera i podmaster'ja* (Masters and apprentices, 1923). While discussing them, I would like to comment on some significant motives and circumstances arising in connection with them. Very little known, the book has never been reprinted in the Soviet Union. Neither has it been translated into English.[4] Subsequently, Kaverin himself dismissed

Masters and Apprentices as "child's play".[5] Perhaps so, but a very bright child's play. The book deserves more than casual interest. It includes six stories: "Carpenters," "Shields (and Candles)," "Engineer Shvarc," "The Chronicle of the City of Leipzig for the Year 18..," "The Purple Palimpsest," "The Fifth Wanderer".[6]

In one respect *Masters and Apprentices* is, to quote Kaverin, "a tribute to my enthusiasm for the German Romantics".[7] In the early twenties there was a rebirth of Hoffmannism among the group of young beginning writers united under the Hoffmannian name of the "Serapion Brothers." Their impassioned "manifesto" "Why We Are Serapion Brothers" exalted Hoffmann's sense of phantasmagoria, which for the Serapions had the additional value of asserting creative freedom. Kaverin, the youngest "brother," gave the most forceful and extravagant expression to this "Hoffmann motive."

The most important aspect of this "Hoffmann motive" is the interlocking of the fantastic and the empirical on the one hand, and the principle of metamorphosis on the other. Hoffmann's art consists in skillfully engineering contacts between the two and transitions from one to the other. Objects can change their substance and switch from one level of existence to the other. This is obviously a characteristic Romantic vision. As a rule the fantastic motive interweaves effortlessly with the "realist" texture of a work by Hoffmann. He motivates this blending of the supernatural with the empirical in different ways. The motivation may be the poetic vision of the subject. For example, all the fantastic adventures the student Anselmus experiences in "The Golden Flower Pot" may have been conjured up by his own turbulently growing poetic vision of the world. Or the motivation can be placed in a different perspective: a universal myth converting its cosmic symbols into the events and beings of empirical reality. The distorted vision of deepening insanity provides another motivation good for fantastic development. For example, Nathanael's obsession with the Sandman and his infatuation with Olimpia may well be the biography of his diseased mind, which even the devoted love of Clara cannot save ("The Sandman"). On the whole, the two areas, the fantastic and the empirical, stand in a clear opposition to each other. Hoffmann eases transitions from one area to the other by conjuring up poetic enchantment and humor. This may especially be the case when no natural empirical motivation can neutralize the supernatural or the empirically impossible, e.g., when man's reflection detaches itself from its owner and remains in the mirror, or when man allows his shadow to emancipate itself from him, as in "A New Year's Adventure."

Kaverin uses the principle of metamorphosis differently. His stories also abound in imaginative situations, but the dramatic potency of his transitions and metamorphoses is quite diluted. His representational material has little actual reference to empirical and historical reality. The stories seem predominantly to reproduce a medieval German setting: craftsmen, scholastics, bürgers, their women, churches, market places and such. However, this setting has virtually nothing historically valid. Nowhere in the stories will the reader find anything remotely similar to the Nuremberg masters and journeymen as they appear in Hoffmann's "Tobias Martin, Master Cooper, and His Men." Perhaps Kaverin turns to this emotionally distant material because it is easier to

experiment with it. He enjoys the advantage of not having to reckon with the resistance his representational material may offer to his manipulation. In any case, all those Leipzig students, medieval craftsmen and wanderers, and even Petrograd of the early 1920s and its Soviet inhabitants seem to be whirling through some kind of never-never land. If so, the essential differentia proper to the fantastic tale is simply missing in these stories: there is no irreconcilable conflict between the "never-never" and the "here and now;" no menace that a rationally unfathomable circumstance, arising in our rational fathomable world, holds for our sense of security. In other words, no morbid fear of ominous mystery.

This over-all absence of depth of representation derives from the comical context of most of these stories. They are written in a jocularly self-parodying and ironic key. Thus Kaverin "discredits" his own representational material. The prevailing self-parody typical of these stories makes all their puppets and goblins look somewhat humorous. Neither the author nor the reader take them seriously. Our potential horror of a two-dimensional monster melts away as soon as we see the monster using cheap tobacco ("Engineer Shvarc"). And how can we esteem a landsknecht who crashes the gates of the never-never land dragging in his old prejudices, who dies there, only to die again, murdered, back in the empirical world ("Shields (and Candles)")? And what should we think of a wooden boy chasing a not so wooden girl and winning her favors ("Carpenters")? In our eyes these all too human foibles of the non-humans strip them of their evil auras.

Whether they assume their "fantastic" shape or their "empirical" one does not matter because the interlocking of the two spheres is not the artistic keystone in these stories. Therefore metamorphoses as such are not the main object of representation either and the main creative tension does not lie between the fantastic and the empirical. The two spheres combine to weave the experimental patterns of the plot. If goblins behave and are willing to support the structure of the plot, let them, the author seems to think slyly. He tests certain ways of plot engineering. With an experimenter's curiosity he tries to ascertain how far plot organization can be strained before it comes to its breaking point.

While none of these stories hides any ominous mystery, each of them seems to set a little riddle. The paradox is that the author does not seem to offer any real solutions. This very absence of solution might have been a sign of greatness in another kind of work. Here, it is more like a petty parody of suspense itself. In this respect, "Shields (and Candles)" is the most tantalizing of the stories. A shoemaker, a carpenter, a dumb man, and a late-comer who turns out to be a soldier all join in a card game called landsknecht. The soldier plainly states the purpose of his coming: he wants to kill the shoemaker because the latter abducted his sister. Both men, however, suspend any possible enmity while the game is on. It is as if they are playing, or staging or rehearsing that which they are going to actualize later. The game lasts the better part of the night, with candles flickering and illuminating the sinister faces of the gamblers. As the first rays of dawn hit the window-pane, the soldier, who seems to be winning, has the card game called off. The hour of retribution has come. The soldier unsheathes his sword to run through the shoemaker in revenge for the disgrace and murder of his sister. But at this point the tide is suddenly reversed. The three other cronies unexpectedly pounce upon the soldier and slay him.

The plot is complicated and rendered virtually unintelligible by the fact that the very cards the four gamblers use in their own game of landsknecht concurrently stage their own play of life and death. Ominous events seem ready to shake the cards' kingdom, persecutions threaten its subjects, and even the kings fear for their lives. The king of clubs has a senate convened at which all the card kings meet and discuss their predicaments. And to make matters worse, the card Emperor, feeling betrayed on all sides, dies at this very session of the senate. The action of the story shifts from one setting to the other. The soldier seems to be a landsknecht; the name of the game is also landsknecht. Through this pun the soldier serves as a precarious link between the two settings. People and cards somehow shape and seal one another's destinies, but the author takes impish delight in setting these interactions at such grotesque cross-purposes that the reader, losing the thread at each twist in the plot, comes to suspect that there is no circumstantial plot consistency. Most likely, the story does not have any coherent plot, unless all inconsistencies are simply disregarded for the sake of interpretation. A kind of "anti-plot" moves the incidents, but in what direction?

The basic element of the plot is quite clear: it is *reversal*. "A" comes to murder "B," but at the end of the plot development "B" murders "A." That much is obvious, but the attending circumstances are not. I would venture the assumption that this story is a play of "pure forms" with no actual reference to circumstantial reality, not even fantastic. In this instance the Russian formalists might have spoken of a story about pure device abstracted from its motivation, e.g., of a story about *peripeteia*, much as Viktor Shklovskij symptomatically entitled his 1966 book *Tales about Prose.*[8] Moreover, Kaverin grotesquely emphasizes the sense of fatality in a "play-within-a-play" situation.

"The Purple Palimpsest" pursues a similar aim. Mr. Wurst, an elderly man of scholastic inclinations, and Kranzer the bookbinder come close to exchanging their characters and situations. They happen to be journeying to each other's cities. At night their coaches collide and they meet. Before long the two travellers resume their trips. However, in the dark they take the wrong coaches so that the next morning they both return to their points of departure, i.e., home. It looks as if something of each personality has rubbed off on the other during their brief meeting. Wurst, the scholar, takes to bookbinding, whereas Kranzer, the bookbinder, cherishes scholarly pursuits. The rest of the story seems to develop two complementary motives. Wurst is deciphering a palimpsest (yellow after sunset, purple after sunrise) which tells two ancient stories, one buried underneath the other, about men caught in the same kind of avocational interchange that links the scholar and the bookbinder. Then the bookbinder is taken over to the scholar's place. In a nocturnal scene which is blurred and incoherent, the bookbinder seems to superimpose himself on the scholar, not unlike the writing of a palimpsest.

This story is about "pure forms" of plot analogous to those of "Shields (and Candles)," namely, double reversal and interchange. As for the narrated incidents and circumstances, they seem to be made intentionally nonsensical. All those "split personalities," mirror reflections, lost shadows, and doubles (rather "part-time" doubles) make little sense. In any case they lack the artistic validity or the psychological and philosophical purposefulness with which Hoffmann invests the same devices. Still, there may be a legitimate purpose in this apparent nonsense – for which the well-intentioned Gorky berated the young author.9 Any reference to meaningful circumstantial reality draws the reader's attention away from what may be hidden behind. By means of its thematic interest, circumstantial reality "reflected" in the narrative blinds the reader's mental eyes to the "abstract" infrastructure of the narrative. Should the author deliberately obscure the circumstantial reality "reflected" in the narrative, the vision of the reader would be deflected toward the "abstract" infrastructure. Unable to make out the circumstantial reality, the reader will have to refocus his mental vision on the over-all design of the plot, which will then stand out the more clearly because the circumstantial details of the narrative are blurred. The creative process itself, in a sense, stands at the center of representation. This may be the reason why Kaverin lapses so readily into the absurd throughout the stories. Absurd circumstantial reality deflects the reader's attention toward the "abstract" "pure forms" underlying the narrative. Kaverin is only modestly successful in doing so in these stories. However, we may wonder whether at that point ("Shields (and Candles)" is dated January 1922) Kaverin was not taking his first timid steps along the road that has brought Pirandello all the way to *Six Characters in Search of an Author* (1921). It is a pity that Kaverin did not have a chance to continue along that road.

In "The Chronicle of the City of Leipzig for the Year 18.." Kaverin chooses to show the "riddle" proper to the story and the "toying" with its plot from a somewhat different angle. The story is about a student, Heinrich Bornholm, who has fallen in love with Gretchen, the daughter of his philosophy professor. Desperate over being rejected, the student takes a vow of silence. A stranger makes him an unusual bargain: in exchange for Bornholm's silence he will give him Gretchen's love and hand. Who would resist such an offer? Inadvertently Bornholm misses his chance. He loses the envelope in which his silence has been sealed. This is, of course, a grotesque way of showing the unreliability of the devil's deal. Silence as such is secondary in the bargain. What the stranger wanted was to have Bornholm violate his pledge, i.e., give up his integrity. Bornholm forfeits the girl, in addition to losing his silence. In utter despair he has himself sculpted into a small bronze statue and ends on an obscure shelf in an antique shop. The one who buys the statuette is an old ugly woman antiquarian who owns the shop. This lady must have migrated from the pages of E.T.A. Hoffmann's "The Golden Flower Pot." There she used to sell apples and cookies. The same lady, still, seems to have moved onto the pages of Kaverin's "Engineer Shvarc." She is as ugly and old as ever; now she peddles tobacco. She is more evil than she looks; she knows more than she acknowledges; she does more than her humble trade lets it suspect.

The very title of "The Chronicle" leads to a riddle. It involves an ironic interplay with the actual structure of the story. The notion of a chronicle is based on consecutive connection in time. Events are recorded as they follow one another, measured solely by the succession of hours, days, months and years. But the structure of this story mocks and utterly annihilates the chronological principle heralded by the title. The story is again a little riddle because its plot is broken up like a sort of jigsaw puzzle. The author has scattered the pieces of the puzzle — the chronological segments of the plot — as if at random, all through the narrative. Therefore, until almost the end the reader does not quite understand the story. Fortunately, the "riddle," at least most of its plot development, is solvable, because almost all pieces of the puzzle are there, and the reader, after some minimal mental gymnastics, can put the pieces back where they belong.

The apparent chaos of the plot structure results from the author's undisguised "tyranny" over his characters and narrative material. This relation of the author to his narrative material harks back to the Sternian, or rather, Shandean tradition of "toying" with plot. The purpose of the narrative is to show how its plot is being constructed. In this connection *Six Characters in Search of an Author* again comes to mind. In this play the actors do not impersonate any people from real life (even if invented) as they are represented in conventional plays. Creative process as such is represented. The actors of Pirandello's play stand for the elusive mental images arising and consolidating into mature stage characters in the mind of the "author". The very title of the play signifies this process. There is some functional similarity between the Director in Pirandello's play and the narrator in Kaverin's story (although the two characters are not really comparable as to their artistic substance). Not unlike the Director, the narrator every now and then interferes with the progress of the action, hesitates as to where it should move, makes arbitrary changes, tricks his characters, incurs their displeasures, and occasionally has to overcome their resistance when he and his independent-minded characters differ on which course to follow. In Kaverin's story, an "omniscient" author reflects on which turn to give to the action of the narrative. At the same time this "omniscient" author doubles as a first-person narrator who takes part in the action, i.e., as one who has only a partial knowledge of the action. For experimental purposes, Kaverin combines the two points of view. This combination turns the story into a sort of narrative madhouse. The first — "omniscient" — point of view puts the author above his characters; it allows him to dispose of them as he wishes. The second — restricted — point of view does the opposite: it makes the first-person narrator consubstantial with his characters; it prevents him from moving them around in the manner of chessmen over a chessboard. Thus, the two contradictory points of view, set head on, tend to reciprocally destroy each other's artistic effect.

This double perspective deprives both the characters and the narrator of any kind of validity and plausibility. Only the jocose tone of the narrative holds this impossible combination together, turning it into something grotesque. Therefore, the only artistically valid factor in the story seems to be the voice of the one we may call "omniscient-author-turned-first-person-narrator." Throughout the story this voice keeps debating which plot incidents to create. The fact of the "omniscient-author-turned-first-person-narrator" reflecting upon the plot comes to the center of artistic representation, while the plot as such recedes to the periphery. This is a typically Shandean situation. Kaverin's story does not stand comparision with *Tristram Shandy's* fireworks, but it applies the same artistic principle: the awareness of the time and energy attached to discoursing on the plot grows at the expense of that attached to the movement of the plot itself. In modern literature this imbalance betrays the growing psychologism and internalization of the narrative. As for Kaverin, he later returned to this double perspective — that of the "omniscient" author and that of the first-person narrator — and used this technique, freed from jocose verbosity, with a great deal of artistic validity.

In these stories Kaverin chooses not to recreate an empirical three-dimensional world. Neither does he represent three-dimensional human beings. He shapes something short of both. Most of the characters who populate the pages of his stories originated in Hoffmann's stories. Occasionally the young author himself airily acknowledges this literary lineage, or at least this dependence on the Hoffmann tradition. In "The Purple Palimpsest" the apprentice Spiegel leaves his reflection in the mirror in the bookbinder Kranzer's house so that his reflection may keep Kranzer's shadow company, and the apprentice also makes the shadow detach itself from Kranzer by slamming the door shut as the latter walks out of his house. The narrator adds: "And the shadow and the reflection in the mirror, uniting in legitimate wedlock, performed a wonderful dance in the honor of Amadeus Hoffmann".[10] What in Hoffmann's "A New Year's Eve Adventure" is a poetic parody of how man is seduced into forfeiting his identity and integrity, becomes in Kaverin's story a matter of flimsy literary play. As they reappear in Kaverin's stories, all these Spikhers, Schlemihls, ugly old women, Olimpias, and automata have lost their complexities and depth. In both "The Chronicle" and "The Purple Palimpsest" Kaverin subjects one of the very solemn motives of Russian literature, the splitting of personality, to a most irreverent treatment. Because of their built-in sub-human limitations, these monsters and goblins naturally suffer centrifugal fates. They naturally tend to fade out. None of the puppets or homunculi Kaverin unleashes in these stories generate any sense of horror or evil. The jocular tone of the narrative, it nothing else, will not allow it. And still, even within these narrow limits they may raise valid problems.

"Carpenters" is Kaverin's interpretation of the "automaton" motive. It tells the story of a wooden boy, Sergej, who has grown to become an expert carpenter in search of a magic plane, the elusive reward of the best among carpenters. His fruitless quest brings him finally to Moscow. Sergej's destiny is somewhat like that of Pinocchio, although Kaverin's spoof and Collodi's diminutive epic are hardly commensurable. Had Kaverin had his puppet follow in Pinocchio's footsteps, or had he simply duplicated any of Hoffmann's automata, his experiment would have been quite worthless. What then is the purpose of the plot in this story? Before leaving in quest of the magic plane, Sergej lives through a strange experience: one night, during a rendezvous with the local priest's maidservant, Sergej catches sight of a statue. Kaverin has a grotesque way of framing Sergej's anxiety. At precisely this amatory moment, the priest, terrorized at the idea of someone prowling through his house, falls back on his meager stock of prayers in Latin, and mutters this piece of wisdom:

"Inter feces and urinam nascimus".[1] Sergej, most likely, does not understand Latin. This suggests, ironically under the circumstances, that Sergej has not come into this world the way in which humankind does, that he is different from the rest of mankind. The quotation offers a riddle, still unsuspected by Sergej, but which guides his steps. In Moscow he again comes across a statue, that of Emperor Alexander. And Sergej again experiences the same chilling feeling that he did with the first statue. At this point, helped by a somewhat enigmatic "old man" who drives his anxieties home, Sergej fully realizes that he has always been inferior to what he believed himself to be, and that, his time running out, he has to revert to his original state. This is an enormously pregnant motive. It can set in motion very different, and each time rewarding, plot developments. In his *Pinocchio*, Collodi chose to impart an idyllic turn to this motive, which leads to a fairytale-like happy ending. On quite a different level, Shaw dramatizes a similar motive of metamorphosis in his *Pygmalion*, emphasizing its self-defeating incompletion. In Kaverin's story, the underlying purpose of the plot seems to be to articulate the peripeties in the life of a puppet which honestly believes itself to be a human being and acts as the best of humankind would: it tries to transcend itself and to reach for an ideal above the human. And then it suddenly realizes it is not more than a puppet, a spurious human, an involuntary imposter on the point of exposure. Another possibility is that the underlying purpose of the plot was to have a puppet, vaguely aware of its inferiority, desperately try to redeem itself and thereby to overcome its inferiority, but it fails, either absolutely or because the stipulated time has run it course. The author does place the essential dramatic signposts pointing in this direction so that the plot may follow it. However, such a truly significant plot plays itself out behind a verbal screen that lets episodic, and somewhat misleading, scenes be projected on its surface. Perhaps the author challenges the reader to guess what the actual behind-the-screen plot moves toward. And this challenge may well be a part of this literary experiment. If so, however, then this actual plot should have been artistically more substantial to be worth solving. If it has been more substantial, this particular "puppet" motive would have grown into a powerful poetic reality, in the province of modern existentialist literature.

In "Engineer Shvarc" Kaverin describes how something unexplainable and eerie seems to be entering our familiar three-dimensional world. A young mathematician Korchaga experiences a strange attraction toward engineer Shvarc. Once at dawn, after a night's study, Korchaga comes across this engineer Shvarc and his coadjutors. To his amazement, Korchaga sees that they are two-dimensional. It turns out that they are all on a friendly mission to the Soviet Union from the Country of Geometrists. Engineer Shvarc, their head, is returning back to his country. He entrusts Korchaga with his notes about the Geometric State. Has it all been a dream at the end of a tiresome sleepless night?

The two incommensurable worlds happen to meet in Petrograd, in the early twenties. Speaking of the city, engineer Shvarc uses its old name: Petersburg. He surely knows that the city was rebaptized "Petrograd" in 1914, even if he is not to be expected to know that it will change to "Leningrad" in 1924. How can this anachronism be explained? Perhaps the author intentionally resurrects the city's old name to conjure up motives proper to the image of the city of Petersburg as it appeared in the 19th-century Russian classical literature. One thinks, namely, of the fantastic motive that Gogol used in Part II of his tale "The Portrait" (the 1835 version): the Evil One visits this world indefatigably, trying to perpetuate his presence by incarnating himself in a human form or by leaving his imprint on some object of human intercourse. In Gogol's tale it happens to be a Petersburg usurer Petromixali and his unfinished portrait through whose lifelike eyes the Evil One asserts his presence in our world.

Might not engineer Shvarc and his coadjutors be such evil spirits, refurbished and trimmed up to catch more skeptical eyes and to captivate more positive minds? Engineer Shvarc is the chief emissary of the Geometric State. He stays provisionally in Petrograd where he meets Korchaga. If one is to judge from the former's confidence and the latter's observations, a friendly invasion has been going on from the Country of Geometrists. Where is this country? Not far from Petrograd, engineer Shvarc says. Without pushing the analogy between the Gogolian motive and the present too far, we still can perceive that engineer Shvarc, or perhaps "the geometrical mug of the engineer," has taken hold of Korchaga's mind. And when engineer Shvarc returns to his Country of Geometrists, Korchaga remains his willing deputy in the Soviet Union. And the "Evil One" has even left his "portrait" to keep his presence alive – a geometrical chart that has suddenly appeared on the wall of Korchaga's room, and "by its general outline and form of lines it was extraordinarily reminiscent of engineer Shvarc to confused Korchaga".[12]

It is perhaps most significant that engineer Shvarc, possibly a modern devil, has chosen to make his way in the modern world through the mind of a mathematician, and not an artist, as old-fashioned devils used to do. And it is equally significant that his presence is conveyed not by an old-fashioned oil portrait but rather by a geometrical chart, perhaps a blueprint, a plan for things to come. Engineer Shvarc may symbolize a totally rationalized world, not unlike the one Zamjatin has shaped in his "anti-utopia" *We*. It turns out that the subjects of this Country of Geometrists possess only two dimensions – width and height; they are denied the third dimension – depth. This third dimension obviously makes all the difference between the abstract vision of a perfect life that engineer Shvarc advocates and the concrete "thick" life, imperfect and live. He observes that his friendly invasion started under favorable auspices. After the 1917 revolution, he says, people in Russia went in for ideas dear to Geometrists. People became nearly two-dimensional, things acquired a new eerie beauty of straight lines, transparent surfaces, clear perspectives, rectilinear polygons, and mathematical curves. Ultimately, however, "two-dimensionality" led to people's disaffection. Therefore engineer Shvarc thinks it no longer useful to stay in Russia, and returns to his Country of Geometrists. This country is everywhere, wherever the abstract vision of life prevails. It is, among other places, in Korchaga's mind. So that, ultimately, engineer Shvarc withdrew, perhaps to where he could have originated, in Korchaga's own mind. Not without reason does engineer Shvarc disappear while Korchaga is sleeping. The engineer then is Korchaga's dream, and a projection of the latter's ambitions. The image of engineer Shvarc may prefigure what Korchaga deep down in his consciousness would like to become: the one giving the ultimate form to the perfect mathematical expression of life, simple, eternal and inhuman. This inhumanity of purpose may best be seen when Korchaga discovers that Shvarc and his coadjutors lack the third dimension. His surprise is only mathematical. For Korchaga it is a strictly scientific question, a problem of defining a geometrical locus when he wants to know where the "two-dimensional" have their hearts. He does not seem to sense any moral implication in his question. So it's all up to what Korchaga will do about his vision of the linear, transparent and two-dimensional Russia. Will he be willing and able to enforce the mathematical formula?

The first-person narrator lets his protagonist Korchaga view the world around him. There is something of Zamjatin's technique in the story: the mathematician, the viewer, tends to simplify and to schematize the picture of the world into a set of geometrical surfaces, angles, squares, straight lines, curves and underlying mathematical formulas. However, in the spirit of all these stories, things should not be taken too seriously. The narrator himself makes his drollish presence felt only enough to tilt those geometrical constructions somewhat. This slightly grotesque deformation "discredits" the mathematical world of Korchaga. In consequence, straight lines go somewhat crooked, rectangles bend into rhombuses, curves bulge out of their pristine sveltness, and geometrical surfaces, besmirched, lose their ideal transparency. As for Korchaga, for the time being the author has him floundering through grotesque misadventures, amidst a whirlwind of phantasmagoria. Perhaps the author tries to reassure the reader: Korchaga will forever lose his game for want of one point.[13]

In "The Fifth Wanderer," the last story of the collection, Kaverin recounts the fate of four brave searchers and wayfarers. The charlatan and clown Hanswurst wanders all over medieval Germany. He earns his and his donkey's keep by staging puppet shows. At one of these he meets Oswald Schwerindoch, "a scholastic and master of many sciences." The two wayfarers set out together and after many days they come to Württemberg. There they meet Johann Faust, doctor and master of philosophy, and Kurt, an artisan of the guild of glaziers. They sign a compact pledging that they will set out on a journey, in quest of solutions to their pursuits. Their quests, enlivened by motley travel adventures, end in failure: none of them find what they have been searching for. It is regrettable that their search fails. It is perhaps even more regrettable that these four searchers turn out to be not people, but mere puppets. This story presents a panorama in which puppets and humans live side by side. It is an unstable co-existence. The demarcation line between the world of puppets and the world of humans is somewhat indistinct and keeps changing. Things seem to come to an inexorable end: everyone in the story turns out to be a puppet, except the enigmatic "fifth wanderer." But who is he?

It is through this puppetry that the author dabbles with his diminutive game of reality and illusion. He faces the difficuly of transcribing one artistic medium in terms of another. Transcribing puppet (stage) drama in terms of (epic) narrative adds something to the latter not present to such a degree in the former. On the face of it, the story gives a not too imaginative version — probably Kaverin's own — of the *Faust*

Puppenspiel. If so, the reality represented should be Germany of the first half of the sixteenth century when the prototype of the Faust legend lived. The frame of the enactment (or the narrative transcription of the enactment) should be set in Germany of the Thirty Years' War and afterward, when the *Faust Puppenspiel* was popular. Kaverin's own inspiration, however, harks back to German Romanticism, when puppets won their grand "rehabilitation." Judging from what Kaverin represents and how he does so, the young author hardly worried about the sense of history or valid characterization.

A puppet-player is performing in an inn. Among the spectators are the hostess, journeymen, merchants, sailors, wenches and the scholastic Oswald Schwerindoch, one of the "wanderers." So logically the puppet-player and spectators stand on an existential level different from that of the puppets (namely, the puppet Pickelhering, which plays the part of the devil). Pickelhering and his consort are puppets, whereas the puppet-player and the audience are people, the former manipulating the puppets, and the latter watching the puppets act on the stage. However, as the story progresses, it turns out that the three other "wanderers," human-like at the beginning, are also puppets who (except for Doctor Faust) end their careers on the bottom of the puppet chest. This should mean that all the people and things that the four "wanderers" meet during their careers also belong to the world of puppets, not of human beings.

Thus the story belongs in the "play-within-a-play" category. The process of "transcription" I mentioned earlier gives the narrative an evocative power which stage enactment cannot do. The convention of stage impersonation cannot escape the spectators' consciousness, because the stage and puppets stand before their eyes reminding them that this is a stage impersonation, that the actors are puppets. But in narrative transcription the stage paraphernalia are only matters of mental representation, not of physical presence. Therefore, as the narrative unfolds, it may neutralize the reader's awareness that what he sees is puppets, especially if the narrator uses stylistic devices which keep emphasizing their human qualities.

The "play-within-a-play" technique disposes plays in concentric circles so that the movement outward increases the sense of reality, whereas the movement inward increases the sense of illusion. In other words, the "inner" play will psychologically seem more of a play-reality than the "outer" from the vantage of the "outer," and *vice versa*. In "The Fifth Wanderer" the puppet-player is a real human being compared with Pickelhering, the hero of the "inner" play-reality. However, as soon as the "fifth wanderer" appears, the puppet-player turns into a puppet engaged in play-reality in relation to the "fifth wanderer," the one of empirical reality. Commenting on this technique of play within a play, Robert J. Nelson observes:

According to such a view of *The Tempest,* Prospero's pageant for the betrothed Ferdinand and Miranda becomes a play within a play. Now, the reflective spectator will regard this triple convolution — indeed, this logically endless series of convolutions — as implicit in the very use of the technique of the play within a play. The unwary, looking upon Bottom's "Pyramus and Thisbe" or Hamlet's "The Murder of Gonzago," cannot believe that those onstage spectators who look at these plays are unreal also, only player kings and player queens.[14] But the more reflective will sense with Fiedler the implications of the double convolution: if the players are but looking at a play, what are we doing but looking at a play, and is there some still more ultimate audience looking upon us and itself being looked upon, *ad infinitum?* The world-stage concept is the very essence of the play-within-a-play idea.[15]

It would be, of course, preposterous to discuss this story on the same footing as Shakespeare's plays. However, it is typical for this and other stories in *Masters and Apprentices* that a flimsy narrative stuffed with extravagance contains some excellent motives and principles of structure. The "play-within-a-play" pattern is a case in point. This over-all design redeems it to some extent. The emotion which this device arouses is similar to the emotion elicited by Romantic irony.

Romantic irony is felt on two levels. First, Kaverin's world of bustling activity and adventures shrinks catastrophically into a paltry contraption of wood, painted paper, and glue. As soon as the "fifth wanderer" steps in, one becomes aware of the cardboard illusion we have been "tricked" into accepting. In a work of Romantic irony the lofty illusion dissolves into vulgar farce. The substitution frustrates one's expectation. This frustrated expectation is weak in Kaverin's story because of the story's flimsiness. In a sense "The Fifth Wanderer" is a persiflage of Romantic irony itself. All four wanderers, on different levels of vulgarity, enact Faust's feat of reaching out for the ultimate (even if it is a donkey's gold excrement bestrewn with precious stones). The author endows with the noblest human virtues creatures which by definition must forever remain gentle caricatures of mankind, the puppets. Does the author mean that the Faustian dream ought to be relegated to the never-never land of the little wooden comedians, or that it should be entrusted to the holy frenzy of the Don Quixote that rescues the fair Melisanda?

All in all, *Masters and Apprentices* is a strange book. A string of spoofs, a take-off on E.T.A. Hoffmann written more against than in behalf of German Romanticism — a parody of uneven taste and quality. But the collection does occasionally exhibit a surprisingly mature treatment of literary construction and representation. We can already see some of the recurrent features of Kaverin's later prose.

Most obvious is Kaverin's predilection for "plot engineering." Already in *Masters and Apprentices* we can observe Kaverin's skill in controlling the representation of the action: bringing several lines of action to a stimulatingly significant confrontation; marshalling characters with a view to giving a most unusual twist to the action; characters popping up and vanishing at the most tantalizing moments; deliberately planting obstacles in the way of a developing action in order to bring a promising development to a flimsy end; letting two lines of action run parallel so that they both emphasize each other's drama and render each other absurd; using dreams to twist the action one way or another; scrambling toward an incongruous end; embroiling time sequences for the sake of suspense and mystery. To be sure these tricks seldom bring about anything beyond farcical action. But they point to the youthful Kaverin's interest in the dynamic design of the action. Later the tricks which proliferate in *Masters and Apprentices* almost for their own sake will evolve into thoughtful devices.

These devices will enable Kaverin's sober and somewhat Romantic narrative to represent living people and the complexities of the world. This narrative will then represent conflicts of will-power and mind locked in a dramatic action marked by suspenseful reversals.

In *Masters and Apprentices* Kaverin takes the mischievous pleasure of dumping together his goblins, puppets, automata, and people in the puppets' image into a merry free-for-all of cardboard and tinsel where the plausible scarcely differs from the implausible. This juvenile exoticism developed into the mature Kaverin's tendency to view life from novel and inventive angles. This enables him to discover new facets of man's personality and to achieve sharpness of representation.

Masters and Apprentices is extremely "literary" in the sense that it is imitative of and committed to literary traditions. The collection betrays Kaverin's lack of experience and maturity. But in his maturity this commitment to literariness helped safeguard his literary culture from non-literature.

CHAPTER TWO

PLOT AND CONTEST

1

The leading Russian literary critics of the twenties[1] agreed that the Russian narrative prose of their time was going through a serious crisis. What shape should a valid Russian prose take at that point? It would be meaningless to duplicate the complex form of L.N. Tolstoy. To write short stories with a psychological point would have been an unoriginal imitation of A. Chekhov's prose.

A measure of success was achieved in narrative prose by the use of the technique of *skaz*. By means of this technique the writer may have aimed to attain the effect of orality in literary narrative. Conventional literary narrative probably loses this effect of orality in the long run. It becomes, as the very word "literature" intimates, a written communication, removed from the presumed original epic situation. The latter represents a community made up of listeners and the live narrator with his oral speech which characterizes him and links them, the narrator and his listeners, together, apropos of an experience or an event to tell. The underlying purpose of *skaz* is probably to re-create such an original epic situation, and thus to revitalize literature as a live oral communication. The reader should not only understand words but also feel, hear and see them, he should sense their emotional charge. Thus literature again creates a new vision — and a new hearing — of the world. It seems that this technique of *skaz* conveys a somewhat myopic vision. It is usually a vision as manifested in the speech of a narrator limited in his awareness of things. The splendid *skaz* of M. Zoshchenko is a case in point. A magnificently crooked vision asserts itself at the expense of its sweep and semantic capacity. A *War and Peace* would hardly be possible in *skaz*. It occurs to me in this connection that Solzhenitsyn has tried this imposible task. He conveys an all-embracing vision of things by means of *skaz,* or by means of a phraseology much akin to *skaz*. This is where Solzhenitsyn's literary originality lies.

Another attempt of revitalizing Russian prose happened to be the writing of "ornamental prose." This somewhat vague term refers to different stylistic phenomena. I would like to point out only A. Belyj's prose. This prose may have been an attempt to widen the scope of linguistic communication. That is, simultaneously to convey the reality, the mental processes pertaining to the reality conveyed, and the peculiarities of the speech conveying both the reality and the mental processes. If so, it was an attempt of conjuring up a kind of total communication. I believe that this is even a more desperate venture than to narrate *War and Peace* in *skaz*.

In the early twenties, a few critics and writers pinned their hopes of the renewal of Russian prose on the development of what Russian criticism calls *sjuzhetnaja proza,* i.e., plot-oriented prose.[2] In the context of the Russian literary criticism of the time and Russian literature, this concept has many literary implications. In Russian critical terminology, there are two concepts which describe narrative prose. One is the concept of "bytopisanie." It stands for the kind of narrative that more or less objectively portrays everyday life and customs. The other is the concept of "sjuzhetnaja proza." "Sjuzhet" as understood in Russian literary criticism basically corresponds to "plot," especially plot under its dynamic and extraordinary aspect. "Sjuzhetnaja proza" approximately means "plot-oriented prose."[3] "Bytopisanie" tends toward documentary writing. "Sjuzhetnaja proza" tends to be identified with fiction.

When discussing the nature of tragedy, Aristotle observed that what action *(praxis)* is to empirical life, plot *(mythos)* is to stage reality. Aristotle intended his definitions for a specific kind of tragedy. However, they may be used effectively in the description of narrative fiction. Action, broadly understood, both generates life and is life's indication. Action externalizes man's mental life. Through action man shows his rational personality. A succession of actions gives expression to man's good or ill fortune. Plot fulfills a similar function in relation to the subjects of artistic representation. Plot is that which imitates the action of empirical reality. Building a plot is synonymous with motivating the representation of a conflict. The author shows why and how the conflict has started, how it goes on, reaches its climax and how it comes to an end. Therefore, plot implies the presence of antagonists or foes at conflict against one another. For this conflictual development to take shape characters must enact their emotions and willpower. When these specific components of narrative structure and representation are at the center of the narrative, Russian literary criticism describes it as "sjuzhetnaja proza" or pattern-plot prose.

The specific genre of the pattern-plot prose of which the critics expected the renewal of Russian prose was the adventure novel. One of the most outspoken ideologists of the adventure novel was Lev Lunc. In his reminiscences of Gorky, K. Fedin gave a picturesque account of Lunc's ideas and feelings about this issue:

My coming to the Serapions was accompanied with a quarrel. [. . .] At the third meeting I gave vent to my settled protest against "play" in defense of "seriousness." Lev Lunc accepted the blow.
The encounter was severe. [. . .]
The argument was pursued thus.
Lunc said: Russian prose has ceased "to move," it "lies," in it nothing happens, nothing is going, in it they either reason or experience feelings, but do not act, do not perform deeds; it must die from an absence of circulation of the blood, of bedsores, of dropsy; it has become a simple reflection of ideologies, programs, a mirror of the journalism of publicists and has ceased existing as art; only plot can save it, plot — a mechanism that will stir it up, will force it to move, to perform volitional acts; the tradition of plot is in the West; we must bring this tradition from there and impregnate with it our recumbent prose, overcoming in ourselves the trivial fear,

inspired by literary uncles, of the novel of adventure, learning from the writer who possesses the secret of action, be it Sterne or Dumas, Stevenson or Conan Doyle; [. . .] [4]

In the Russian literary awareness the genre of the adventure novel was connected with the names of Western writers. For example, in his "Manifesto" Lunc mentions, among other names, those of A. Dumas father and Robert L. Stevenson: "[. . .] Stevenson, an author of novels about robbers, is a great writer; [. . .] Dumas is classic like Dostoyevsky."[5] Shklovskij states that "[. . .] Kaverin is rather interested in Stevenson, Sterne and Conan Doyle."[6] K. Paustovskij too refers to his boyhood *Treasure Island* syndrome.[7] In his autobiography, A. Grin says that T. Mayne Reid, G. Aimard, Jules Verne, L. Jacolliot were his "indispensable vital reading."[8] Actually, some of these authors of adventure novels, such as L. Jacolliot or T. Mayne Reid, may have found, at the turn of the century, a more responsive audience in Russia than in their native environment. For example, L. Jacolliot's name does not even appear in *The Oxford Companion to French Literature* (1959 edition), whereas *Kratkaja Literaturnaja Ènciklopedija* (1962-72) devotes 34 lines and bibliography[9] to this forgotten French writer of adventure novels. Likewise, T. Mayne Reid may have attained a greater popularity with the Russian reading public than with the Anglo-Saxon. Examples could be multiplied to greater length. In 1925 Gorky complained that the exotic plots of Western writers such as Jack London, Conrad, O. Henry found a greater favor with the Russian reading public than the native writings on contemporary topics.[10] N. Aseev worried about the Russian literary market being "colonized" by the translated western literature of suspense and adventure.[11] A. Slonimskij chimed in by acknowledging that the pattern-plot quality and the sense of suspense of the contemporary Russian literature had declined to the point of being rejected by the Russian reading public. And the public was right, he conceded.[12] Lending libraries and railroad newsstands bore an emphatic testimony to the same effect.[13] By the mid-twenties, the topical and ideologically desirable literature concocted by the proletarian writers came to be sold by the pound.[14] All these facts corroborate the hypothesis that in Russian literature the adventure novel as a literary genre has spontaneously been taken for a foreign literary product.

The modern adventure novel seems to have appeared in connection with the colonial expansion that European nations had undertaken overseas. This has determined its intensely exotic setting: Kipling's India; Haggard's Africa; Ch. Kingsley's South America; the tropical islands with their bright colors as they appear in J. Conrad's novels; Jack London's rigorous reaches of Alaska and northern seas. Such are some of the typical far-flung settings of the novel of adventure. It is a world of external actions, often violent and impetuous, and external pursuits. In this world energetic characters set off in quest of treasures and good fortune. And since in their quest energetic characters unavoidably enter into the land of the unknown, they encounter unexpected situations and dangers with which they must cope in order to pursue their quest. Therefore they travel much, scouring all over continents and seas. This activity goes on in the objective, empirical world. The emphasis on external achievement directs the protagonist's mind almost exclusively to overcoming external obstacles and attaining external aims. For this reason it precludes such mental activities as self-reflection and introspection. At most, the latter go only as far as external action motivates. Therefore, nothing is probably as alien to the representation of the novel of adventure as the irresolute self-reflecting intellectual of the Russian psychological novel. As a rule, no metaphysical doubts assail the minds of the protagonists. On the contrary, the main virtues in this world of the adventure novel consist in individual daring, enterprise and a certain carefree lightheartedness coupled with a cool lookout for danger. To great extent, R.L. Stevenson's comment on romance holds true here: the interest of the adventure novel bears on "[. . .] the problems of the body and of the practical intelligence, in clean, open-air adventure [. . .] [14a]

In Russian literature the Caucasus supplied the "colonial romanticism" similar in its function to India in the works of R. Kipling, or to the American frontier in those of J.F. Cooper. Action, violence, abduction, exotic passions may look kindred in both *A Hero of Our Time* and *The Last of The Mohicans.* What sets these two works significantly apart is the protagonists' (and the authors') attitudes toward external action. For Pechorin, external action does not matter as such, it does not have its own essential validity. It serves only as an "ad hoc" resource whose sole purpose is to feed Pechorin's introspection of the moment. If so, the action of *A Hero of Our Time* is not of the kind proper to the adventure novel, whereas that of *The Last of The Mohicans* may be so. These energetic characters in quest of good fortune and treasure encounter many people of every description, often bizarre and enigmatic, which generates a sense of mystery. When they encounter adversaries, they come to grips with them; they try to defeat them by either force or stratagem. This struggle develops reversals — sudden changes of situation. Typically, the protagonist faces a challenging situation and ends in a deadly impasse. Only an extraordinary coincidence or a daredevil rescue reverses the plight and saves him from doom. Which means that a tight plot dominates the narrative. Its reversals create a sense of suspense. What makes this kind of literature attractive is its sense of play: in it, men are playing an absorbing game, both rewarding and deadly.

Thus defined, the adventure novel is a prose work with self-contained narrative interest. It does not purport more than it says, e.g., as in *Treasure Island*. It is "serious," as opposed to satirical bias. Its actions are oriented toward explainable empirical reality. If irrationality exists at all, it is still treated as an object and part of man's rational action, e.g., the enigmatic Ayesha in H.R. Haggard's novel *She* (1887). External action prevails over internal; the describing of events matters more than probing into characters. This presupposes an articulate plot with a special emphasis on reversals. The latter generate the effect of energetic and violent incidents. The characters draw their validity from both the validity of the plot and the novel's dimension of psychological plausibility. However, they mostly do not grow beyond the framework of their narrated adventure. In terms of this definition, the adventure novel belongs to the 18th and 19th century literature, especially the Anglo-Saxon.

2

In the previous chapter I already referred to Kaverin's inclination to "toy" with the plot. The author takes pleasure in giving unexpected twists to the patterns of the conflict; he playfully cancels out one point of view with another; he intentionally blurs the representation to the point of dislocating empirical reality; he does not allow one particular incident or situation to stay long at the center of the narrative. In experimenting so, Kaverin betrayed his heightened awareness of the plot and its manipulation. This early predilection for the manipulation of the plots of his stories earned him the reputation of a plot-oriented writer (*sjuzhetnyj pisatel'*), and for which he was often censured by Soviet critics.[15] Now, the adventure novel was felt to be a particularly emphatic form of the pattern-plot prose. Therefore, Kaverin's early inclination brought him, as it were, naturally to writing works with underlying patterns of the adventure novel. In addition to this motivating literary temperament, this trend toward the adventure novel may also have been Kaverin's own response to the literary debates of the time. In his early biographical note Kaverin declared that he would try to put into effect the literary principles advocated by Lunc.[16] That meant, in the first place, to create the Russian adventure novel. Indeed, Kaverin's works of the twenties are brimful of action, sense of reversal, suspense and mystery, i.e., of those elements which make up the adventure novel.

We may speak of Kaverin's "binary" plot, i.e., the kind of plot in which the two adversaries confront each other as if in a duel over a certain period of time, and try to defeat each other. This is the prevailing mode of Kaverin's plots. What varies is the level or the nature of the conflict.

At the least substantial level, the conflict unfolds in the flimsily exotic setting of far-away countries, international intelligence agents and their derrings-do, gangsters, attempts of spectacular robberies and other deeds of this nature. A good deal of the works Kaverin wrote in the twenties belong to this category: "Kutumskie chasovshchiki" (The clockmakers of Kutum, 1924); "Bochka" (The cask, 1924); *Konec xazy* (The end of the gang, 1925); *Bol'shaja igra* (The great game, 1925); "Drug Mikado" (The friend of the Mikado, 1927); "Goluboe solnce" (The sky-blue sun, 1927); "Segodnja utrom" (This morning, 1927).

"The Clockmakers of Kutum" is an amusing picaresque tale. In it, the author builds a plot about a crook who builds a plot to hoodwink provincial clockmakers. The setting is a provincial Ukrainian town during the NEP. A crook, under the assumed identity of a foreign watch-company representative, tries to dupe the local clockmakers into buying and paying in advance for nonexistent clocks. He updates Chichikov's trick: the "dead souls" at least existed. The crook exhibits the ways of an important metropolitan businessman and worms his way into the family of the local moneyman and, what is even more important, into the heart of the moneyman's overripe sister. At the height of his success, his schemes go awry, owing to most untimely coincidences and indiscretions. Unmasked, the former foreign watch-company representative decamps hastily. The author narrates the whole rogue's adventure with his tongue in his cheek. How much importance the author attaches to the engineering of the plot can be seen from a detail toward the end of the story. A character within the story condemns the crook in these words: "[. . .] there are different frauds, but this one is simply poorly thought out (ploxo pridumano)."[17] The crook is condemned not so much for the wrongdoing as such as he is for the poor execution of his swindle. The crook is condemned on aesthetic grounds. Himself a professional literary plot-builder, the author has the crook put to shame for poor "craftsmanship" above any other reason.

To some of these works, Kaverin tried to give a "foreign" mark. In "The Cask" and *The Great Game* Kaverin imitated the Anglo-Saxon literature of adventure, fantasy and romance. "The Cask" is a strange combination of mystery tale and science fiction, perhaps rather pseudo-science fiction. The author sets its action in London, remotely reminiscent of the London of R.L. Stevenson's *The Dynamiter*. He neutralizes the depth of representation for the sake of narrative stylization. The adventure of "The Cask" revolves around a considerable fortune bequeathed by Reginald Stejfors,[18] a mathematician of note. In his will Reginald set down a bizarre stipulation: twenty-four hours after his death all newspapers were to announce that a vast amount of money and precious stones had been buried in a place which Reginald had taken the trouble to indicate exactly. A gang of felons, among whom is Reginald's brother, stole the will before its newspaper announcement. They immediately set off for the location in order to take possession of the treasure. However, the first to read Reginald's will was his father, also a famous mathematician. Along with the bequest, he took notice of a diagram and its accompanying mathematical computation. From the latter the old mathematician understood the real significance of his son's bequest. The diagram and the mathematical formula set down on the reverse of the will announced a fantastic discovery: the city of London and its adjacent districts lie on the inner side of an immense wine cask which rolls along on some kind of hard surface. The location of the treasure, at the bottom of a pit, is the place where people can reach the very wall of the very cask inside of which the city of London is situated. The felons, victims of greed, and the mathematician, moved by scientific curiosity, met at that spot. They were even able to smell the odor of wine, as if in a wine celler . . . With a dynamite charge, the old mathematician blew up an opening in the wall of the cask and then the whole group crawled out into the outer world through the hole bristling, on its edges, with splintered wood and rusty wires. Neither greed, nor scientific curiosity was rewarded, however. The cask had rolled over them and killed them before they had time to escape into the extra-cask world.

In this tale, similarly to all others of this description, the author combines those motives, characters and situations that make up the novel of adventure. The early hint at some fantastic scientific discovery creates an atmosphere of mystery and suspense, whereas the presence of ruffians who will stop at no wrong-doing to take hold of the treasure, promises energetic actions, reversals and struggle. No wonder that these two lines of action originate from a fairly conventional source: two brothers, of whom one, the mathematician, makes the discovery, the other, the thief, initiates the treasure hunt. It is somewhat less conventional that their common father should eventually unite the scientific venture and the wrongdoer's search for the treasure. Partially, the incidents of the narrative occur in a dive, taverns and streets of London astir with motley human fauna, volatile and quick to go on rampage. This last motive obviously provides an exotic "foreign" setting, so desirable for the novel of adventure.

All this comes to rather a grotesque resolution. The initial prospect of some postulated scientific breakthrough affecting the life of mankind foreshortens itself into a tongue-in-cheek fantasy devoid of the earnestness of true science fiction. The youthful author seems to experience a peculiar fascination for wine casks, as if they offered some special source of inspiration. The original text of the tale[19] is graced by the diagram of an excellent wine cask gently reposing on the x-axis of a coordinate system and supported by lengthy mathematical symbols. Later, in *Artist Unknown*, the narrator whom we may legitimately identify with the author, acknowledges:

As a youth who had read his fill of Edgar Poe and who had taken every cask for the Cask of Amontillado, I once diligently studied the cheerless dives of Leningrad.[20]

An additional touch of humor coloring the resolution of the tale can be detected in the fact that the felons' trouble has gone for nothing. There has not been any treasure. Thus the tale has deviated from the traditional pattern of romance in which the villainous brother tries to despoil his unselfish sibling of the material benefit deriving from the latter's scientific discovery.

The Great Game represents another bizarre mixture of crime-detection tale, colonial romanticism from R. Kipling and the fantastic fiction of *The Queen of Spades*. It appears quite obvious that Kaverin borrowed the prime motivation of his tale, as well as its title, from Kipling's novel *Kim*. One of the epigraphs, taken from the text of Kipling's novel, clearly testifies to this indebtedness. In the language of the characters of Kipling's novel, the "Great Game" was the game of intelligence and counter-intelligence in which different powers joined throughout the British India. This, then, is the game at whose representation Kaverin dabbles in his tale, only shifting the setting from India to Ethiopia and Russia and turning the episodic Anglo-Russian duel of *Kim* into the leading motive of his *The Great Game*.

For a present-day reader, *The Great Game*, as a spy story, will appear singularly unsophisticated. In this kind of literature a present-day reader relishes an imaginatively thought-out scheme whose articulations click flawlessly; a coordination of actions demanding sleight and breathtaking nerve, an ingenious network of communication, elegance of performance of the scheme, a sudden threat of failure overcome by the hero's ultimate inventiveness and sangfroid. Neither does Kaverin's work generate the tingling suspense and the lightning action of counter-intelligence novels such as *Message from Malaga* or any other by Helen MacInnes. All these prerequisites of the genre are mostly missing in Kaverin's tale. Nor does the spy demonstrate any faculty of keen observation to uncover clues unnoticed by a simple mortal. He is not endowed with the ability of meticulous deductive thinking which constitutes the main literary asset of E.A. Poe's Dupin or A.C. Doyle's Sherlock

Holmes, not to mention the "little gray cells" of Hercule Poirot . . .

As an imitation of R. Kipling's *Kim, The Great Game* is rather pale. However, the tale has a curious asset, again pertaining to its overall design. In *Kim,* the dynamics of the plot resides in the somewhat incongruous contradiction between Kim's counter-intelligence schooling (an activity as attached to and engaged in sansara as anything possibly can be) and his devotion to his lama, the very embodiment of nirvana.

The dialectics in *The Great Game* appears more rewarding artistically, in spite of the author falling short of a full-bodied representation. While most likely borrowing the title of his story from Kipling's novel, Kaverin adds to its rather restricted and specific meaning another dimension. Kaverin's tale is about the antagonism of two men, a British intelligence agent and his Russian counterpart Panaev. Their activity is, in the last analysis, motivated by their thirst to dominate. Wood, the British agent, betrays his thirst in his mad project of blessing mankind with the "Regensdorf jail system." Panaev seems to receive a similar gratification from pipe-dreaming. He is a strange figure. Kaverin depicts him rather sparingly, as if reluctantly. The potency of this character may lie precisely in this. Panaev seems sluggish, reluctant to act and even to live conventionally. He is rather a contemplative kind of man, a somewhat enigmatic figure blurred amidst the clouds of opium smoke. His actions appear all the more irrevocable for this reluctance. It is also somewhat unusual that this non-conformist intelligence agent should be a professional philologist and a university professor. These features remind one of the Russian journalist, critic, editor and orientalist Osip Senkovskij (1800-1858). It would not be surprising if Kaverin, who made a study of Senkovskij in the mid-twenties (1926), used this controversial 19th-century character as a prototype for his Panaev.

The duel between the two antagonists unfolds on two levels. On the "lower" level, the two agents, engaged in a cloak-and-dagger game, dispute a choice prize of international imperialism (nothing less than the testament of the Emperor of Ethiopia). In this game, Wood, a supremely resourceful prestidigitator, outwits the somewhat sluggish Panaev. Although this contest takes up the most part of the story, it is somewhat preparatory to another game which irresistibly draws Wood and Panaev together and pits the two against each other, as it were, on a "cosmic" level. On this higher, "cosmic," level, they play for quite different stakes. At this point, the author introduces the motive of gambling.

The gambling motive appears in a number of Kaverin's early works. His first story, "The Eleventh Axiom," deals with a student who gambles away everything at cards. The motive also appears in "Shields (and Candles)," "The Friend of the Mikado," "This Morning," and "Vorob'inaja noch'" (Short summer night).[21]

"The Friend of the Mikado" supposedly describes the lore of the Samurais, their loyalty to the Emperor unto death, and how European environment can affect it. Kato Sadao, an old friend of the Mikado, has just received the news of the Emperor's demise. For two decades he has been a diplomatic representative of Japan in a Western capital. And now, bound by the ancient Samurai code of honor, he has to follow his Emperor. His lengthy exposure to Western ways has not gone without impunity: it has eroded his Samurai integrity. He is now unable and unwilling to disembowel himself just because an Emperor has died. He confides his bewilderment to his secretary Matamura, who performs the part of an "Eminence Grise" toward Kato. Matamura urges Kato in no ambiguous terms to discharge his Samurai's duty, and even hints that he would be willing to help, for the sake of the deceased Emperor's honor. Nonetheless, Kato surrenders all his duties and privileges to Matamura, and leaves the residence as a private person about to get lost in the anonymous crowd of the Western capital. At that point, Kato betrays the traditional code of honor of the Samurai; he betrays the deceased Emperor; he betrays Japan and even Matamura. As for the latter, he is the one who, at that point, upholds the honor of Japan. He is the only one that can now avenge the vile insult by killing Kato. He pulls out a revolver from his pocket; the back of departing Kato offers an easy target. Still, something worries Matamura. He has not slept several nights and some important happening haunts his memory; in vain does he try to call it to mind. At this point, when Matamura's finger comes to fondle the trigger ready to avenge Japan's honor and to punish the traitor, Matamura remembers that last night he sold off all Japanese documents and papers and gambled away everything. He too faces a certain death, unless he joins Kato in a common flight.

Kaverin puts this gambling motive at the heart of his story "This Morning." Skal'kovskij shoots his wife in what seems to be a drama of jealousy. He then betakes himself to a gambling-house and there he loses all his money. He deplores his bad luck in both love and cards, and to make matters worse, a woman mistakes him for a thief and raises an alarm. Guilty of quite another misdeed, Skal'kovskij dashes out of the gambling-house, and makes off as fast as his legs can carry him. An ambulance comes across his way. He manages to jump aboard. Inside, he discovers a mortally wounded man. It turns out that a most extraordinary bond connects him to the latter. Skal'kovskij infers from the wounded man's words that the latter has probably been his wife's lover whom he shot accidentally while aiming at his own wife, this very morning. The wounded man thinks that he already met Skal'kovskij before, probably in school, and that he even owed him some money, which he makes it a point to return at once and Skal'kovskij finds it imposible to refuse under the circumstances. A little later, we find Skal'kovskij again in the gambling-house, betting the few rubles received from the man he shot. This time, gambler's luck singles him out. At each game he stakes all he has, and each time the right card unavoidably comes to him, until Skal'kovskij wins all that there is to win. Surrounded with awed attention, he walks out with a bundle of bills. Presently, he returns and pours out a bizarre public confession: he mortally wounded a man this morning; he used the latter's money to amass his astounding winnings a short while ago at cards; by now, the wounded man must be dead; Skal'kovskij has just despatched all the money won to the latter's old mother whose support the dead man was; what a good fortune, anyway, that he, Skal'kovskij, missed his wife at whom he had aimed. A police-officer charitably gives him a glass of water before arresting him for murder.

In all these stories, the gambling motive performs a decisive function in the development of the plot. It may testify to the lingering impact of German Romanticism and the latter's Russian parallel manifestations, such as Pushkin's *The*

Queen of Spades. One of the Romantic motives is that of the unusual, superior, personality, as it manifests itself at grips with the games of chance. In the above-mentioned stories this Romantic motive may have preserved its afterglow. To be sure, none of the characters in these stories stands out as a significant figure of literary representation. The reader would rather remember them as concisely sketched figures caught in a stream of crisply changing situations. Speaking schematically, the characters draw their validity from the organization of the plot, as it often occurs in Kaverin's works. But in their minor way, they convey that which fascinated E.T.A. Hoffmann's Menars (*Spielerglück,* 1819), Pushkin's German, or Dostoyevsky's Alexej, the gambler (*The Gambler*), and wrecked their lives. At the green table, a gambler must experience most complex emotions. He must experience the thrill of working out a shortcut toward riches and pleasures on one turn of the card. This is a sufficiently attractive perspective for Matamura to sell off Japanese diplomatic documents, thereby sealing his own fate. For a compulsive gambler, such as Skal'kovskij, gambling is a haven where he can forget his other worries, a pleasure free of greed, of winning for winning's sake. Or it is a sort of solemn ritual, as in "Shields (and Candles)," where it leads to a murder. And the higher the stakes, the greater the awareness of fate.

The reader can feel this awareness of fate best in *The Great Game.* Wood and Panaev are gamblers in the most selective sense. In this selective sense, the "great game" means that either of them enters a kind of magic sphere in which by gambling for high stakes either usurps and wields some essential prerogatives of Fate: from amidst absolute contingency either omnipotently designates one irrevocable option that determines the whole subsequent course of life. At the fall of the card either dominates Fate, or even identifies himself with omnipotent Fate. This euphoria of the imminent Fate-designated win is undoubtedly the strongest emotion of them all, stronger even than "the seduction of philandering," as Pushkin chastely observes in *The Queen of Spades.* Thus, at their ultimate encounter over the liturgical green cloth and pack of cards, Wood and Panaev meet to decide who will dominate Fate, Fate in its purest, "mathematical" expression abstracted from the workaday toil and trouble of practical life. It is like an encounter on a battlefield. The author signals this by symbolically covering the green cloth of the gambling table with hostile troops at war against one another. One of the two men must needs eliminate the other, since two different men cannot dominate Fate at the same time. To outwit Panaev, Wood dips into his bag of proven tricks, but they all fail against something superior. Wood does not understand that this is no longer a game of petty deception or sleight of hand. There is just no outwitting Fate and in Panaev Wood meets his Fate and Fate steamrollers Wood to death together with his bag of tricks and all.

In the works subsequent to the enumerated, the gambling motive not only does not stand at the center of the plot, but does not even appear. It may well signify that by 1927 Kaverin gave up this powerful Romantic motivation.

I would like to mention still another story which, like "The Friend of the Mikado," and perhaps not quite coincidentally, bears on the ultimate testing of loyalty. "The Sky-Blue Sun" narrates an episode in the life of a colonel of the Chinese

National Army. Confined to his bed by severe illness, he has an interview with his ward, now a grown-up son of another famous revolutionary leader. The ward does not compare favorably with his heroic father executed by the enemy. He shows no interest in the fate of his country. The colonel feels desperate at the sight of his good-for-nothing ward. He devises one last test to probe his ward's moral fiber. He falsely confesses to having been a British spy for a decade. However, his ward responds with complete unconcern to this confession of treason, and after a while politely withdraws. Such an utter lack of civic fervor drives the colonel to despair. There is no one to hand down to the fruits and the challenges of a lifetime of struggle and self-denial, his own as well as that of his comrades-in-arms. The revolution has failed if this young apathetic opium smoker is its successor. The colonel lapses into sleep. When he wakes up, he sees his ward's face bent over him, asking whether his confession is true. The colonel reaffirms it. The ward swiftly pulls out a knife from underneath his coat-breast and swings the razor-edged blade down to plunge it into the colonel's chest. The colonel escapes death by only a hairbreadth, flinging himself out of his bed. But he is overjoyed, since his ward has passed his test. What the colonel took for unconcern in his ward had turned out to be self-control. The ward ran out to buy a knife with his last money in order to kill the one whom he has believed to be a traitor to the Chinese revolution.

Foreign narrative material enframed in a tale of adventure must have been believed to generate the greatest sense of the exotic. However, during the same period Kaverin also resorted to Rusian material. In a few of his works the author conjures up the people and the events of contemporary Russia. I would like to refer to two of them: *Konec xazy* (The end of the gang, 1925) and *Devjat' desjatyx sud'by* (The nine tenths of fate, 1925). In these works, too, we can detect an underlying concern for the exotic, the out-of-the-ordinary and romance. The first tale narrates the misdoings and the destruction of a gang of Petrograd robbers.

In the twenties, the "underworld motive" caught the eye of a few notable writers willing to deal with this motive in their prose. One immediately thinks of I. Babel's *Tales of Odessa* (1923-24) and L. Leonov's *The Thief* (1927). Kaverin's tale does not compare to the best advantage with those works. Babel says less and conveys more. Kaverin's ways in his tale work in reverse. Neither is the tale a match to Leonov's monumental undertaking, even if a monumental blunder. In his autobiographical notes, Kaverin gives a few details describing how this work came about:

[. . .] The tale *The End of the Gang* [literally: end of a robbers' den] was the first, for the time being still very timid, withdrawal from this circle of narrowly literary representation; a tale in which I attemped to depict the bandits and robbers of the NEP years, the "thieves' world" [*blatnoj mir*] of Leningrad. Collecting material for *The End of a Gang,* I read the criminal chronicle, went to court sessions, and, occasionally, I spent evenings in low-class hangouts, of which at that time there was still quite a number. I was preparing for the work just as my older friends would do, who repeatedly and justly reproached me for not knowing life, for my striving to shelter myself from it behind the walls of a student's room, piled up with books on the history of literature. And nonetheless, almost all that I had succeeded in learning about robbers and bandits had remained in my notebook, whereas the tale was written by dint of "ready-made patterns" and youthful imagination. Only one of its aspects slightly opened the peculiarity of the "thieves' world" – the language of the robbers, the thieves' cant in which I took interest as a linguist.

The tale had success – a *succès de scandale,* though. One of the reviews was entitled: "[A review] on how Gosizdat [State Publishing Office] has printed a handbook on hoodlumism."[22]

Two "ready-made patterns" combine to animate the plot: robbers' adventures and robbers' romance, The former provides the apparent prime motivation. Shmerl the Turkish Drum, as he himself proudly acknowledges, is an "organizer." His concern for modern efficient business management is surely funny under the circumstances. However, his amusing malapropisms conceal the idea dear to the author: just as in actions of life, the plot of literary representation should be a well-thought-up and coherent play. The Turkish Drum is the "intellectual," the one-man "brain trust" who thinks up the whole "plot" and organizes its execution. He has not planned well and therefore ultimately loses his game. Or perhaps he has done so well enough, only his intellectual scheme fell through when it ran against the emotional reefs that intellect by its very nature cannot register. A certain "play-reality" dissolves when exposed to "life-reality." The latter is ushered in by the second motive: that of the passion of two men for one woman. It provides the underlying dramatic substance and actually brings about the ultimate reversal.

"Ready-made patterns" or motives thread their way through the whole story. They are all the traditional motives of the novel of adventure and romance, such as abduction and kidnapping; escape from prison (for woman's sake); mistaken identities; a duel (for women's sake); the help of a compassionate prostitute. If they do not appear too tired, it is because Kaverin treats them in an ironic key, in the manner of parody. The villain boils with unreciprocated passion for the girl and she is abducted but it all occurs somewhat unromantically: a girl stenographer is hunting for a job and walks straight into the trap; the villain has her taken to his "castle", a dilapidated structure as condemned as its inmates. The author handles the jailbreak motive also with tongue in cheek: Travin escapes from prison also quite unroman- tically via the latrine and on his way to freedom has only to take an easy swim across a peaceful rivulet in which children dabble all day long and women rinse their laundry – surely an idyllic way for the Soviet government to treat its prisoners.

In the literature of adventure the motive of mistaken identity holds an important place. In this connection, I can hardly think of a happier example than Jules Verne's enchanting, even if somewhat lengthy, adventure novel *The Children of Captain Grant* (1868). In it, mistaken identifications that Paganel makes form the dramatic backbone of the whole quest, supply the novel's suspense and comic verve. And Paganel's ultimate misidentification, so sorely vexacious for the French geographer, contributes to the triumphant success of the whole enterprise. Things take quite a different, reverse, turn in Kaverin's tale. The gang kidnaps the wrong Pineta and thereby dooms its "affair on a large scale" (i.e., cracking the safe of the State Bank) to certain failure. Pjatak murders the wrong girl and thereby ruins the whole romance of the thieves' loves, jealousies, and retributions of passion. Thus the motive carries some overtones of parody: everything develops *as if* it were the "real thing" (skillfully engineered burglary; thieves' drama of jealousy), but it all turns out to be only a semblance of the real thing. The tale imparts to the action an illusory nature. The whole plot is a colossal mistake all along. What may contribute to this illusiveness is the fact that the woman primarily responsible for the whole mess barely appears in the tale, and when she does eventually, she is dead. And what is one to think about the duel between the two bums? The ancient connoisseurs of this lofty art of squaring accounts would surely not recognize its plebeian caricature in which more verbal abuse is exchanged than bullets and the victorious duelist robs his killed opponent. And finally, the help of the charitable prostitute does not help anything, it only muddles things to the ultimate disaster. The irony of the situation is that she wants to help save others at the risk of her own doom. But her help actually dooms others and probably saves her. This recurrent lapse into parody deprives the characters of their apparent sting. The author may have intended Shmerl the Turkish Drum and his coadjutors to be dangerous criminals very much wanted by the police. But, somehow, the reader does not feel this danger in his bones . . .

Unlike in other aforementioned works of this period, in *The Nine Tenths of Fate* Kaverin turns away from experimental plots, foreign exoticism, fantastic motives, or even the unconventional Russian material such as that of *The End of the Gang*. This time, the most vital and dramatic events of the epoch form the very framework of the novel: the capture of the Winter Palace, the seat of the Russian Provisional Government in Petrograd, by the Red guards on October 26, 1917, which laid the foundation of the Soviet State; the subsequent armed actions between the Bolshevik troops and the counter-revolutionary forces for the control of the region adjoining Petrograd; and the victory of the Bolshevik troops over counter-revolutionary forces in those early days of the Civil War.

This most up-to-date narrative material comes in conjunction with the most involved plot development. The main line of the plot, involving Shaxov and Galja, offers a string of intriguing encounters, suspense-provoking hints, thrilling recognitions, tense confrontations, bitter disappointments, unhoped-for good fortune, and reversals, both catastrophic and providential. The reader would certainly not deny to this kind of development a great wealth of spectacular actions bordering on melodrama.

The dramatic developments actually narrated in the novel cover only a few days in the life of Shaxov. They start early in the morning on October 25, 1917, when, frustrated, lovelorn and lonely, Shaxov arrives at Petrograd. They last for about two weeks, at the end of which Shaxov, regenerated, leaves Petrograd, at the head of his Red Guard outfit.

During this action-packed fortnight Shaxov solves his personal problems. They result from the combination of the motive of long repressed love emotion with the motive of unconfessed guilt, both placed in the exceptional setting of political revolution. Actually, only thanks to the latter can Shaxov solve his personal problems at all. It is Shaxov's love for Galja that brings him to Petrograd in the first place. After a long separation Shaxov comes all the way from Siberia to meet his love Galja. Instead of reunion, he nearly kills her, now his political enemy, in a gun fight with her. This melodramatic shooting confrontation between them stems from their dedication to opposed political camps. Shaxov spontaneously embraces the Bolshevik cause, whereas Galja goes to the melodramatic length of disguising herself as "ensign Miller" in her armed support of the Provisional Government. It is likely, however, that through this political militancy both of them (especially Galja) try to solve their love dilemma. Shaxov subconsciously hopes to regain her love in the way of heroism, whereas Galja directs her love frustration into the most provocative channel of political activism, hence her short-lived soldiering for the Provisional Government.

He saves Galja anyway, only to be rewarded with her alienation. His passion for her is even more exasperated by the appearance of Tarxanov, a handsome Guards officer, in whom Shaxov senses a rival for Galja's love. This game of love and politics develops a triangle in which Shaxov and Tarxanov hate each other as much for political reasons as for the reason of their conflicting love for Galja. The two men meet at Galja's house and signify to each other in no ambiguous terms that in the forthcoming armed conflict between the enemy camps they will wage a ruthless war against each other. They don't say it, but both understand, that it will also be a ruthless war for Galja.

In the first round, when Shaxov is taken prisoner by counter-revolutionary forces, Tarxanov, who confronts him as the winner, is going to have him executed. Only the timely rescue of the Red guards saves Shaxov from death. In the second round, the tables are turned. The Red troops capture Tarxanov and he is convicted of counter-revolutionary activity. Shaxov, however, cannot enjoy the triumph of a live confrontation with Tarxanov because the latter had chosen suicide to ease himself out of his humiliating impasse.

Thus, objective political and military events, well beyond the two rivals' control, have undone the love triangle (if, however, there has ever been any). When Galja learns about Shaxov's imminent execution, she undergoes a dramatic change of heart: she sets out immediately to the war zone, defying danger to save him. Again, objective political and military events make their paths cross, in full war action, she, a changed and loving woman, oblivious of her previous political sentiments, and this time, shooting from the same side of the barricade.

It would seem that at this point all obstacles in the way to their reunion in love have vanished. However, the logic of Shaxov's biography has interposed another, ultimate, obstacle which not only threatens their love fulfillment, but even exposes Shaxov's very life to a danger even more ominous than those that he has so far weathered. The danger in question is his ancient transgression, unexpiated, and therefore a source of ever-present sense of guilt in Shaxov.

In this regard the actual plot is a sort of denouement of or answer to the plight that Shaxov inflicted on himself by his unmanly behavior. This development, however, well predates the events of the actual plot of the novel and the author chooses to leave it outside the latter.

In solving the problem of Shaxov's life, the author follows the technique of mystery tales. All the complications and perplexing anxieties besetting the protagonist derive from a certain original situation that the author chooses to leave totally mysterious at the outset of the narrative. For this reason, Shaxov's background remains intriguingly enigmatic and he steps into the plot as an unknown quantity. As the plot develops the original mystery is gradually revealed. From the end of his very first day in Petrograd, Shaxov's obsession of the past wrong starts plaguing his mind. It does so with renewed pain after he suddenly meets one Glaveckij, the villainous witness of Shaxov's past infamy. Curiously enough, the plot of the novel has a sort of "looking backward" orientation. Insofar as Shaxov stands at the center, the up-to-date plot is geared toward his freeing himself from the burden of a past transgression. At the crucial points of the plot, this ever-present prehistory makes inroads into the plot in the form of flashbacks conveying the vision of the gallows, their trappings and a figure swinging at the end of the rope.

Above, I pointed out that the dynamics of this story derives from the concurrence of three motives: love, guilt and revolution. Shaxov is something of a guilt-ridden intellectual who in his heart harbors a great love for a woman. He believes that his guilt denies him the right ever to deserve or claim her love. Nonetheless, he sets out on the journey at whose end he hopes to reach her. It most likely is not political passion or class hatred that constitute the driving force behind Shaxov's behavior. It is rather his concern for universally clear conscience, passion for a woman, and taste for action. He states during the nocturnal political discussion in the train: "I am not a Bolshevik, [...] I am a person very much aloof from politics,"[23] although under the circumstances he supports the Bolsheviks. Therefore, when he takes such an unstinting and active part in the Bolsheviks' revolutionary operations, we may legitimately assume that this activity is for him first of all a chance to rehabilitate himself in his own eyes and thus to break down the moral wall that, he feels, separates him from Galja and other people. He must subconsciously feel that only heroic life, and, possibly, heroic death, will gain him the rehabilitation. Shaxov overcomes his obsession and feels released from his guilt after he fights gallantly in Bolshevik ranks, escapes death, becomes himself a trusted Bolshevik leader and, most of all, after he finds Galja and wins back her love.

It is quite in the spirit of Kaverin's dramatic sense of timing that the ultimate catastrophe should overwhelm the protagonist at the moment of his triumph. His sudden arrest dashes all Shaxov's hopes and achievements and leaves him again dishonored, a fugitive from revolutionary justice at last delivered to retribution. Here lies the most important point of the story. As the train is approaching Petrograd at night, Shaxov has an ugly dream. Lying on the floor with his arms wide outspread, Shaxov observes a rather short-statured man walk into his compartment and put his heavy-booted foot on Shaxov's chest so that its tip presses against Shaxov's chin. He distinctly notices the man's striped tee shirt. He requests him to withdraw his foot. The man complies and sits down on the bench. He suddenly expresses his commiseration for Shaxov's "glassy fate" and, producing some child's toy, he voices his willingness to arrange things. At close quarters, the child's toy turns out to be a huge revolver suffused with the lilac gleam of steel. The revolver suddenly remains in the air. At this point Shaxov wakes up. The dream is prophetic. It prefigures almost point for point the scene, toward the end of the novel, of Shaxov's arrest which is to pave the way to his trial and death: close to his face, almost point-blank, over a same striped tee shirt, a revolver, suddenly suspended in the air, and lighted up with lilac gleam of steel.

Kaverin's motives may be viewed in a context somewhat common with Tolstoyan "correspondences." The afore-mentioned dream spontaneously reminds one of the young Grinev's prophetic dream in *Captain's Daughter* of Pushkin, or of the premonitory accident at the beginning of *Anna Karenina.* They all are those irrational and subconscious "correspondences" that explain and foreshadow a fate and impart a certain symbolic value to the representation.

Not unlike in *Anna Karenina,* the opening scene in *The Nine Tenths of Fate* symbolically illuminates Shaxov's whole fate and its meaning. Shaxov wants to gain his rehabilitation without true expiation, i.e., without humbly submitting his transgression to the judgment of good people, no matter what their verdict may be. The prophetic meaning of his nightmare in the opening scene consists in portending that Shaxov's whole fate hinges on such a trial, that is, arrest and trial. For better or worse, only this alternative will restore the integrity of his fate. Even heroism in revolutionary combats proves too cheap a price to pay for the restoration. Nothing short of public penance would return him his honor, unless it sends him to the gallows.

This dialectic of transgression and expiation places Shaxov in a situation somewhat reminiscent of Raskol'nikov's. Their attitudes, however, differ. Raskol'nikov's dilemma in its artistic representation centers on establishing whether his murdering the old pawn-broker is morally wrong under the particular circumstances of his life. The major controversies of the novel tend to conclude that it is. Once Raskol'nikov appears to acknowledge that there is a moral *corpus delicti* in his doing, he sets out toward public penance, of his own, albeit reluctant, accord. Thus, Sonja seems to have prevailed upon Raskol'nikov to extinguish his guilt, in the spirit of Christian ethics, through atonement, public penance and resorting to the merciful judgment of his fellow men. Shaxov is acutely aware of the evil of his transgression. The implicit controversy pertains to expiation. Differing completely from Raskol'nikov on this issue, Shaxov totally resists exposing himself to public penance and judgment. He does everything to avoid the trial and even goes to the length of murdering his blackmailer, probably with a view to eliminate the only surviving witness of his disgrace. The ruthless logic of circumstances has forced Shaxov to the point to which Raskol'nikov has come out of his own moral conviction. However, it would probably be too far-fetched to draw any close parallels between the two works. The sense of guilt that Kaverin deals with is quite different from the one that Dostoyevsky concerns himself with. All in all, *Crime and Punishment* rests on the stable Christian notions of man's free choice, responsibility and atonement. It would be misplaced to expect Dostoyevsky's Christian phraseology or symbolism in a work such as *The Nine Tenths of Fate.* If we were to emphasize the latter's importance, we would have ascribed to it certain existentialist dimensions: because of the lack of the essential and stable scale of values, man becomes guilty against his own choice to be so. The absurdity of circumstances inflicts on him a punishment for the crime that he has not intended and he is saved by blind chance too.

The author seems to lay the greatest emphasis on the plotting of individual destinies and on the depiction of subjective values. Objective political circumstances, no matter how important, mostly serve the purpose of occasioning bizarre coincidences and reversals of the plot. For example, were it not for these objective political circumstances, the plot could not materially have ended in the melodramatic resolution of the conflict (the one believed long dead stepping in person into the court-room scene). Under the czar's rule Shaxov was not shouldering any legal guilt. It took a political revolution for his commutation to become a legal crime for which Shaxov could have been put to public shame and to something even worse. And it is this fear of public shame that constitutes the mainspring of the plot. There may be something self-defeating in this arrangement. The author's heavy emphasis on love, reversal and suspense requires the somewhat melodramatic climax. The latter, however, may belie whatever there is of a real drama throughout the story and thus belittle the whole action. For this reason what often appears in this story as a drama of conscience loses something of its validity.

These stories seem still to be to some extent experimental. The author concerns himself predominantly with the mechanics of the dynamic plot, and takes less interest in the plausibility of the setting. Now, the most dynamic component of the plot is peripeteia, which Aristotle defines as "a change by which the action veers round to its opposite."[24] This reversal of the situation is the very manifestation of dramatic action. It is this reversal – peripeteia – that produces the greatest emotional impact on the spectator or the reader. Therefore Aristotle believed peripeteia to be essential for tragedy. It is no less essential for the plot of narrative fiction. The underlying deftness of the reversal will serve as the principal measure of the ingenuity of the plot. And this is what seems to matter most in all these stories: the author's main purpose is to practice his reversals, so to speak. In some of these works the plot shrinks to a minimum. What does this minimum of plot mean? We define plot as a purposeful action or conflict, external or internal, which throughout the narrative comes to its ultimate reversal. This ultimate reversal winds up the whole action and gives the latter its definitive, and sometimes unexpected, meaning. The modern short story often shuns the formal mechanism of the beginning, development, and end of the plot, i.e., the noeud, the development of the struggle and the denouement. The short stories of Maupassant, O. Henry and Chekhov are of this kind. In them, only the ultimate reversal is treated. Thus, by minimal plot I mean that the author represents some motive and its ultimate reversal and little beyond that. Other components of the plot are either not represented or treated marginally.

Therefore, if the setting is the main weakness in the above-mentioned stories of Kaverin, the stories with minimal plots enjoy more validity because they have to cope with minimal settings. For this reason, the two shorter works "The Friend of the Mikado" and "The Sky-Blue Sun" seem to be the most valid among all the above-mentioned works. Both stories have self-contained narrative interest. The reversal is dramatically jolting. It unexpectedly shifts the dramatic center of the narrative. The secondary character is suddenly projected to the foreground and becomes the primary, and *vice versa*. This reversal considerably magnifies the characterization. It serves a significant artistic purpose. The flimsiness of the setting is more perceptible in longer works, e.g., *The Great Game* or *The End of the Gang*. There are not enough *realia* in the settings of these works. The settings are not tangible enough, not enough in the round. All in all, it is a colorless world. In spite of intricate plots, characters are moving, to use Koestler's phrase, "through a frictionless universe."[25] We could hardly expect Kaverin to know the intimate life of the emperor of Ethiopia, or the routine of the British intelligence service, or the inside life of the Petrograd robbers. And because of this lack of knowledge of the "material," the settings that the author produces are rooted very little in "real life."

In the above-mentioned writings Kaverin does not quite succeed in creating valid adventure novels or tales. That is, the adventure novel as defined in the terms above, as a Romantic, "colonial" vision of objective actions in an empirical world. In certain cases, this lack of success derives from the effect of the "resistance of the material." For example, *The Nine Tenths of Fate* seems to suffer from this kind of liability. A certain brutal magnitude of the events characterizing the October Revolution does not let itself be readily molded into the conventions of the traditional adventure novel, especially of one with melodramatic design. In the process, the great reality of human life and passions shrinks somewhat, as if through the effect of a distance which comes to separate a real duel from its enactment on stage. Curiously enough, in *The Nine Tenths of Fate* comparisons and imagery contribute to this effect of staginess and reduction. Not a few times does the author represent people as if acting on stage, or as if engaged in a game or as if being less than lifesize, somewhat puppet-like. It is true that this effect of staginess and reduction clings prevailingly to the adversaries of the Revolution. In that much it may convey satirical purpose. The difficulty here may lie in the fact that topical material does not lend itself easily to fictionalization. Topical material is more receptive to documentary writing, that is, the writing that is cast in documentary form. This is the approach that Kaverin took in *Artist Unknown*, *Double Portrait*, or even "The Seven Pairs of the Impure Ones." And this is why these works are successful, although they deal with no less topical material than that of *The Nine Tenths of Fate*.

Sometimes, the message of these stories seems to grow well beyond their narrative purport. This may be the case of *The Great Game*. At the end, the story turns into a multilevel phantasmagoria about who dominates fate and how. This hardly is a "clean, open-air adventure."[26] In "The Cask" the author distorts his Romantic vision into a kind of literary joke. His ironic play dissolves the validity of the adventure. It is perhaps with a view to give some objective validity to this story that the author appends a postscript in its 1930 version to the effect that the whole adventure is the product of the oppressed imagination of a young mathematician.[27]

It is my assumption that irony and jocularity dissolve the substance of adventure novel. At the same time, they may establish another kind of validity, the one in terms of which there is no need for *realia*, or objective and "true-to-life" setting. A certain representation distorted by irony and jocular vision in itself becomes valid. In this respect "Revizor" (Inspector General, 1926) and "Vorob'inaja noch'" (Short summer night, 1927) occupy a special place among these works of the twenties.

"Inspector General" and "Short Summer Night" share in common the grotesque picaresqueness of the narrative and the protagonists. Both of these stories somewhat hark back to Gogol's and Dostoyevsky's stories of "civic sentimentalism," although Kaverin displays more mocking irony than compassionate sentiment toward his hapless characters. What the titular counselor symbolizes in the works of Gogol and Dostoyevsky, the cashier and the bookkeeper do in these two stories of Kaverin. The cashier and the bookkeeper embody the mediocrity that vaguely aspires after some more exalted station in life and even takes a few inept steps toward fulfilling their intimate wish.

The bookkeeper Chuchugin of "Revizor" seems to be a mental patient. One day he escapes from the asylum he is committed to, and takes refuge in a public bath-house. He is mistaken for one of the customers. Exposed to hot steam amidst numerous naked customers and overhearing their conversations, Chuchugin seems to sink into a paranoiac dream before he is caught and returned to his asylum. It probably would not be an exaggeration to state that this dream combines Major Kovalev's particular alienation with Jakov Goljadkin's anxiety. From what can be gathered from the intentionally blurred narrative, we suspect that Chuchugin assumes the personality of the Finance Inspector Galaev as well as the latter's official responsibilities and worldly privileges and possessions including Galaev's not unattractive wife. Galaev himself seems to replace Chuchugin in the lunatic asylum. Is this not a Gogolian grotesque "anthropomorphic" projection (separation of parts of body) carried out in a Dostoyevskian, psychological, "split personality" fashion? Is it not the highest fulfillment for a common bookkeeper to become a Finance Inspector? An advancement he may have dreamt of in his most cherished dreams? And apparently no one has noticed the double substitution, not even the wife. Perhaps by sloughing off his original self Chuchugin has freed himself from another liability. Major Kovalev's own nose broke loose from Kovalev's person and paraded all over Petersburg in the uniform of a State Counselor. To this already ambiguous motive in Gogol's story Kaverin gives an obscene, as it were, terminal twist. The "trivial personality" does not even bother to put anything on, let alone a handsome uniform. Chuchugin states that this "trivial personality" had run away from its owner, i.e., the "former" Galaev, on its own initiative and that such an important civil servant as Galaev could not have been implicated in such an unheard-of wrongdoing. Chuchugin must have had some sexual inadequacy and this turns out to be a good opportunity for him to get rid of it at the expense of the "former" Galaev. When the whole adventure has run its course, Chuchugin ends up where he has always been: in his lonely cell of the lunatic asylum. Apart from his old abortive attempt to escape and the commotion he made in the public bathhouse, the whole drama seems to have occurred inside his enfeebled mind. However, not enfeebled enough not to attempt another escape, it seems.

If the bookkeeper Chuchugin spends most of his time in paranoiac dreams, the cashier Martyn Zezjulin of "Short Summer Night" at least happens to be undone by real action, an action commensurate to his personality, it should be conceded. This cashier also longs for a life more exciting than the one that has fallen to his lot thus far. He believes himself to have all the mettle of a great man. He only has not yet chanced upon his splendid opportunity that will transform and exalt his life far above its present mediocrity. One night, at a card game with a travelling salesman Vas'ka Goloshein our cashier Zezjulin wins a substantial amount of money from the outset. Zezjulin feels his long-awaited opportunity of a lifetime at last smiling on him. He feels that this win inaugurates his new splendid life of victories and romantic adventures. In reality, it initiates Zezjulin's pitiful undoing. Enticed by his first easy win, Zezjulin continues gambling, and by dawn, predictably, he has lost everything, including the funds of the co-operative society he has been working for. This pathetic reversal has foreclosed any honorable return to his past or even present. Now, only one way remains open to the former cashier aspiring after high-style life: the road of high adventure. Since Vas'ka Goloshein is the only man that Zezjulin has seen living in high style, the latter fraudulently takes up the identity of the former and undertakes to retrace Goloshein's footsteps, i.e., as it were, Zezjulin undertakes to re-live Goloshein's life in reverse. In the trivial phraseology of the participants in this story, Zezjulin collects, along this road, all the thorns of all the roses that Vas'ka Goloshein has plucked for his own pleasure. Zezjulin's grotesque misadventures come to an early end. At the end of a nocturnal pursuit, when he tries to run away, naked, from a stone-throwing mob in a small provincial town, he commits suicide by leaping from a bridge.

These two stories depict the very reverse of what the adventure story or novel do. The latter evolve and expand in a both exotic and tangible setting, and reach some tangible results which render the protagonists richer in some respects than they were at the outset. The plots of "Inspector General" and "Short Summer Night" follow an opposite course. They involute and shrink. If anything, they are parodies of the adventure narrative. The action bogs down into apathetic trifles, it becomes paltrier and more inane. The protagonists are no conquistadors, but rather the embodiments of what is superficial and mediocre about man. They end in ignominious failure. In both tales the narrator holds the ironic perspective to the very end. This is why he does not need any particular "true-to-life" setting. Only at the point of ultimate reversal does the narrator disclose his formally concealed meaning. At that point the ironic perspective disappears, of course. However, the story is then over, and therefore no problem of setting arises.

3

When we compare Kaverin's works of the twenties with those of the subsequent decades, we may notice that much of the adventure novel pattern still underlies Kaverin's works, although the works themselves are something more than mere adventure novels or tales as I define them above.[28] Let us consider Kaverin's three major novels: *Ispolnenie zhelanij* (Fulfillment of desires, 1934-36), *Dva kapitana* (Two captains, 1938-44), and *Otkrytaja kniga* (Open Book, 1949-52-56).

The principle underlying these novels is the motive of treasure-hunting, both literal and figurative. This principle postulates the attributes of the adventure novel. The author cultivates his art of story telling often in the first-person narrative. This technique entails the restricted vision of a participant who witnesses the events. It also contributes to creating an effect of mystery and suspense.

The beginnings of Kaverin's novels seem to announce traditional adventures extraordinary and Romantic. In *Two Captains* the motive of treasure-hunting enters the novel at the very beginning. Two hardy little boys, stirred up by their juvenile reading, venture on a desperate escapade. The little Sanja Grigor'ev, now a complete orphan, oppressed by his life of drabness, lets himself be talked into running away to Turkestan by his little friend Pet'ka Skovorodnikov. In Pet'ka's words, Turkestan is an enchanted city where pears, apples and oranges grow in the very streets and anyone may partake of them with impunity. This first adventurous dream sustains the little boys, turned into *besprizornye* (homeless children), on their march through Russia to Moscow, the first leg of their journey to the fabulous Turkestan. In *Open Book* the author plays on the traditional motives of romance, mystery or exoticism when he reviews the heroine's childhood, adolescence and early student experiences: Tat'jana's being shot and wounded by a stray bullet from the pistol of a hot-headed gymnasium-boy fighting a duel with his school-mate over a girl; the abduction of the girl by one of the two boys in question; their fortune told from cards; strange books with mysterious titles; the old doctor's enigmatic antecedents. All these motives are topped off by Tat'jana's ambition to become a movie star with which intent she sets off for Petrograd. Likewise, in the introductory pages of *Fulfillment of Desires* the author describes out-of-the-way little shops dealing in antiques, second-hand objects of every description, old books, rare manuscripts and other exotic goods. All this bric-a-brac from the very start evokes an atmosphere of strangeness which stimulates the sense of Romantic adventure.[29]

Now, all these traditional motives and rather Romantic paraphernalia come to an early dead end. In *Two Captains* the author's ironic tone at every turn "exposes" the puerile nature of the boys' venture, their pathetic hardships notwithstanding. In comparison, David Copperfield's flight to Dover, or Oliver Twist's to London were intended in dead earnest. As to Sanja and Petja, the author emphasizes his tenderly ironic attitude toward their flight by making it look like a literary reminiscence of Chekhov's "Mal'chiki" (The boys). In this connection, Kaverin even conjures up the Indian name that Chekhov's boy gave to himself — "Montigomo Jastrebinyj Kogot'" (Montigomo the Hawk's Talon). Quite characteristically, in Kaverin's fiction this gentle Romantic fancy of boyhood subsequently causes a tragic death. In *Open Book* the heroine also comes soon to the end of her early Romantic treasure-hunt: once in Petrograd, she fails miserably in trying to become a movie star. Disappointed, she takes a more prosaic course in life: she enrolls in Medical School. *Fulfillment of Desires* in this respect stands somewhat apart. There is no early "exposure" of Trubachevskij's misdirected quest. This determines a different line of dramatic development.

To the Romantic adventure, mystery and exoticism that the author produces at this early stage of the game he resorts not without gentle irony. These adventure-like motives relate to the plots of Kaverin's novels in a manner of slight parody. The author, as it were, forewarns the reader not to take this romance or this adventure at its face value.

Kaverin re-interprets the patterns of the novel of adventure on his own terms. He tries to "elevate" the traditional novel of adventure to the level of a work of literary representation dealing with intellectual quest and scientific discovery. The treasure-hunting motive changes, as it were, from literal meaning to figurative. This kind of primary motivation appeals rather to the intellect than to mere curiosity. Thus in the three novels, *Fulfillment of Desires*, *Two Captains*, and *Open Book*, the primary motivations assume the forms of, respectively, a philological problem; a historical and geographical problem; a microbiological problem. Motivations of that kind unavoidably entail the rethinking of how to use the traditional motives that make up the traditional novel of adventure.

The primary motivation in these novels being the solution of an intellectual or scientific problem, Kaverin does not need to assemble his novel around the traditional "mystery" motive. In Dickensian tradition this sense of mystery and the ensuing adventure often derive from some initial misconception of people's relations. Frequently, this misconception pertains to the hero's birth and wealth. This "birth-mystery" motive creates a situation in which the character, because of the uncertainty of his identity, is denied the inheritance, the station in life and emotional attachments that are rightfully his and that the unfolding plot will restore to this unsuspecting lawful beneficiary, e.g., in *Oliver Twist*.[30] Neither does Kaverin use the "wealth" motive in relation to his main characters. If at all, the author resorts to this motive for negative characterization. This is the case in *Fulfillment of Desires*, where the motive of apportionment of property turns up episodically after the death of Professor Bauer. The author avoids the motive of accumulation of wealth or that of venomous fight for inheritance. He may do so for ideological reasons. What traditional "mystery" there is in Kaverin's novel relates to the villain. It remains secondary in regard to the main, scientific and intellectual, enigma. The latter relates to the hero. For example, in *Two Captains* the primary, scientific and intellectual enigma consists in the unaccounted-for circumstances under which the polar expedition of Captain Tatarinov vanished somewhere in the Arctic Ocean. The secondary, traditional "mystery" lies in the suspicious antecedents of Nikolaj Antonovich Tatarinov, the villain, and his doings toward his cousin the Captain.

Inasmuch as scientific and intellectual issues motivate the plots, we may expect Kaverin to cultivate the genre of the "production novel" (*proizvodstvennyj roman*) of Soviet "documentary literature." That is, the kind of Soviet literature in which the writer tries to translate into the language of belles-lettres the problems of industrial growth, technology, planning and scientific research; or the novel in which it is shown how different teams vie with one another in friendly contest or co-operation toward an industrial breakthrough or a common scientific discovery. And indeed, such situations arise, for example, in *Open Book* when Tat'jana Vlasenkova works as a medical doctor on a State farm newly set up in Southern Russia, or when she later devotes her professional talents to scientific research at a microbiological institute in Moscow, or when she and her colleagues work frantically toward manufacturing penicillin. This aspect of the plot matters because it allows the author artistically to represent the psychology of scientific thinking. Important as this genre of "con-flictless" literature may be, it does not hold the vital part of the novel. Why should Kaverin avoid putting the representation of friendly contest or socialist competition at the center of his novel? For example, one good biologist honestly competing with another good biologist for common welfare? The crux of the problem here seems to lie in the fact that the representation of Socialist competition evolves, or degenerates — as the case may be — into "documentary" literature. In its most literal sense this "documentary" literature professes factually to record socialist construction in the appropriate ideological light.[31] The essential — or at least the traditional — dramatic ingredient is gone from this "documentary" literature: the reader has no opportunity to fear for the good hero since no "villain" threatens the latter's safety. Here may lie one of the weaknesses of the "conflictless" literature: it lacks a real sense of empathy; the reader does not experience any psychologically compelling reason to identify himself with its hero. Another reason for this weakness may lie in its frequent artistic ineptness.[32]

The real dynamics of Kaverin's novels lie in the acute sense of conflict. In them, the hero and the villain — and their respective followings — remain locked in conflict against one another all throughout the narrated time until one or the other wins out. Confrontation over a scientific or intellectual issue becomes at the same time a ruthless duel between a good person and a evil person.

The nature of the conflict depends mostly on the personality of the villain, since he usually initiates hostilities. The hero only defends his rightful own. In *Fulfillment of Desires* Nevorozhin, the villain, wants to rob Professor Bauer of his valuable manuscripts. Trubachevskij is Nevorozhin's victim, his involuntary tool to carry out his fraudulent schemes. The drama derives from Trubachevskij's "frailty:" because of his youthful inexperience and his mistaking his bookish world for everyday reality, Trubachevskij lets himself be caught, without even realizing it, in Nevorozhin's conspiracy. Nevorozhin soon guesses Trubachevskij's merits and weaknesses and manipulates them for his own evil purposes. To begin with, intellectual curiosity and quest for celebrity in Trubachevskij somewhat blunts his sense of ends and means. Trubachevskij is unquestionably an honest young man and he would not employ impeachable means either to gratify his intellectual curiosity or to attain celebrity. However, he experiences some fleeting moments of hesitation when a glorious and glamorous end makes him forget the questionable nature of the means. Does he not immerse himself in the study of an unpublished manuscript, with the vision of his second, much talked-about, book glimmering before his eyes, and forget that the manuscript is unlawfully in his possession? In his mind, he overcomes the temptation. However, the few fleeting moments of hesitation open a crack in his moral integrity, a minute crack, to be sure, but sufficient to prevent him from doing the only thing that moral integrity commands: to notify Bauer at once of the conspiracy. His failure to do so brings about the subsequent catastrophe: his being publicly accused of stealing Professor Bauer's manuscripts and ejected from the latter's home. In the novel, Kaverin applies his creative power to showing how Nevorozhin succeeds in dampening Trubachevskij's hard-working scholastic ardor and luring him into the fluid world of superficial social success. In due course, Trubachevskij is infatuated with a beautiful but loose woman whom Nevorozhin has planted in his way for this purpose. Trubachevskij drifts away from his sober scholastic occupations and starts neglecting his duties, namely, his duties toward Professor Bauer. Kaverin skillfully represents how Trubachevskij — because of his own weaknesses, Nevorozhin's intrigues, untoward circumstances such as Professor Bauer's illness — falls from his prime glory to his catastrophic disgrace. Trubachevskij, to be sure, fights back as hard as he can but his guileless doings cannot match the intelligently foul play of Nevorozhin.

Nevorozhin is a somewhat unusual figure for a villain. He operates under somewhat unusual circumstances, too. He works in the bookselling business. In his own way, he is a literary scholar and certainly a connoisseur of books. His are the qualities that make the first-rate thief and swindler: a high degree of intelligence, quiet courage in carrying out one's schemes, ability to penetrate other people's interests and temperaments and putting them to use without scruple. Thus, realizing the literary ambitions of Trubachevskij, he addresses to him insinuating flatteries interspersed with pertinent observations on Trubachevskij's literary discovery. The subtle poison of Nevorozhin's message has sunk deeper in Trubachevskij's mind than the latter realizes and attains its intended effect. Later, when Nevorozhin needs to discredit Trubachevskij, he reviews the latter's work in an article devastating in its negative judgment. Both actions are well timed, both sound plausible, betoken the thorough thinking-out of the scheme. Kaverin's villain at his best is a truly substantial figure, free from conventionality, as Dickensian Villains tend to be, convincing in his human stature and villainy. In *Fulfillment of Desires* the contest is not actually a suspense-filled duel between the hero and the villain, evenly matched and alternately prevailing over each other. The drama of the novel centers about the undoing of Trubachevskij's vain ambitions and his subsequent frantic efforts to redeem himself out of the ensuing adversity. He struggles against heavy odds and, on the whole, fails, within the dramatic framework of the novel.

In *Two Captains* the contest is much more a collision between the hero striving toward a lofty aim and the villain who stands in the way and tries to pervert the hero's course. All throughout his narrated autobiography Sanja Grigor'ev obstinately pursues his object and meets no less obstinate resistance from his enemies. There are two of them: Romashka, his school-mate, and Nikolaj Antonovich, his school-director. The two villains team up to undo Sanja. Romashka does so out of envy and jealousy. Nikolaj Antonovich has more vital reasons to destroy Sanja: if Sanja attains his aim, he will find out the truth damning for Nikolaj Antonovich.

Of the three novels the plot of *Two Captains* seems the most seasoned with peripeties. Sanja's move toward the final resolution of the mystery at once brings about a decisive countermove from his foes, so that from move to move the final resolution is postponed for years in view of recurring obstacles. Therefore the reader's expectation remains keyed-up. However, these peripeties lose some dramatic tension because of the form that the author chose for his novel. This novel is presented as a first-person narrative. Sanja and his wife Katja, alternately, tell the story of their lives in memoir form. Plot and unity of action somewhat suffer from the limitations of the first-person narrative. For example, several times Sanja and Katja succeed in persuading the Government to have an expedition equipped and sent in search of Captain Tatarinov. Each time, at the last minute, the expedition is cancelled. The last cancellation especially hurts Sanja. To top off his frustration, the Government re-assigns him to another employment, much less attractive for him: spraying crops with pesticide. Both Sanja and Katja accept these reversals as so much of bad luck in their lives. They have no way of knowing, or even suspecting, that this "bad luck" springs from the consistent intrigues that their foes contrive against them. Thus, the tension of the conflict is somewhat blunted because the reader can see only the moves of the hero, whereas the intrigues of the villains remain in the shade, and become known only once the game is over, from the confession of the villain himself.

It is *Open Book*, however, that develops the fiercest sense of contest. The duel between Vlasenkova and Kramov takes place on a high level of tension because it is intellectual in its nature. They know each other well and can set the right value on each other's talents. Therefore, they can anticipate each other's moves. Thus, throughout the plot the contending parties remain on the stage, in close touch, locked in bitter conflict, all the time. They plot their blows, and anticipate counterblows. And they do exchange blows. Tat'jana Vlasenkova suffers her bitterest defeat at a public discussion in her Institute when Kramov justifies his having eliminated her experiments on penicillium from the research program of the Institute and publicly derides her work. However, Vlasenkova continues her research. Five years later comes her triumphant victory over Kramov. Vlasenkova does develop penicillin and does prove its therapeutic value. At a point when Vlaskenkova's penicillin is gaining official recognition, Kramov and his party try to discredit her product and to prove it inferior to the British penicillin. For this purpose, Kramov suggests the idea of testing the product under clinical observation. He does so with a hope that Vlasenkova's product will lose the contest. However, it wins. At another public meeting honoring her discovery, she plays Kramov's treachery against him. Vlasenkova in her turn publicly humiliates Kramov. In a fit of bitter irony she points to Kramov's having misunderstood and misjudged the whole new theory of antibiotics. This charge nearly gives him a heart attack. It may have been the only time when Kramov loses his self-control, so crushing is Vlasenkova's scientific victory in her contest with Kramov. This is what decides him to deal the ultimate blow that will ruin Vlasenkova's life. Together with his henchmen Kramov trumps up a denunciation against her husband, falsely accusing him of sabotage. An unexpected, although logical, development of the plot offsets the "tactical" advantage that villainy may hold over decency: Kramov's wife betrays her husband at the critical moment of the struggle. Therefore Vlasenkova has a chance for countermove. All this generates the novel's fierce sense of contest, all the more effective because of its catastrophic end. Security police arrest Tat'jana's husband. He is sentenced to a long term of hard labor.

The proponents of Socialist Realism may look with disapproval on such a negative end. The doctrine of Socialist Realism expects a victorious end, no matter how small. The "happy end" is one of the most persistent stereotypes of Soviet literature. Kaverin avoids it. How much importance he attached to the catastrophic impasse as a final motive in the structure of *Open Book* may be seen from the history of the composition of the novel. The very first version of the novel (the one that started appearing in *Novyj Mir* in 1949) begins with an "Introduction" (Vstuplenie) in which the heroine, at the height of her career shortly after the end of the war in 1945, views in retrospect her previous years. Thus the whole novel assumes the form of emphatic reminiscing and its chronologically final, triumphal, point stands at the beginning of the novel as an introduction. In the 1956 version which the author himself declares to be definitive in an initial note, the climax changes both in its nature and place: the "Introduction" is missing altogether; the development advances from the initial chronological point to the chronological end. The climax stands at this final point. Far from being a point of triumph in the heroine's biography, this end is a point of unrelieved, catastrophic, reversal.

Kaverin likewise neutralizes the stereotype of the "happy end" in *Fulfillment of Desires*. In this novel it is the story of the protagonist's "misstep" that constitutes the novel's dramatic substance. In terms of dramatic development, there is scarcely any prescribed "happy end" in the destiny of the most significant character of the novel. The author achieves genuine drama through chronological limitation of the development.

Now, in both novels the author devised an Epilogue which briefly tells of the protagonist's "rehabilitation." Trubachevskij, after working for two years at Dneprostroj, comes to life again, and it is intimated that he has found a new lease on life in his unselfish participation in socialist construction. Let it be observed that in the 1964 edition of *Fulfillment of Desires* the author carries the motive of "rehabilitation" a little further: Trubachevskij is called to restore Professor Bauer's archives for the dilapidation of which he feels somewhat responsible. From the Epilogue appended to *Open Book* the reader learns that Andrej had survived to see better times. After at least seven years of imprisonment, Andrej was released from the concentration camp, rehabilitated, and restored to his former civil and professional status. Ever since, Andrej and Tat'jana and the rest of the family lived happily.

I call these Epilogues "false endings" because they are somewhat alien from the novels' dramatic substance. As such, they do not conclude the dramatic development. It has already been concluded. They do not add anything significant to the artistic value of the dramatic development. At best, they belong to this dramatic development only marginally. Things happen as if these "false endings" were used in order to comply with the prescribed pattern. The latter demands "rehabilitation" as a form of the "happy end." This "rehabilitation" may be a concession to political censorship. It does not result from the internal necessity of the artistic organization of the material. Therefore it cannot avoid assuming a mostly declarative form, which means that this "rehabilitation" of the protagonist cannot be woven into the artistic texture; it stands outside the dramatic development of the novel in the form of an epilogue. The artistic form — as opposed to the novel's de-emphasized declarative form — conflicts with any "rehabilitation," or "happy end" agreeable to the prescribed pattern. Thus, Kaverin's first novel conceals a subtle paradox: the author has the story somewhat ironically belie its title — in terms of artistic representation there is hardly any "fulfillment of desires" in this *Fulfillment of Desires.*

In this respect, *Two Captains* differs from the two other novels. In it, along with the sturdy plot of adventure and action, a thread of something is working its way on that we may call Dickensian sentimentalism, almost melodrama. At a school ball, at a point when the puppy love between Sanja Grigor'ev and Katja Tatarinova is growing into a mature emotion, she catches sight of Sanja's schoolfellow Romashka. The latter at once elicits her aversion. She observes to Sanja that Romashka looks like Uriah Heep. Indeed, the author almost duplicates Uriah Heep in the character of Romashka. Kaverin endows the latter with the repulsive features related to those of the Dickensian villain. Likewise, Romashka's dramatic function follows a pattern of plot almost identical with the one that Uriah Heep pursues in *David Copperfield.* Like Uriah Heep, Romashka would "umble" himself to please his patron of the day Nikolaj Antonovich, preparatory to victimizing him and using him as a springboard for his next move. In school, Romashka turns informer against his schoolmates on behalf of the school director Nikolaj Antonovich the more decisively to earn his director's goodwill. This unenviable co-operation continues long after, Romashka gaining the upper hand in the game. Like Uriah, Romashka too plots to impose his influence on Nikolaj Antonovich in order to worm himself into the latter's family and with his support marry his niece Katja, Romashka's coveted prize, just as Agnes is Uriah's. Just as Uriah Heep hates the good boy — David Copperfield — and out of jealousy and envy tries to harm him, so Romashka hates Sanja and out of jealousy and envy tries to ruin his career. Both good boys despise the villains and at the end expose them and triumph over their conspiracies. So, the plots run quite parallel in both stories. In a Dickensian vein, the "happy end" in this novel is not only victory over wicked foes, it is also fulfillment of "family happiness." After being separated by war and at one time believing each other forever lost, Sanja and Katja at last find each other, a little bit providentially, north of the Polar Circle, in the closing pages of the novel.

All these novels develop binary plots in more than one regard. These binary plots appear the most obviously in the form of hostile conflicts. In the three major novels the fundamental polarization is of a moral nature. The "positive character" stands up to the "villain." This pattern is, of course, profoundly traditional. Kaverin has not been spared Soviet critics' disapproval for identifying the contest over scientific issues with the traditional "good-versus-evil" motivation. One Soviet critic even went as far as calling Kaverin's prose "archaic."[33] Kaverin may want to preserve this traditional sense of drama and its emphatic "literariness" in order to safeguard his artistic prose against the potential amorphousness of "conflictless" or "documentary" literature. In a broader context, commitment to literary traditionalism may be a means of keeping his artistic prose out of the realm of non-literature.

This "hero-versus-villain" motivation may offer another artistic dimension of Kaverin's novels. The conflictual material seems to conceal some ambiguity. On the one hand, it conveys a certain outward meaning emphasizing the destinies of rather successful positive heroes. This aspect of the novels presents rather a conventional setup. It conforms to the prescribed pattern of Socialist Realism. On the other hand, the conflictual material implies a certain inner meaning somewhat in disagreement with the outward. From this angle, villains are the principal heroes in Kaverin's novels, whereas positive heroes' presence only measures the degree to which the villains succeed. This ambiguity of the conflictual material can be best seen in *Open Book*. The heroine wins in the sense that she attains her unselfish purpose. However, she does so at the cost of appalling personal adversity. As for the villains, their conspiracy fails on one particular point, but none of them suffers any ultimate punishment. Likewise, if the dramatic substance of *Fulfillment of Desires* consists in the conflict between Trubachevskij and Nevorozhin, its only vital consequence is the defeat of the former. The way in which the villain fades out is not too convincing; neither does the retribution ensue from the main conflict. All in all, this aspect of Kaverin's novels complies less with the copybook morality of Socialist Realism. This ambiguity is perhaps a more or less spontaneous response by means of which the author's creative mind shields the artistic integrity of its product from the infringement of political censorship.

The binary plot of Kaverin's novels does not concern only the "hero-versus-villain" pattern. The polarization is not only of a moral nature. It may also be complementary. For example, *Fulfillment of Desires* is the story of the parallel development of two young students at the University of Leningrad during the crucial period of their lives and that of their society: on the threshold of the First Five-Year Plan, in the years 1927, '28 and '29. Trubachevskij, who came from a family of musicians, is a student in literature and history. His friend Kartashixin, a son of medical doctors, is a biology student. Trubachevskij's personality is in full formation: he is rather extroverted; in his character a youthful enthusiasm for history bubbles side by side with his worldly aspiration for celebrity; his intense intellectual curiosity feeds on his love for literature; he is not immune to flattery; on him a beautiful woman can exert an infinite fascination. Kartashixin is in some respect Trubachevskij's opposite: he is rather an introvert; in him, deliberateness combines with the gift of purposeful observation; superior to his friend in willpower, Kartashixin lacks his friend's spontaneity and exuberance. The author has the two friends engaged in a sort of friendly contest: Kartashixin "corrects" Trubachevskij; he succeeds where the latter fails. Trubachevskij succumbs to the lures of an "evil" woman; Kartashixin withstands the same temptation. Trubachevskij "drops out" of the University; Kartashixin successfully completes his studies. Trubachevskij gives up the good girl; Kartashixin wins her.[34] However, the character of Trubachevskij succeeds better artistically.

The very title *Two Captains* points to a similar binary pattern in this novel. From his early childhood, unwittingly, Sanja Grigor'ev enters upon and follows the path of Captain Tatarinov, the long dead explorer who vanished with his crew and ship somewhere in the Arctic Ocean shortly before the First World War. The young captain emulates the old. In a sense, through his destiny the young captain redeems the destiny of the old captain, and, as it were, improves on it. Likewise, the two brothers L'vov of *Open Book* also work their way in life as a team. The level-headedness of the young brother Andrej tempers the impulsiveness of the older Dmitri. In return, the unconventional creative intellect of the latter opens the way where the former is trapped in a dead end. Such examples could be multiplied. Even a title such as *Double Portrait* hints at such a binary correlation. In all these cases, the binary patterns of plot serve as a means of characterization, as a comparative study of personalities.

4

I believe that the most remarkable case of such a binary plot is *Xudozhnik neizvesten* (Artist unknown, 1931). Although small in size, the novel deals with a wide range of stimulating problems. First, the novel develops a thematic conflict, a conflict of two distinct characters. The author dramatizes this conflict in the form of a philosophical confrontation between two opponents: Shpektorov, an engineer, and Arximedov, an artist. To this philosophical confrontation a personal drama adds another dimension. A woman and child give a human depth to the philosophical antagonism between the two men. Second, the story reveals, on another level, a conflict in the techniques of representation. This is the conflict between the narrator of the story and an "anti-narrator." Metaphorically speaking, we could compare the first conflict to the warp of the representational texture. The second conflict forms its woof. Viewed from a certain philosophical angle, the novel rests on the opposition between play-reality and serious reality, very much as J. Huizinga understands this opposition.

Arximedov is the central character of the story. In this complex personality three different selves stand in opposition: a quixotic self, a "sane" man, and an artist. His quixotic self comes out in his personality as a social and moral reformer. It never completely dominates his "sane" personality, i.e., that of a man of everyday life who loves his wife and child. The artist in Arximedov remains subdued throughout the story, perhaps intentionally so. Life puts a brutal end to Arximedov's quixotic career. Then, it steamrollers a tragically forlorn man. Only the artist, or rather the artistic message left by Arximedov, survives.

It is Arximedov's quixotic personality that has the greatest dramatic value in the novel. His destiny is to a degree that of Don Quixote. Arximedov cherishes a certain ethical vision of the world — the vision of medieval guilds as generators of professional honesty and dedication in labor. This vision absorbs him totally. Adapted to and actualized in modern conditions, it would usher in the Golden Age. And some such Golden Age of valor in labor, rather poetically evoked than conceptually defined,

Arximedov wants to bring to life. And in this he resembles Don Quixote, with his vision of the Golden Age of knight-errantry revived.

Arximedov chooses a theater for his stronghold whence he goes on his "sallies." This choice is significant. It means that Arximedov is engaged in a play − a play at combatting "hypocrisy, dishonor, meanness and boredom" − whose rules his own ideal vision of the world has devised. The theater, then, is the most appropriate "play ground" for Arximedov, since in it fantasy can cast time and space in any mold. In the theater a Don Quixote can feel most at home because there he meets the least resistance to his lying down his rules of the game, thus rendering his play meaningful. There, he also can more easily find like-minded persons. And indeed, in the School Young People's theater Arximedov wins his two and only disciples Zhaba and Vizel'.

The narrator encounters them in the theater on the day when he brings Èsfir' to her husband Arximedov, who has left her and has taken away their child. The teacher and his two disciples have been gathering in one of the workshops of the theater cluttered up with props of every description. The theatrical setting and atmosphere make their activity appear artificial, like "some kind of play, half childish, half theatrical."[35] Such is also the high-flown speech delivered by Zhaba, in which he obviously echoes Arximedov's ideas. As a "play-community," the three initiates display a certain reticence, if not hostility, toward the "outsider," that is, toward the narrator, who does not participate in their play. To top off the effect of the encounter, Arximedov invests himself with the insignia of Don Quixote − a jam pot for the headgear, a frying pan for the shield, and an oven fork for the lance; even Rosinante is not missing − a tricycle with the gaunt head of a horse. Arximedov does all this as if in reply to some question that he has been brooding over. But it makes the narrator wonder whether he has not in vain been looking for the "features of a reformer in this Soviet Don Quixote."[36]

Frustrations beset Arximedov when he steps out of his own "play ground" in order to impose his rules upon his contemporaries. The latter have their own rules of the game, and they therefore reject his. This rejection need not be to their credit, since Arximedov may well be a genius and prophet who understands more and sees farther than his contemporaries. From this clash between Arximedov's "stage reality" and his contemporaries' "life reality" emerges a sense of the ludicrous and of parody. One "sally" that Arximedov undertakes from his stronghold is quite striking in this respect. From a friend, the narrator heard about how Arximedov had interceded with law-enforcement officers on behalf of the young tramps living in the heating pipes beneath a busy street of Leningrad. Police are ousting them from their subterranean residence. A strange man, looking like both "a novice and a Jacobin," wearing an old-fashioned jacket and glasses, forty years old in his bearing and seventeen in his speech, unexpectedly makes his appearance and, raising his hand, "votes for confidence" in those juvenile delinquents. In a lofty piece of rhetoric in their defense, he reproaches the policemen with "not trusting the poor" and interlards his exhortations with nobility, morality and stars. One after the other the juvenile delinquents emerge from the hatch and form a crowd, while Arximedov stands at their head like the Pied Piper. "It was almost a theatrical scene," the eye-witness comments.37 Here Arximedov shows himself in an intensely quixotic situation. He miserably fails to bridge the gap between his lofty vision and its fulfillment because he resorts to absurd means in order to actualize his vision. A lofty sentiment materialized in the wrong way toward the wrong people turns out to be inept. In the above-mentioned incident Arximedov's conduct is as mad and ludicrous as Don Quixote's when the latter frees the convicts on their way to the galleys. To that extent Arximedov follows in Don Quixote's footsteps.

Don Quixote is an essentially comic character. What saves him from succumbing to tragic destiny is his wisdom in remaining in the mad world of his own making throughout. Thus his "madness" prevents him both from coming into touch with the real world and from becoming aware of the absurdity of his behavior. It favors him with a sort of immunity. This immunity derives from prosopopoeic forms of thought. To liken a windmill to a giant is a matter of poetic awareness. The "madness" starts when Don Quixote acts accordingly and imposes his vision on others.

Arximedov follows a similar course. He acts irrationally. Insofar as his adult and "sane" contemporaries reject him, he cannot help resorting to prosopopoeic forms of thought. The narrator wants to signal that because Arximedov cannot communicate meaningfully with his adult and "sane" contemporaries he communicates with something lesser, attributing to this "something lesser" the capacity of understanding him that he does not find in his adult, "sane" contemporaries. This is a dangerous path: it may lead to schizophrenia. Arximedov seems to be taking a few steps along this path as the frustration of his apostleship deepens. For lack of a human being to take counsel with, Arximedov turns to the statue of Lasalle for advice. When he comes to despair of conveying his message to his contemporaries, he starts arguing with imaginary people, against imaginary enemies. Even his own disciple Zhaba realizes at one point that Arximedov has not been able to do anything with his ideas: "He choked in his ideas, so much was he immersed in them. It was difficult to listen to him. Maybe guessing it, he kept on in jest addressing his words to the puppets hanging on strings along walls . . ."38 Puppets at least seemed to understand Arximedov. Such an extremity might make us fear for his state of mind — or that of his contemporaries. Is Arximedov a Don Quixote-like lunatic, losing communication with sane society? Or, conversely, is he a philosopher who has the vision and the courage to speak the simple truth to his mentally blinded brethren?

The narrator does not attribute to Arximedov's "prosopopoeic behavior" the dimensions of Don Quixote's. Arximedov stands on this side of sanity. Therefrom comes his trouble. He does not enjoy the kind of "immunity" that Don Quixote does. Quixotic spirit can thrive only on "stage reality:" its "rules of the game" tolerate only the sham death of the stage, angels with painted wings, and emperors with tinsel crowns. Don Quixote, through his "madness," transmogrifies all this whirl of props, cardboard, and tinsel into meaningful reality, that is, play reality. In contact with "life reality" the quixotic world of ludicrous and painless "madness" crumbles. It crumbles, namely, when real death steps into the play. Then the hero foresees a tragic reversal. His wife Êsfir''s self-inflicted death brings about such a tragic reversal in Arximedov's destiny. The tragic reversal exposes the unreality of his quixotic career and thereby puts an end to it.

Thus, Arximedov's destiny is that of a reformer whose endeavors turn more and more illusory. One should expect that, when Arximedov reaches the height of his quixotic career, he also reaches the height of his grotesqueness. Because of his "madness" he stands more and more alienated from others and ends up in total loneliness. At this point of total loneliness, Arximedov becomes a different figure: after rising to the climax of quixotism and grotesqueness his destiny takes a tragic fall.

The climax and the tragic anti-climax in Arximedov's destiny is recorded in the Eighth Encounter ("You Have Lost Your Face"). It is a masterful piece of representation. In this chapter of the book Zhaba recounts to the narrator the circumstances that decided him to desert Arximedov. The latter, disheartened after the death of his wife, spent all his time in the School Young People's Theater. One night turmoil shook the theater. Vizel' had sent the old puppets for salvage, and for this reason he was dismissed from his job as a propman, whereupon he caused a riotous brawl and wrecked property. Arximedov and Zhaba joined Vizel'. They were pursued all over the theater and finally surrounded in the gallery above the stage. Vizel' decided, "We will meet them with weapons in our hands." While the director, the prompter, and the booking clerks were closing in upon the small gang − the teacher and his two disciples −, Vizel' handed Arximedov a sword: a long sword of dark steel, with half a mug instead of the ordinary guard and with a blue and pink ribbon wound around the handle.

And he took it in his hands and, walking under the low arches of the gallery, he stopped on the first step of the staircase, with his feet planted apart, squinting his eyes. He was listening intently: from all sides was coming the measured beat of approaching footsteps, from East, West, North and South.

And the theater kept repeating their echoes in the empty spaces of scenes, staircases, corridors, halls.

An army was marching.

It seemed somewhere already rose the shrill whistle of flutes; drumsticks were beating against the calfskin of drums.

And the footsteps became more and more resounding, more and more distinct, more and more accurate.

An army was marching.

And now, squaring his shoulders, holding out his arm with the sword, Arximedov stepped out to meet it.

Now he was on the offensive − alone but in such a way as if the knights of all latitudes marched behind him, crying "Joy" and clanging their weapons.[39]

In this excerpt, Kaverin neutralizes the borderline between circumstantial reality and pure fantasy. For a short while the author chooses − through Zhaba's testimony − to halo a petty detail of a scandalous brawl with the dignity of an epic battle. The author isolates this piece of fantasy from the antecedent circumstantial reality by inserting another piece of even greater fantasy − Arximedov's dream − so that the subsequent lesser piece of fantasy stands out somewhat more credibly against the background of a "dream." Even more effectual is the power of the poetic evocation. As if under the stress of a poetic "blackout," Zhaba momentarily forgets actual causes and agents and replaces them in his representation by their effects, namely, their auditory effects, which he can interpret according to what he himself chooses to hear or to see. In the above-quoted excerpt, the key effect is the sound of footsteps produced by people tramping up the stairs. The hollow spaces of the theater widen immeasurably — "East, West, North, and South" — and immeasurably amplify the footfalls, so that the willing ear perceives the formidable rumble of an army on the march, the flutes whistling, the drums beating. Next, the poetic logic associates this impression with the image of the hero — Arximedov — standing up to this army. This appears to be the highest point of the knight's self-fulfillment: a champion among the knights, alone, heroic, to the viril strains of martial music, confronts the enemy host with the might of his sword. Arximedov has suddenly attained the apotheosis of chivalry.

But this poetic "blackout" vanishes as soon as the actual cause comes to belie an imaginary effect. The footsteps are those of Shpektorov, and here he appears in person. Under his sobering gaze people and things again resume their ordinary shape: the propman Vizel', sitting on the steps and disturbed at being fired from his job; Arximedov in a shabby dark-brown suit, for some reason holding a toy sword. Harsh reality deals an irreparable blow to Arximedov's "madness."

Zhaba winds up his fanciful tale with a last "fib:" as Arximedov and Shpektorov stand facing each other on the top floor of the School Young People's Theater, they engage in a grand colloquy that sets off the grievous defeat of the one against the unmerciful triumph of the other. A grand colloquy,

such, — Zhaba said, — as if there never had been a woman whom they both loved, as if it was not people who stood against each other but two minds.

— I remember, you wanted to rebuild the world, to give new names to things, — Shpektorov allegedly asked, — well, have you succeeded?

And Arximedov answered:

— I wanted to make labor an act of valor, and tiredness a joy. — You? — Shpektorov allegedly asked then, — you are the book that our elder brothers read in their childhood, is that that you wanted? I remember it. You were portrayed on the cover, encased in a coat of mail, an armor, and the gear of the Middle Ages which you now propose to include in the Five-Year plan.

And so Arximedov raised at him his tired thoughtful eyes.

—So what, the Middle Ages, — he allegedly said, — don't we really have the right to take from any epoch what may prove useful for us? Hasn't history really left us this choice?

Then Shpektorov burst out laughing and planted himself in front of him spreading out his large arms.

—It has left us only one choice — to win or to lose, — he allegedly said. — And every day we choose the first.[40] We who are playing the great game. So, put your sword in the corner, give it to actors or children. Go and register with an employment office, at one time, it seems, you worked in a pharmacy. Take advantage of your days off, learn how to draw. Perhaps time will come when we call you to color our banners . . .[41]

Zhaba and the narrator bear conflicting testimonies as to the end of Arximedov's career. The "fibber" reports a noble romantic end, perhaps as a philosopher turned poet might imagine it — uplifting even in Arximedov's failure. The narrator is a witness — literally, a legal witness — of the actual end of Arximedov's career. The last, real encounter between Arximedov and Shpektorov occurred later, at an hour woefully evil for unfortunate Arximedov.

But how different it looked from that which he [Zhaba] recounted to me. It was quiet, simple. And one could not hear the mysterious footsteps behind the walls of the Department of Children's Welfare, the resounding footsteps coming from East, North, West, and South! And there was not any colloquy with an ancient book which our elder brothers used to read in their childhood, a lofty colloquy about valor, labor, and the right for existence.

The talk was different, a very clear one.

In linen soiled by wear, in a long-lapped overcoat, a stooping shaggy ragamuffin was sitting at an office desk and writing up a document to dictation; in it he was renouncing what remained after he had lost everything else — his son.

And there was not any sword. A pen-holder stained with ink was sticking between his weak fingers, he was writing in a child's hand, and after every word he lifted up his myopic blue eyes and looked at Shpektorov — Shpektorov was dictating a document.[42]

The narrator, in a dingy office at the Department of Children's Welfare, sees the squalid and lost Arximedov sign — to Shpektorov's dictation — his ultimate defeat and then sink into ultimate despair.

The structure of the story rests on this principle of conflicting testimonies. These conflicting testimonies account for Arximedov's very special stature. Without them, Arximedov would not be what he is. Kaverin chooses to shape the representation from the restricted point of view of a narrator — a chronicler — who observes and records everyday reality. At one point of the story when the drama has not yet run its course, the narrator describes his chronicle in these words: ". . . This book appeared to me as a coolly expounded contest between 'counting on romanticism' and 'romanticism of accounting,' whereas only the name of the author on the title page had to testify to my participation in this contest."[43] In fact, the narrator fails to display the disengaged curiosity of a cool observer. It becomes a matter of intensely personal concern for the narrator to get to know and to understand the destinies of Arximedov, Ėsfir', and Shpektorov. The narrator relates step by step his own experiences, encounters, thoughts, and impressions as they occur while he witnesses the unfolding drama. Thus the presence of the narrator infuses a sense of reality into the story. And the story itself appears as a piece of the narrator's own autobiography. The narrator happens to be at the same time a professional litterateur. What constitutes the driving motivation throughout the novel is the fact that this litterateur wants to solve a riddle, to penetrate the mystery enveloping the destinies of Shpektorov, Ėsfir', and Arximedov.

In trying to solve the riddle of Arximedov's destiny the narrator sees his efforts more than once frustrated and several times the narrator has given up the idea of bringing his chronicle to a meaningful end. The sober toil of the builders of socialist construction, the suicide of Èsfir', and the very degradation of Arximedov make his dreamy orations appear so unsubstantial that the narrator, disillusioned with his chronicle, thinks of not continuing it. Let it be observed, however, that after each such disillusionment the narrator resumes his chronicle with a maturer insight. And the story would have come to nothing, the narrator maintains, were it not for Zhaba, who brings the story out of oblivion.

The novel is presented as if the very process of its creation was going on before the reader. It is a novel about a novel in the making. At any moment of the action the narrator does not know what will happen next; he can only guess. In anticipating events, as in experiencing them, he holds no advantage over the characters of the story since he is one of them.[44] For the same reason, he is as much limited in his resources. In a sense, the character who is the narrator — and because he is the narrator — subjects himself to certain limitations that other characters in the story need not heed. The narrator is committed to circumstantial truth; other characters need not be so. This inequality adds a far-reaching dimension to the novel.

The sense of movement and the fulfillment of the artistic purpose in this story result from the tension between the two poles of representation. One pole is that of objective representation; the other pole counteracts it. The conflict thus generated sets the circumstantial truth against phantasmagoria or *vran'e* (fibbing), the objective representation of a man or a situation against the parody or caricature of the same man or situation. It opposes "seriousness" to "playfulness" and "life reality" to "stage reality."

These contrasting attitudes alternately prevail throughout the story and correspondingly determine the tenor of the representation. One attitude results from the restricted and objective vision of the narrator, the "eye-witness" who maintains the sense of reality. The other attitude derives from the unrestricted and uncontrolled vision of the "anti-narrator," one who, as it were, distorts the objective reality of the main conflict as recorded by the narrator. The "anti-narrator's" interferences tend to dissolve the realistic motivation of the story. They replace the objective reality with phantasmagoric situations which have never actually occurred. These two attitudes do not stand in absolute contrast to each other. Neither do they mark a character totally or exclusively.

Thus Zhaba's, that is to say, the "anti-narrator's," function strangely supplements that of the narrator. The latter conducts his search on the level of circumstantial truth. The "anti-narrator" tends to annihilate this circumstantial truth. It is perhaps significant that when Zhaba makes his first appearance in the story, the narrator mistakes him for a bear. Thus tending to annihilate the circumstantial truth, the "anti-narrator" achieves a double result.

On the one hand, he attains an effect of parody. In conferring his boisterous allegiance on Arximedov and becoming his enthusiastic follower, Zhaba unwittingly parodies Arximedov's struggle against "hypocrisy, dishonor, meanness, and boredom." Above all, Zhaba parodies Arximedov's quixotic ineffectuality: he gives striking prominence to the ineptness of Arximedov's means by driving them to the point of absurdity. For example, when Zhaba proposes in his bombastic speech "to repaint the world," he garbles, in the manner of parody, the message of his teacher about the wholesome impact that harmoniously distributed colors and well-shaped objects communicate to people at work or rest. Zhaba parodies Arximedov's intuitions of industrial aesthetics.

Zhaba's account of the final encounter between Arximedov and Shpektorov tends to render Arximedov's image insubstantial. This happens because this image is projected into the world of "stage reality," a cardboard reality in which Arximedov only plays himself. It should also be observed that Arximedov's battle royal that was not had a parodistic cause too. Arximedov thought that whatever was made unconscientiously and carelessly — be it a coat of arms or a law — bears the hidden seeds of evil. His other disciple Vizel' assimilated this idea but applied it on the wrong occasion: he discarded all the old puppets of the School Young People's Theater "because they were saboteurs!" This brought about the brawl that elevated Arximedov to his illusory and short-lived glory. Thus, through an unwitting parody Zhaba "lowers" Arximedov in the sense in which a caricature or parody "lowers" objective representation. Arximedov's image has its validity jeopardized in terms of life reality and circumstantial truth. It is for this reason that Zhaba finds it so easy to dissociate himself from Arximedov. The narrator, for his part, does not challenge this validity. He merely tries to understand who Arximedov is.

There is a certain parallelism between the narrator and the "anti-narrator" in point of "lowering" their objects. If the "anti-narrator" tends to "lower" Arximedov from "life reality" to "stage reality," the narrator operates in the reverse direction when dealing with Shpektorov. He "lowers" Shpektorov from a certain "stage reality" (Shpektorov, in his own words, is "playing the great game") to "life reality." Shpektorov, in relation to Arximedov, appears surrounded with a somewhat affected intellectual glamor, somewhat superhuman, as a formidable force of socialist trans- formation. But the perceptive narrator sees Shpektorov's weaknesses, detects his misjudgments, witnesses his shy tenderness toward the beloved woman, and comprehends his ever agonizing frustration. So the narrator "lowers" Shpektorov in the sense that he returns to Shpektorov his common human and everyday dimension. This situation is motivated by the fact that the narrator and Shpektorov have been friends since their early childhood. Contrariwise, Arximedov, at the beginning of the story, represents an almost completely unknown quantity for the narrator. In this respect, too, the narrator asserts the sense of reality.

On the other hand, in tending to annihilate the circumstantial truth, the "anti-narrator" gains the intuition of an essential truth of the representation, beyond the circumstantial truth. This "fibber with unerring taste"[45] at once comprehends the true value and the magnitude of Arximedov's personality. He is the one who explains to the narrator that Arximedov is a great man, a great artist, a bold innovator concerned with the ethical and social problems of his time. Then, parody assumes a new dimension. "According to what astonishing laws is fibbing built up . . . if, raised to the level of a system, it unwittingly comes to the truth that is unknown to it?" the narrator wonders when listening to Zhaba's account.[46] We cannot really tell whether it is true, we cannot ascertain whether Arximedov actually took the sword in his hand and stepped out to meet the enemy host; whether, at the sight of Shpektorov, Arximedov tumbled from the height of his heroic delusion down into disenchantingly base reality. Fibber that he is, Zhaba may have made it all up from beginning to end. We know positively that "the grand colloquy with quotations from *Don Quixote*" never occurred between Shpektorov and Arximedov on the night of the brawl at the School Young People's Theater. The narrator learns subsequently from Shpektorov that the latter did not even have a chance to speak to Arximedov at that juncture. However, Zhaba senses that it all ought to have happened.

The essential truth of the matter is archetypal. Arximedov is a Don Quixote but, unlike his archetype, he lives and acts in an utterly unquixotic world. Such an alienation could find its expression only in a grotesque confrontation of that which ought to be with that which is. It ought to be the last, heroic square of the last battle for a noble but forlorn cause. It is a silly brawl in which a gang of cranks squabble, up in the gallery above the stage, wielding toy weapons against imaginary enemies. The lofty illusion emerges in the "anti-narrator's" intuition. It clashes with the base reality that the narrator witnesses.

Only from such a violent head-on collision between the lofty illusion and the base reality can Arximedov, a Don Quixote deprived of his madness, evolve into an original tragic character. The dramatically conflicting testimonies of both the "anti-narrator" and the narrator magnify the reversal of Arximedov's destiny to the point of lending to this reversal of Arximedov's destiny a tragic dimension. Should only one testimony be present, this tragic dimension would virtually vanish. The "anti-narrator's" testimony alone would not provide the sense of actual catastrophe in a good man's fate. The reader would not realize the measure of the depth of the protagonist's fall. The sole record of the narrator would not go far beyond a sad story of a misfit. It would not generate enough power to stimulate the sense of tragic awe because the sole record of the narrator would not bring the protagonist to an elevation high enough for a tragic hero to fall from. Arximedov owes his superior, tragic stature to this subtle conflict of vision which both divides and unites the narrator and the "anti-narrator."

Thus, on the thematic level, Shpektorov and Arximedov, the "two minds," confront each other in an ideological conflict. Both fail to measure up to their original expectation. A child and a woman add to this ideological conflict an intensely human, emotional dimension. All this constitutes the "what" of the representation, its external dynamics. On the level of the techniques of representation another conflict sets in competition with each other the narrator and the "anti-narrator." This conflict involves the "how" of the representation, its internal dynamics. Each of them has his own way of viewing and understanding the struggle between Shpektorov and Arximedov. Depending on who does the viewing, the representation oscillates between objectivity and distortion, between circumstantial truth and phantasmagoria. The interest of the novel lies in this simultaneous conflict both on the thematic level and on the level of the techniques of representation.

PART TWO

REPRESENTATION

CHAPTER THREE

FORMATION OF YOUTHFUL PERSONALITY

1

Kaverin's prose fiction centers, with a good deal of recurrence, on the destinies of young people. In his longer narrative works such as *Chernovik cheloveka* (the rough draft of man, 1931), *Fulfillment of Desires* (1934-36), *Two Captains* (1938-44) and *Open Book* (1949-52-56), the novelist represents the panoramas of the ways in which the lives of young people develop from their childhood. In his shorter works, "Kusok stekla" (A piece of glass, 1960), "Kosoj dozhd'" (Slanting rain, 1962), and "Shkol'nyj spektakl'" (A school play, 1968), the author depicts some striking experiences reaching deep into their minds. In both cases, Kaverin lays artistic emphasis on youth as the most formative period of life.

This emphasis on the literary representation of the formative value of youth points to the European narrative prose that describes the formation of a youthful personality, namely, the subject's intelligence, sensibility and willpower, its cultural and moral development. Such a common generic denominator would bring to some unity such different works as *Wilhelm Meister's Apprenticeship*, *Green Henry, David Copperfield*, *Oliver Twist*, *The Red and the Black*, *A Sentimental Education* and a host of others.

In this very comprehensive family of prose works, the European *Bildungsroman* may well hold the most genteel place. Susanne Howe points to the very complex background of this genre as exemplified in *Wilhelm Meister's Apprenticeship*: it absorbs the tradition of the moral allegory, the picaresque novel, the ideal of the "universal man" of the Renaissance, and "[. . .] the shadow of a still remote ancestor, Parsifal, 'the brave man slowly wise' [. . .]"[1]

One of the most distinguishing features of the *Bildungsroman* seems to be the protagonist's pursuit of individual development, his conscious effort toward self-culture. In modern European narrative tradition the roots of this genre go into the culture of the 18th-century individualism, with *Wilhelm Meister's Apprenticeship* as its most exalted paragon. The sense of personal self-fulfillment is the stable property of the *Bildungsroman*. To form one's personality, to acquire education and culture becomes both the means and the aim of one's purposeful activity. The subject applies all his striving and reflection to chiseling out his own life into a work of art. The *Bildungsroman* tells the story of a young man's commitment to thoroughly developing his abilities. It traces his course, through disappointments and achievements, toward the aim of his endeavors. This aim is to reach a degree of wordly wisdom and self-knowledge higher than the one from which he has started. And the young man places this journey through life, from error to truth, from confusion to clarity, on the highest level of awareness. For this reason, an experience in his eyes assumes some special quality. It is not something simply to live through or overcome, and then to be discarded from one's awareness. Rather, it is felt and taken as a formative or educational event with universal lifelong implications. The world then is a school of life from which he is continuously learning. The trials and sufferings the young man encounters on his journey through this world increase his edifying experience and maturity. Therefore, these trials and sufferings make sense. The worldly wisdom and self-knowledge the subject thus achieves will then maintain his sense of harmony with the world, which, for this very reason, will not offer any threat for him.

The *Bildungsroman* represents youth and the formation of youthful personality. The biography of the *Bildungsroman* subject unfolds in different stages[2]: the stage of "apprenticeship" and "travel," and the stage of maturity. The *Bildungsroman* subject leaves his home to confront the world on his own and learn from his experiences. At this travel stage the *Bildungsroman* subject purposefully strives for a certain universal development of his personality. He frequents various places, people and institutions, he falls in love with women, strikes up friendships, engages in business occupations, devotes himself to art, theater, poetry or philosophical pursuits, or may live through some religious experience. The locus of these experiences is this empirical world looked upon as a school of life. And then comes the stage when the young subject's *Bildung* (formation and education) comes to its completion and he enters upon the mature and error-free understanding of his own self, the world and his mission in this world. For Wilhelm Meister this moment comes at Lothario's castle when the abbé hands him his Indenture thereby signaling that Wilhelm's Apprenticeship has successfully ended. Heinrich Lee reaches this point of salvation when, weary, cold and hungry, he stumbles on Count Dietrich von W . . . berg's castle.

What characterizes the movement of the subject in the *Bildungsroman* is his constant awareness of the aim he is pursuing. The classical subject of the *Bildungsroman*, a Wilhelm Meister, is a centripetal character in the sense that his own individual *Bildung* — formation and education — is both the means and the aim of his activity. He achieves both through his own reflection and under his own spiritual power. With him, society as such, objectively, abstracted from his own self, does not seem to count. His environment and the society amid which he lives perform mostly a symbolic function. They owe their validity mostly to this symbolic function through which they contribute to the formation and education of the subject of the *Bildungsroman*. This lengthy educational and formative process results in the emergence of a more or less universal man, world-wise and humane, at peace and harmony with the world.

This philosophical and pedagogical individualism is already dissolving in *Green Henry*. Here, the *Bildungsroman* subject's self-culture is no longer amenable just to his own individual self. Environment and society hold as much validity as the subject of the *Bildungsroman* himself does. In Dickens' narrative prose the *Bildungsroman* substantially changes: education and formation is no longer either the means or the aim of the subject's activity. David Copperfield no longer particularly worries about his all-around culture. When he teaches himself stenography, it obviously is not for the sake of self-culture. Self-culture yields place to the acquisition of a special skill that David can trade for his own support and that of his child-wife. Thus, society and environment become a hard unyielding reality that one has to overcome in hard struggle in order to survive. Leisurely self-education and self-culture perforce give way to acquired skill toward external action. Thus, in regard to the classical *Bildungsroman* and its subject, this genre in its subsequent development, as evolved in the narrative prose of Dickens, responds in the way of the "empiricism" of the English *Bildungsroman*: the young man facing the world at the beginning of his journey through life cannot quite afford devoting his exclusive endeavors to self-culture, to refining his life into a work of art. Environment and society are rather hostile. He has to break through its not always well-wishing medium. How does he pick his way through his novelistic biography? He may have to acquire special skills which he has to do at the expense of self-culture. In the Dickensian world, more often than not, the young man has to live through an intricate plot of adventures, mysteries and action. Amidst the wickedness of many, there is, however, the courageous honor and gentle goodwill of a few. These good souls do help. And because the young protagonist himself does not lack in virtue, he finally overcomes difficulties and fares rather well in his life. However, struggle for survival and concern for doing well in practical life may somewhat impair his higher sense of philosophical integrity. Does he attain the ultimate faith, purification and sense of unity and harmony with the world that the classical subject of the *Bildungsroman* is supposed to? Does not the Dickensian "apprentice" emerge, at the end of his "apprenticeship," with some sense of scepticism and uncertainty?

2

It would most likely be a mistake to postulate any direct genetic links between the classical *Bildungsroman* and Kaverin's above-mentioned works about the formation and education of youth, especially his three major novels, *Fulfillment of Desires*, *Two Captains* and *Open Book*. I find it convenient to use this concept because it helps pinpoint certain specific features of Kaverin's novels. Nor is this comparison arbitrary since the latter and the *Bildungsroman* have some comparable points. Moreover, when discussing these specific novels, we should do so with their historical context in mind, that is, within the Soviet literary environment of the time. The latter had its own specific requirements and aims. Kaverin could not have disregarded them.

One of the fundamental aims of Soviet literature has been to create the image of the New Soviet Man and Woman at their best, to show their formation and education, the new environment they grow in, the new society and the country they build. As molded by the tenets of Socialist Realism, Soviet literature pursues educational and pedagogic purposes. The educational purpose of this literature manifests itself on two levels simultaneously: first, the fictional character within the narrative lives through the appropriate educational process, and second, this educational process represented is intended to exert a formative influence on the reader.

At its dogmatic extreme, this literature should depict typical characters under typical circumstances; "typical characters" and "typical circumstances" being those that represent the main tendencies of reality; the "main tendencies of reality" being those that lead to the triumph of socialism or, in the longer range, communism. The "typical character" may be complex in its diversity, insofar as anthropomorphized inventories of virtues and features of character may be complex and diverse. The personality features may vary a great deal. Their range may fan out from the inflexible ethical code of the ruthlessly purposeful revolutionary like Nechaev, such as Pavel Vlasov or Pavel Korchagin[3] to the generous self-effacement of an aging actress as in B. Polevoj's "Moskvichka." By definition, "typical" are those people and circumstances that lead toward the ultimate triumph of socialism or communism. Therefore, among the most abiding virtues that grace the "typical character" should be singled out his purposeful service to communist ideals as interpreted by the Communist Party. This entails his total loyalty and obedience to the Communist Party leadership, a loyalty that subordinates conventional morality to political expediency. This original quality postulates a certain number of other kindred qualities. For example, qualities of leadership, such as ability to evaluate and anticipate the public impact of his actions. In a sense, a "typical character" never relaxes a certain political vigilance. This also means that his public concerns dominate his private, individual self. Such a constitution predisposes the "typical character" to external action, thus heavily taxing his intellect and willpower, while possibly impeding his affective life, namely, uncontrolled emotions toward women. Since intellect and willpower are the primary tools of his impact on his environment, he will develop them to the utmost. Therefore, the "typical character" keeps improving his intellectual proficiency, his technical skills, and trains his willpower. It would be futile to try to enumerate all these qualities. This "typical character" increasingly becomes the image of the New Soviet Man which in its turn is identifiable with that of the "positive hero." The latter is endowed with the most humane and praiseworthy, even saintly features of personality.

Soviet literature should be imbued with the Party spirit, it should be devoted to the Party and Party policies. This literature should not shy from anticipating the prospective communist millenium: there is nothing wrong in the Soviet writer's reading the features of the prospective communist millenium already in the Soviet reality of to-day and to represent them somewhat magnified. There is nothing wrong in this practice because these somewhat magnified features of the future lie in the line of the main tendencies of life. In evoking a certain picture of life, more or less plausibly conveying an idealized image of the socialist or communist way of life, a Soviet writer is simply prefiguring the shape of things to come. For the same reason, it is no use dwelling at any great length on the seamy sides of the present-day Soviet reality. These seamy sides will disappear, and therefore they do not lie in the line of the main tendencies of life. To insist much on them is false realism. Thus, in substance, runs the official commentary.

It is therefore in keeping with the tenets of Socialist Realism for the Soviet writer to emphasize the cheerful, optimistic sides of life. Typically, he will depict the locus wherein socialism is being built, for example, a construction site of a prospective factory or powerplant, a collective farm, a State grain farm, a research institute and such. In this locus, the Soviet writer shows toiling masses building socialism, with dedication and enthusiasm, under the direction of the positive heroes, most likely Party members or prospective Party members who are the driving force of the socialist construction. The leaders, while overcoming technical difficulties and fulfilling or, most likely, overfulfilling, their production quotas, re-educate and win over the skeptics and, should the need arise, expose the saboteurs, just a handful of despicable scoundrels, and have them punished. This unfailing optimism, the "life-asserting" principle of Socialist Realism finds its most tangible testimony in the *unambiguous happy end* which crowns any work of Socialist Realism worth its salt: the builders have accomplished their mission; the heroine has married the positive hero after having, possibly, been attracted toward the skeptic or even the saboteur; another step has successfully been taken toward the ultimate triumph of communism. At this point of the happy denouement, the initial awareness of the purpose — which has always been present in the mind of the positive hero — reaches a higher stage of awareness. Thanks to the latter, the positive hero can see the purpose in a perspective more far-reaching than the daily routine of his assignment may hitherto have allowed him to do. Such is, for example, the experience of Gleb Chumalov of Gladkov's novel *Cement* at the successful end of his deed. Similar, although more complex and confusing, is the experience of Kurilov in L. Leonov's novel *Doroga na okean* (Road to the ocean). At this terminal point of resolution, the individual destiny of the positive hero more fully articulates with that of the collective, possibly, with that of the nation. All that may hitherto have appeared accidental and contingent, attains the character of necessity.

Kaverin's above-mentioned novels about the formation and education of youth seem in certain respects akin to the European *Bildungsroman* and in certain other respects fulfill some of the requirements of Socialist Realism. In a sense, the novels under study are products of compromise.

The very nature of the genre of the *Bildungsroman* compels the writer to represent a subject endowed with a personality above the average. A mediocre character simply would not qualify to perform all the tasks required by the nature of the *Bildungsroman*. Wilhelm Meister's personality undergoes rapid emotional development soon matched by his worldly wisdom. Heinrich Lee's more or less imagined talent for painting uproots him from his native soil, brings him to the verge of starvation abroad, only to land him miraculously at the castle of Count Dietrich von W...berg. Julien Sorel's crafty willpower lifts him first to a pinnacle of power and glory, and then dooms him to his execution.

The subjects of Kaverin's novels are also of this above-the-average kind. It certainly is not accidental that in Kaverin's three major novels virtually all the leading characters become orphans at their early age. Trubachevskij's family fell apart while he was still in a tender age: his mother divorced his father and went abroad where she died. His nonentity of a father, with whom the young Trubachevskij lives, has nothing to offer to his son. He does not exert any formative influence on him and the son responds with a somewhat commiserating tolerance. Kartashixin has been complete orphan since almost his infancy. Even Masha Bauer, the girl whose life has so significantly interacted with those of Trubachevskij and Kartashixin, comes from a decaying family. Her father, distinguished historian as he is, somehow has not managed to found a well-knit family with a warmhearted and devoted mother at its center. Likewise, Sanja Grigor'ev lost both parents in early childhood and best remembers his step-father's brutalities. Actually, the whole generation of his co-evals as they appear in the novel are "detdomovskie," i.e., from a children's home, orphans too. Katja Tatarinova, the daughter of the polar explorer, knows her father only from her childhood recollections. Her childhood and then her adolescence have gone on in an increasingly oppressive atmosphere of family insecurity, insulting sanc-timoniousness of her step-father, and reach their catastrophic point when her mother commits suicide. Tat'jana Vlasenkova comes from what may be described as a broken home. Her drifter of a father, a jack-of-all-trades, is really good at none. His being an alcoholic obviously does not help their family prosperity. Actually, the seven-year-old Tanja and her mother's bad times hardly worsen when, abandoning his family, he departs for Kamchatka shortly before World War I. Tanja and her mother continue eking out their drab existence. The October Revolution brings a relief but Tanja's mother survives the change for the better only a couple of years. To complete the picture, even the two brothers L'vov (of whom Tanja eventually marries the younger) became orphans in their childhood. Their father, a well-known lawyer, had been assassinated by one of the Black Hundreds.

The recurrence of this orphanhood motive in the biographies of Kaverin's protagonists betrays in more than one regard the author's attitude toward their formation and education. Their liability, i.e., their being orphans at an early age, turns out to be their very asset. Deprived of paternal support or maternal tenderness, or of both, these youngsters had precociously to develop some protective faculties of their own for the sake of their own survival since they had to depend on their own wits and strengths to protect themselves. This motive of early orphanhood justifies in Kaverin's novels his youngsters' early maturity and earnestness toward life, which characterizes the *Bildungsroman* subjects.

Kaverin's youngsters enter quite early, or rather are born into, a sobering school of survival. The aleatory nature of the latter is less secure than the school of life or "apprenticeship" proper to the experience of Wilhelm Meister or even to that of Heinrich Lee. The school Kaverin's youngsters live through is more like the school of life the Dickensian children are forced into from their tender age. The orphanhood motive gives a certain brutal quality to the school of life allotted to many youngsters in the prose fiction of Dickens and Kaverin. Through this motive the author emphasizes the awareness of the presence of society in the protagonist's life. Especially, this motive points out how much exposed the protagonist may become to society's cruelties and injustices, how defenseless he may stand against them.

There may be another dimension at the bottom of this motive. It would correspond to the scheme of things in line with the tenets of Socialist Realism. The traditional motive of orphanhood gains political pointedness. In this respect the Soviet version of the *Bildungsroman* differs from the previous European tradition. For example, the fate of Mignon in *Wilhelm Meister's Apprenticeship* has a very different dimension. Her abduction, destitution and orphanhood do not seem to be intended as a condemnation pronounced against some and as a meed of praise paid to those who have redressed some of these wrongs. Her pathetic fate merely contributes to Wilhelm's formation and education, and it does so in the manner of a universal parable. Here, prose fiction does not seem to even intend to convey the agonizing problem of social injustices and cruelties. The latter do not seem to matter for Wilhelm in themselves, as objective phenomena for the sake of which he should abandon his personal pursuit of self-education and self-culture. In Dickens' prose fiction this motive carries a distinct social ring, the ring awakening one to social injustices accumulated in British society toward the middle of the 19th century.

It is this distinct social ring, politically and ideologically sharpened, that reverberates through the motive of orphanhood in the Soviet version of the *Bildungsroman*. And it is in conjunction with the Revolution that this orphanhood motive makes best sense within socialist-realism context. Let it be observed that in his first major novel *Fulfillment of Desires* Kaverin chooses not yet to lend political coloring to the orphanhood motive. Only in his subsequent novels, *Two Captains* and *Open Book*, does Kaverin place this orphanhood motive in what might be interpreted as politically tendentious contrast. Kaverin may have done so in order to comply with the increased pressure of Socialist Realism. The fundamental thesis to be illustrated through the medium of literary representation postulates that without the Revolution countless underprivileged children, orphaned or deserted, would remain doomed to their degrading existence. What symbolizes social injustices more incisively than an ill-treated orphan child or a deserted child not taken care of? The Tsarist Russia ill-treated its underprivileged orphans or its deserted ones such as little Sanja Grigor'ev or little Tanja Vlasenkova. The new Soviet order has stretched forth a helping hand to these little waifs and strays, has secured shelter for them and given them nourishment and a new lease on life. How more positively to assert the benefit of the Revolution? How more emphatically to illustrate the superiority of the new Soviet order over the old Tsarist Russia? Here than is a rich mine of literary motives for the socialist-realist writer to exploit.

How does Kaverin proceed in this regard? The young people he represents prove to be nearly the ideal human material reaching the educational machinery of the Communist Revolution. They are young enough at the time of the Revolution to spontaneously identify with the new-born Soviet order. So do Trubachevskij and Kartashixin of *Fulfillment of Desires*. Kartashixin's both parents were active bolsheviks who fought and died for the Revolution. The Revolution is the earliest experience that his childhood awareness registers and ever since, throughout his student years and his early scientific maturity, he has espoused the purposes of the

Revolution — namely, the Five-Year-Plan — as his own. Trubachevskij is more individualistic and less disciplined. These flaws cause his early misfortune. He overcomes his reverses and disappointments by actively taking part in socialist construction and dedicating himself to the vital interests and aspirations that animate most Soviet people. The protagonists of his subsequent novels come from ideologically more desirable backgrounds. Both Trubachevskij and Kartashixin are of middle-class origin, which, however, does not prevent them from totally identifying with the Soviet system. Sanja Grigor'ev of *Two Captains* and Tat'jana Vlasenkova of *Open Book* come from very humble social backgrounds, practically, the proletarian one. This should significantly advance their chances to become the New Soviet Men and Women. Sanja Grigor'ev was born into a poor family of a harbor worker and a washerwoman. Tat'jana Vlasenkova also originates from a lowly family, tottering on the verge of utter destitution. Tat'jana's mother was one of the children of a factory worker; she became a dressmaker's shop hand, later eking out her and her daughter's drab existence with casual seamstressing and fortune-telling. Kaverin uses some somber colors in describing the oppressed childhood of tongue-tied Sanja: his helpless desperation at the arrest of his father whom he knows to be innocent but cannot prove it because of his speech deficiency; his ill-treatment at the hand of his scoundrel of a step-father and finally his mother's death. Similar oppressive effect is brought about by the picture of little Tanja's debuts as a kitchenmaid, rag-picking and scullioning in order to prop up her family's meager finances. What future would have been theirs, had it not been for the Revolution? Such a beginning obviously at once demonstrates the full measure of their good fortune of being born into the Revolution. What has opened out in front of them are unlimited vistas of opportunities for education, culture, self-improvement, achievements and progress. Kaverin's prose fiction stands, thus far, quite in line with the tenets of Socialist Realism. At the same time, Kaverin does not take any vital interest in the Revolution as such, as an object of creative description and literary investigation. In regard to young people's experiences and formation its place might even appear narrowly functional. It signifies little beyond its literal meaning: it revolves the stage.

The fact of his protagonists' being born into the Revolution enables Kaverin to bypass another literary reef. His youth were not old enough in 1917 fully to understand the magnitude of the events and to participate in them actively. Still less would they have been able, of course, gradually to embrace the Bolshevik Revolution during the pre-revolutionary decades. Now, the motive of the conversion to the Revolution is one of the most stereotype-ridden in Soviet literature. Inasmuch as thoughts and attitudes in this regard are prescribed and thoroughly predictable, this motive is almost fatally standardized. Perhaps the paradox of such a stereotype is L. Leonov's *Russkij les* (Russian forest). In depicting the gradual and universal progression toward and conversion to the Revolution Leonov displays an astonishing linguistic versatility, a sort of afterglow of epic poetry. But it all still seems to be an immense and motionless cliché in which magnificent words do not do justice to complex human realities.

Kaverin spares himself this kind of stereotype and standardization thanks to the age of his youthful heroes. The main source of the stereotype here consists in a prerequisite political awareness. Kaverin does not need this prerequisite because it is children who are watching the events. In the first place, there are not too many of these events, since children would not naturally witness them. Little Sanja Grigor'ev witnesses the Revolution during the burial of his mother. The grief sharpens his perception. It also blurs his normal associations. He meets the Revolution perched on the hearse that is taking his dead mother to the cemetery. In his consciousness trivial boy's thoughts alternate with his grief. He wakes up to reality only when stray bullets come buzzing around and the coachman whips up the jade so that the hearse quite indecorously darts off, leaving behind the pedestrian funeral procession. Little Kartashixin's first acquaintance with the Revolution, if not so "untypical," is no less "made strange." He is not over nine years old at the height of the Civil War. Both his parents take part in it: his father as a brilliant bolshevik general, leading the revolutionary troops to victory; his mother as a military doctor. They both fall in action. The little boy happens to accompany his mother and witnesses some of the battles, including the one in which she dies. The boy observes the action from the window of a train and does not understand what is going on around him. Gunfire, soldiers, burning houses, all these paraphernalia of warfare stand beyond the reach of the little boy's understanding. This technique resembles the one that Tolstoy uses in his description of war scenes. And its effect is similar. Kaverin most likely does not want to discredit the epic of warfare, as Tolstoy may. However, Kaverin removes the conventional glamor from the epic of the Civil War. In *Open Book* Kaverin gives a humorous interpretation to this prime awareness of the Revolution. Little Tanja Vlasenkova overhears the grown-ups conversing about the purpose of the Revolution: whom has the Revolution been made for? And the interlocutor points to little Tanja: it is for her, Tanja, that the Revolution has been made, so that she may go to school instead of scullioning and rag-picking. Tanja, not unlike Dickensian children, ascribes literal meaning to a figurative statement. How could she then avoid reveling in pride and carrying her head high to the point of not seeing underfoot, since the whole Revolution has been made for her little person? Thus, revolutionary events become "untypical," or "made strange," or humorously interpreted. They acquire some poetic value. In this particular refraction, these marginal events endow the Revolution with a sense of actually experienced human drama that, for example, the verbose rhetoric of Leonov falls short of achieving.

   In none of his major novels has Kaverin undertaken to narrate the story of the griefs and ill-fortunes of an orphan child. This "Dickensian motive" only sets the initial situation for the main action of the novel to take its start from. This initial situation will serve as a sort of point of reference as to how far the young protagonist will have gone and how well he will have succeeded in life. *Two Captains* ends in such a self-evaluatory look back at the initial point of reference. It also supplies the novel with its initial political and ideological motivation. However, such an orphanhood motive in its Dickensian dramatic significance does not preoccupy Kaverin too much. It clearly stands at the periphery of Kaverin's novels, not at their center. In a sense, Kaverin's novels start where Dickens' leave off. A good case in point is the way in which the two authors treat a similar motive in the novelistic biographies of, respectively, Oliver Twist and Sanja Grigor'ev. At the end of his flight to London, Oliver is trapped in the conspiracy of a gang of malefactors. Oliver's life with the gang and his attempt to break loose from it fill the greatest part of his destiny within the novel. The situation seems typically Dickensian: against the coarsely ruthless wickedness of evil is pitted an utterly defenseless delicate boy pathetically lonely in his innocent virtue and naiveté. He lives through a truly brutal school of life in which he learns the rudimentary art, that of bare survival; and "apprenticeship" in simply not going under. It takes quite a strain of sentimentalism combined with a near miraculous development of the plot to avert the ultimate catastrophe. And this sentimentalism of characterization and intricacy of plot seem to be the idiosyncrasy of Dickens' novels. Now, Sanja Grigor'ev also becomes involved with a gang of shady dealers when he lands in Moscow after his flight from his native town. However, what in Dickens' novels constitutes the very core of the plot, in Kaverin's novel shrinks to a fleeting episode in the life of the protagonist, an episode preparatory to the actual story.

Kaverin spares himself any vital dependence on the Dickensian tradition of the *Bildungsroman* by imparting a historical dimension to his novels. He does not need Dickens' sentimentalism of characterization or intricacy of plot in order to bring his young protagonists out of distress. History itself moves to their rescue: the Communist Revolution breaks out when his young protagonists are still children and its tidal wave carries these underprivileged youngsters away from their sordid beginnings. The Revolution is both the agent and the measure of the astonishing improvement these little waifs and strays experience in their lot almost overnight. The Dickensian poor orphan has to have his mysterious parentage unexpectedly revealed, or must meet a kindly old gentleman, or come into an unexpected inheritance, or unsuspectingly meet his yet unknown relatives, friends and enemies, in order to have his fate changed from the worst to the best. Within the framework of his narrative, Kaverin brings in the biggest *deus ex machina* of them all: the Revolution. Isn't this global impersonal event an even more contrived and more artificial device to solve apparently insoluble personal difficulties than Dickens' stock-in-trade of plot-making? And yet it enjoys the advantage of total plausibility and of politically most desirable motivation. Thanks to the almost miraculous disappearance of the old degrading setting to which Kaverin's orphans seemed otherwise condemned, they very promptly live through the purely "Dickensian" stage of hardships in the "apprenticeship" period of their lives and enter upon another stage of their formation and education, the one to whose representation Kaverin devotes his novels.

3

What most emphatically characterizes Kaverin's young protagonists is their drive for education. *Fulfillment of Desires* describes the critical student years in the lives of Trubachevskij and Kartashixin. The novel naturally centers its narrative on their intellectual pursuits. Trubachevskij intellectually relives the experiences of the

Decembrists and, from the point of view of a young Soviet historian of literature, tries to interpret the epoch of Pushkin. Kartashixin is a biologist and physiologist and already in his student years tries to design experiments elucidating the physiology of hearing and blood circulation. So the very substance of the representation in this novel consists in dramatizing the ways in which a young literary scholar and a biologist study toward their university degrees and engage in research with a view to making new discoveries in their respective fields. The novel pursues the aim of showing how the young people try to gain and expand scholarly and scientific knowledge about man and his environment. Their intellectual activity, however, is not devoted to the exclusive pursuit of detached pure science and neutral truth. They intend their discoveries to promptly serve people, to exert beneficial impact on the lives of their fellow men, expecially, their countrymen. The other young protagonists in Kaverin's novels live through even more illuminating educational experience. From their Dickensian "school of life" they switch over to the Soviet life of school. Sanja Grigor'ev, first arrested with other profiteers, and then freed, is given a new lease on life. He becomes an ordinary schoolboy. In school, where his mind opens to better and higher concerns of life, he can develop his temperament of an explorer and discover his vocation of a polar aviator. Likewise, in *Open Book* the Communist Revolution enables Tat'jana Vlasenkova to enter secondary school, and subsequently to enroll in Medical School.

It is in this respect of education and formation of personality that Kaverin's novels articulate with the *Bildungsroman*. Just as the *Bildungsroman* subjects, Kaverin's young protagonists commit themselves very early in their biographies to the aim of acquiring education and of developing their abilities. At the same time, however, when the author shapes the educational experience of the young protagonists of his novels, he more or less conspicuously follows a certain blueprint implicit in the tenets of Socialist Realism. The young people's education is actualized in terms of manpower, especially the manpower qualified to effect and to control environment. For this reason, perhaps, Kaverin denies Tat'jana Vlasenkova her erstwhile ambition to become a movie actress, and has her enroll reluctantly in Medical School, work as a general medical doctor at a State grain farm and eventually embrace the career of a microbiologist. Sanja Grigor'ev becomes a polar pilot and at different points of his aviator's career flies mail, equipment and personnel between different cities and regions of the Soviet Union, and sprays crops with pesticide from low-flying airplanes. Here we can recognize the motive of the communist builders and specialists participating in socialist construction. A friend of Tat'jana Vlasenkova spells this motive out when he says "raz"ezzhaemsja v pjatiletku" (we are departing for [the different areas of] the Five-Year-Plan). The Revolution has saved all these former orphans, waifs and strays, and has given them a chance to become useful and respected members of the new socialist society. And now that they have graduated from universities and institutes, they are expected to repay their debts to the Revolution by contributing, in their respective fields, to the welfare and the might of their socialist fatherland.

Schools see to these youngsters' character building so as to train them into exemplary good citizens. *Two Captains* stands out in this respect among Kaverin's three major novels. To a great extent this novel belongs to juvenile literature. The very motto threading its way all throughout the novel, "to struggle and to quest, to find and not to surrender," reads not unlike a boy scout's rule of behavior. Little Sanja Grigor'ev, in response to his teacher's rebuke, starts developing and training his willpower. He devises or adopts rules for the development of his willpower and forces himself into observing them while carrying out numerous elaborate exercises destined to steel his willpower. For example, in order to train and test his complete self-control he lets another boy slash his fingers with a penknife during class-hour. He forces himself into taking the habit of setting up his order of the day in the morning and then firmly abiding by it; Sanja remarks that he has pursued this habit all his life ever since. As to the main rule of the development of willpower: "To keep in mind the aim of one's existence," Sanja had never experienced any difficulty in observing it because that aim was clear for him at that time already. Later, when he makes up his mind to enroll in a pilots' school, he sets in motion all his willpower and intelligence toward the admission: he commands himself into rigorous physical training, through hard work he substantially improves his school grades, he studies on his own the theory of airplane building, although much of the theory is still above the level of his comprehension at the time. And after his admission to the pilots' school, he chooses the hardest assignments for the sake of the most arduous training. Kartashixin of *Fulfillment of Desires* likewise demonstrates a high degree of self-control. Self-discipline with him occasionally reaches truly brahmanic proportions: full of sap as he is, he can, confronting a beautiful temptress, order himself not to think of her and steels himself against temptation by taking cold showers. His friend Trubachevskij, caught in the same whirl, throws his self-control to the four winds . . .

This community of life also enables the young protagonists to take part in public affairs beyond the walls of their class-rooms and laboratories. Thus, in *Open Book* Tanja Vlasenkova and her other schoolmates help the local government in feeding, disinfecting and finding shelter for a large group of men, women and children who arrived at their town from the famine-stricken Volga region threatened with typhus epidemic. Later, in Medical School it has become an unwritten rule for students to participate in general student affairs, and to take active organized attitudes toward public issues. After one student meeting, another girl invites Tat'jana to work with her to prove by their activity that no gap separates the intelligentsia from communist youth, as it has been pointed out by the speaker. At another juncture, Tat'jana, too much absorbed in her medical studies and research, incurs the displeasure of the student committee secretary for her inactivity in public affairs. Different communist youth organizations mesh with the general student body and their officers see to it that students do not neglect their public duties. Thus, Kaverin represents schools as performing a double function in the education and formation of these young people. In schools, they are taught their future skills. Moreover, once in schools, they learn a protracted lesson in the *Lebensgemeinschaft* of the new social system.

The author devotes a good deal of his art to representing the growth of scientific awareness in his young protagonists. He tries to show how they become thoughtful scholars and scientists bent on unraveling the clues to the riddles of nature, unknown regions and man's cultural heritage. Some of the most valuable pages to be read in his novels show the mental process whereby a scientific breakthrough and discovery is achieved. These pages convey a good deal of dramatic tension and suspense, as well as humor. The young philologist Trubachevskij reaches a precocious intellectual maturity in his scholarly field, too precocious for his own good. He tries to crack the code in which one of Pushkin's manuscripts is written. The mysterious text haunts his mind day and night. It roots itself deep in his consciousness and he gains a thorough mastery over its undecoded aggregate of words. Days and nights of fruitless reconstructions, elaborate guesses, all this high-strung intellectual exertion coupled with his upstirring emotional experience, his ever-busy intuition all conspire toward the ultimate scene. Trubachevskij is watching a silent movie with Masha: on the screen, a train is rolling into the station, the bright spots of its windows gliding along the platform one after the other, just as the syllables and lines of the mysterious text have been doing lately in his mind. And at that fraction of time, from this coincidence of the motion picture and his mental image of Pushkin's lines, in a flash of hard-earned inspiration, he suddenly understands the hitherto undeciphered poem. This rapid intellectual growth of the young philologist with its occasional illuminations is artistically all the more valid because the author weaves it extra-ordinarily tightly into the overall development of Trubachevskij's personality, and even turns it into one of the factors of Trubachevskij's youthful tragedy: the rest of his personality lags behind his precocious intellectual maturity; for this reason, his scholarly integrity yields, with disastrous results, to his misdirected worldly ambitions.

From his earliest works, Kaverin has kept devoting a major part of his creative effort to representing the fate of the scholar and the scientist. Already in his earliest experimental tales the various medieval figures of "scholastics" and "masters of many sciences," itinerant or settled, hold a noticeable place. These figures are only flimsy puppets without any depth of representation or psychological substance. Their lives and adventures offer a fancy Romantic picture of their assumed magic experience, a picture sprinkled with the author's irony. In "The Cask" and *The Great Game* the setting shifts from the never-never land to recognizable sites. The latter still display a good deal of fancy exotic features (for example, all those numerous Chinese smoking opium in a Petrograd den in *The Great Game*). The mathematician and the philologist of these two tales grow to reach all three dimensions. Conceived in the spirit of the Anglo-Saxon "colonial" Romanticism, crime-detection tale and tale of fantasy, "The Cask" and *The Great Game* mostly describe physical adventures, external to the mathematician's and the philologist's scientific pursuits. Strictly speaking, they do not have any scientific pursuits worth mentioning. To be sure, the mathematician descends to the bottom of a chasm in order to test a scientific theory. But the scientific theory is preposterous, so that we can speak of the theory, its testing and the pursuit pertaining to it only in the manner of a jest. As for Panaev, he either wastes his scientific training altogether (he does not need to be a philologist in order to gamble and to smoke opium), or he uses it for purposes alien to scientific pursuit. Kaverin's subsequent works will tend to "internalize" a scholar's or a scientist's adventures. They will both embark on adventures within their own sphere of activity.

It is in *Open Book* that Kaverin draws the most comprehensive portrayal of the formation and education of a scientist. The scientist in question is Tat'jana Vlasenkova, a woman microbiologist. The author links the growth of her professional expertness and of her personality to the birth of the Soviet penicillin. This particular motive of the novel poses a problem which within the framework of this study about Kaverin's prose fiction I find sufficient to point out without attempting to study in depth.

In his previous two novels Kaverin ascribes an actual discovery or breakthrough made by an actual person to his fictitious characters. The deciphering of what has been described as fragments of the Tenth Chapter of *Evgenij Onegin* was done by P.O. Morozov in 1910. Severnaja Zemlja was discovered by A.I. Vil'kickij in 1913. Kaverin ascribes the two discoveries to his fictitious heroes Trubachevskij and Captain Tatarinov respectively. These "misascriptions" are a matter of artistic convention which motivates the action of narrative fiction. As such, as a method of acknowledged creative fiction, they cannot give reasons for any legitimate objections. In *Open Book* the author refers to specific circumstances concerning the theory, the discovery and the manufacture of penicillin by the pre-Soviet and the Soviet biologists. These circumstances are factual enough to give to the narrative the dimensions of actual history. Likewise, the tone and the drift of the narrative seem to claim that this literary work conveys facts of empirical reality. The novel asserts, and somewhat polemically so, that Soviet biologists – represented by the symbolic figure of Tat'jana Vlasenkova – discovered and produced penicillin about the same time as Western biologists did and its quality turned out to be superior to the British penicillin. Only destructive rivalries among Soviet biologists, intrigues of which the drug had become the object, and appalling red-tape prevented the Soviet biologists from obtaining the credit of being the first in the world to have developed and produced penicillin. This study deals primarily with Kaverin's art of narrative fiction. How the subject matter of this novel refers to historical reality is, of course, entirely the responsibility of the author of the novel.

The *Bildungsroman* population differs from other figures of narrative prose fiction about young people by its reflective and purposeful attitude toward experience. This attitude sets the *Bildungsroman* characters apart from the young characters of picaresque tradition. The former possess a sort of spiritual profundity and psychological complexity. The latter seem to lack such a profundity and complexity; in their representation the point of interest centers more on the art of external movement and circumstances. Now, Kaverin's young protagonists are akin to the former. His young subject takes a global view of his or her life, and judges it in terms of its consecutive achievements and failures and its ultimate purpose. It is an earnest and reflective view of a young person who can revel in life but can also take a detached and judging view of it. Perhaps it would be no exaggeration to state that such earnestness about life and reflective view of it belong to most major protagonists of Russian literature. In another sense it also belongs to the protagonists of the literature of Socialist Realism.

A critic reproached Kaverin with conveying in his novel *Open Book* only a very rudimentary kind of information, one that we can find in any "meager little pamphlet about penicillin." Such criticism misses the purpose of scientific activity as an object of representation in artistic prose. Kaverin himself explains the problem:

[...] Working on *Two Captains* I surrounded myself with books on aviation and the history of the Arctic. Now, their place was taken by works on microbiology, and this, unfortunately, turned out to be much more complex. First of all it was necessary to learn to read these works in a way different from the one in which scientists themselves read them.

To reconstitute the train of thought of the scientist, to read behind the dry short lines of a scholarly article what this man lived by, to understand the story and the meaning of his struggle against enemies (and sometimes even against friends), which almost always is present in scientific work, — this is the task without the fulfillment of which there is no sense even to undertake to write on such a theme. It was necessary to know how to understand that which the scientist factors out [vynosit za skobki] : the psychology of his creation [...] [4]

Thus, what matters in such a work of narrative fiction is scientific research or scientific discovery in terms of its human interest. The author represents scientific quest as it affects not only scientifc problems as such or man's intellect, but also as it affects the total development of man's personality, emotions and total human destiny within its historical context.

Tat'jana Vlasenkova symbolizes the Russian scientist at his or her best, the one who devotes to his scientific pursuit his whole life and whole personality, and whose scientific and intellectual integrity never allows him to accept easy routine for the sake of worldly security. Many features make up her personality of a scientist. She has understood, first intuitively and then consciously, the best and the most daring in the biological thinking of the previous generation of scientists. In the novel, the author shows this scientific continuity in adolescent Tanja's befriending an old biologist, the uncle of the two brothers L'vov, whom hardly anyone takes seriously, although he is a far-sighted biologist. In a makeshift course of lectures intended for youngsters around him he conveys his theory of what subsequently will become known as anti-biotics. Tat'jana writes down these ideas under his dictation without yet being able, just as anyone else, to understand them. Only later, when as a microbiology student she undertakes her first assigned research into diphtheria bacilli, does the significance of the old biologist's ideas dawn on her. This idea of cultural, scientific and intellectual continuity lies deep in all three novels of Kaverin. It distinctly characterizes his young scholars and scientists. For Tat'jana, for example, her dogged quest for penicillin is to great extent a matter of her urge to bring to reality the prophetic vision of the old biologist, to redress the wrongs done to him and his memory, to acknowledge her personal gratitude. And it is also a matter of continuity, albeit of another kind, that, just as the old biologist of the previous generation, Tat'jana should suffer from other people's ill will and that scheming mediocrities should attempt to ridicule and discredit her pioneering scientific work. Hers is a sort of intuitive insight into yet undiscovered scientific truths. In the course of her lifelong research, throughout her successes and failures, her thinking keeps moving with almost maniacal stubbornness toward the theory and practice of anti-biotics. She never entirely parts with the thought of the green mold. She often remembers the old biologist's room always smelling a little of mold, with its perennial piece of mold-grown bread or orange-peel lying in an old cracked glass. Later, when she works as a general medical doctor at a State grain farm in Southern Russia, she again obstinately reverts to this green mold, analyzing the medicinal qualities of its different samples: in her makeshift laboratory she succeeds in controlling a certain kind of vibrio with her culture of mold; so diligently does she apply herself to this task that she ends by smelling herself of mold, thus repelling people around her. This interest in the fungus that grows as green mold on stale bread she brings along to Biochemistry Institute in Moscow where she starts her career of a microbiologist. She realizes that her accumulated experience is not enough. She has to learn a far more sophisticated art of how to use her hands to perform delicate experiments, how to observe, how to doubt creatively, how to acknowledge and concede an error, this especially since her first research work at the Institute ends in a painful failure. However, her renewed work with her new expert team already brings about tangible results. It has shown that the fungus of green mold neutralizes certain kinds of streptococci. At this point, when Tat'jana had actually made a very significant step forward toward the discovery and production of penicillin, Kramov, the director of the Institute, eliminates this project from the Institute's official program of research and publicly ridicules her pursuit. Has it been a piece of catastrophic misjudgment on his part? Or, perhaps, an obscure feeling that Tat'jana's line of research is progressing along a collision course with his own theories of immunity?

While she is still working on her first student project in biology without success, her professor suggests that she read *Don Quixote* in order to carry through her project. So she does, and most likely has understood the message. Subsequently, she fights with a sort of quixotic obstinacy if not frenzy against the obstacles she encounters in her life of a Soviet scientist. In her life she endures more frustration than she experiences satisfaction. Even the obstacles interposed in her path display something of quixotic magic elusiveness: the ubiquitous obstructions of red-tape and pitfalls of slander provided against her by her enemies.

This noble dedication to her profession, synonymous with scientific integrity, at times causes her amusingly inept predicaments, and it always keeps sharp her sense of purposeful observation: once, she keeps buying caviar from a food store with her own – very limited – petty cash while conducting experiments on caviar for the Ministry of Fisheries which, because of some bureaucratic oversight, has failed to supply her with caviar of its own. On another occasion, upset to tears over her rift with her husband, she starts wondering, in the very process of crying, whether tears do not contain the chemical substance she has in vain been searching for, which very thought dries up her tears precisely when she needs them for microbiological testing.

Ultimately, her scientific integrity dooms her to her tragic fate.

Her being a woman biologist may add still other dimensions to the development of her personality. Undoubtedly, Tat'jana Vlasenkova has become a microbiologist by vocation, the vocation awakened by the old biologist. However, some emotional motivation may also have underlain her decisions. The real great, unfulfilled love of her life is the older brother L'vov, the nephew of the old biologist. He attracted her to biological studies emotionally. Subsequently, she marries the younger brother. She surely loves her husband, but the incompleteness of her emotional self-fulfillment keeps betraying itself in her recurrent and blurred thoughts of the older brother, in her unconscious yearning for romance, e.g., when she meets her former school-mate Vladimir Lukashevich. Tat'jana becomes a recognized microbiologist. She wages a resolute struggle for the integrity of Soviet microbiology. However, perhaps by this very striving she also fills in some gap in her emotional being. Otherwise how to explain the fact that she is able to rationalize the very tears she is shedding a propos of her husband and at the very moment of shedding them? For this reason, perhaps, she allows such a mediocre place in her narrative to her attitudes of a wife, of a homemaker. It is also strange to read that she does not always carry the picture of her little boy in her wallet when she travels. Perhaps her selfless dedication to her laboratory work somehow makes up for her fundamental emotional failure. At the end, Tat'jana loses even that humble share of her family happiness. Even her Pushkin's namesake fares better.

4

At its dogmatic extreme, the literature of Socialist Realism entertains a certain abstract notion of man — the Communist Man — which is the anthropomorphic figuration of communist ideals and aspirations. Abram Tertz has written a very incisive commentary of this abstract man, the "positive hero:"

The positive hero is not simply a good man. He is a hero illuminated by the light of the most ideal of all ideals. Leonid Leonov called his positive hero "a peak of humanity from whose height the future can be seen." He has either no faults at all or else a few of them — for example, he sometimes loses his temper a little. These faults have a twofold function. They help the hero to preserve a certain likeness to real men, and they provide something to overcome as he raises himself ever higher on the ladder of political morality. However, these faults must be slight or else they would run counter to his basic qualities. It is not easy to enumerate these basic qualities of the positive hero: ideological conviction, courage, intelligence, will power, patriotism, respect for women, self-sacrifice, etc. etc. [...] [5]

An art figuring such an abstract man must evolve in a very special medium if it wants to survive and be taken seriously: in a medium akin to medieval hagiographic fervor. It should take a great deal of faith, of aggressive emotion in order to keep imparting to this art its sense of validity. Pavel Korchagin, among others, may have come nearest to this ideal of the positive hero. He employs all his resources toward external action, in the unconditional service of political dogma. His literary brethren do alike. They may have inherited something of the ruthless singlemindedness of the persecuted conspirators of another age, of Raxmetov, Nechaev, Pavel Vlasov. Although supremely powerful individuals, they are not individualistic in the sense that they set their personal selves apart from the object they pursue, i.e., apart from the society they try to influence. They have no other problem, their personalities are totally absorbed by their socio-political mission. Their own personal selves, their endeavor and the society to which their endeavor is applied blend into one, the one that justifies their struggle and entirely takes up their awareness.

The positive heroes of Socialist Realism display total permeability to the morality of the group, of life of school, or public indoctrination, of which they may then become heroic champions. This total permeability enables the positive heroes or prospective positive heroes to undergo total pedagogic transformation, should a need for it arise. This possibility of total pedagogic transformation matters vitally because it opens the way for devising the desirable norm of behavior. This means that the primary purpose of the Soviet version of the *Bildungsroman*, inasmuch as it follows the tenets of Socialist Realism, is pedagogic. Its representation of the education and formation of a young man or woman will in the last analysis consecrate this desirable norm of behavior.

Pedagogic purpose need not preclude the aesthetic quality of the given work. However, the two are not necessarily synonymous. In an ultimate case, and not only in an ultimate case, the author may grant predominance to one over the other. For example, he may let predominate the expediency of pedagogic means at the expense of a certain detachment and disengagement of aesthetic perception. For example, a critic berated Kaverin for having endowed Tat'jana Vlasenkova with such a shabby papa and pressed the author to assign to such a distinguished Soviet mircrobiologist a more typical, that is, more respectable father.[6] Here, the critic reasons from the point of view of pedagogic expediency, whereas the author has decided for creating a more elusive aesthetic effect.

At a certain level of discourse, pedagogic expediency becomes synonymous with political propaganda and indoctrination, one determined by the current needs of censorship. And at the level of political propaganda and indoctrination literary representation is or may be felt to become a rickety art or no art at all. A few examples may clarify the issue. V. Azhaev's novel *Daleko ot Moskvy* (Far from Moscow, 1948), S. Babaevskij's *Kavaler zolotoj zvezdy* (The knight of the golden star, 1947) or P. Pavlenko's *Schast'e* (Happiness, (1947) all grace Socialist Realism as its classics, in testimony of which they were all awarded Stalin Prizes. They appeared in the same decade as parts of *Two Captains*[7] and *Open Book*, and in about the same creative atmosphere. In them pedagogic purpose reaches the level of political propaganda and indoctrination. Since they were written in rigid conformity to the requirements of Socialist Realism, they all display the same prescribed attitudes, the same prescribed virtues, the same prescribed vices, the same prescribed emotions, the same prescribed thoughts, to the point of working out one immutable threadbare stereotype. They all suffer from declarativeness. The author simply states the characters' emotions and thoughts instead of showing them through artistically selected details. Thus the reader is reduced to taking the author at his word rather than seeing for himself. Characters speak mostly in political slogans as if they were reciting by rote pages from an ideological journal. Living human beings hardly speak so in spontaneous situations, unless they are joking or parodying some official ideological phraseology. Hence a depersonalizing effect of this phraseology: rather than evoke live human experiences, it inventories these in journalistic clichés borrowed from the routine of politics, economy and labor. In his *Artist Unknown* Kaverin throws upon the stage a curious character, Zhaba, a sort of brilliant linguist *manqué*, who, at one point of the action, delivers a public lecture on "The Bureaucratization of Language" (bjurokratizacija jazyka). In a sense, Zhaba's mixed-up pronouncements turn out to have inadvertently given forth a prophetic ring. The bureaucratic lingo in which the novels of the Stalin-prize vintage were written stifles any valid characterization out of existence. It simply inventories characters. Therefore the characters convey the impression of being human automata "programmed" by not too sophisticated a wordmonger to utter words of dedication to the motherland and socialist labor, high-sounding words to be sure but distressingly deprived of validity and sincerity. And since they all speak the same words in the same way, the strength of characterization of these words is nil. Differences between characters tend to wear off. Instead of producing a gallery of well-individualized characters, the writer postulates dull interchangeable units of speech.

Declarativeness generates the crudeness of the device. Let me discuss one typical example. One of the deuteragonists of *Far from Moscow*, tractor driver Silin, decides to donate his savings to buy a tank. His superiors approve the idea, and one of them even voices his willingness himself to contribute to the purchase. Silin and his wife are young, they have no children. He wants to buy the tank and go to the front in it with his wife. So, he and his wife donate their savings for the purchase of the tank and some time later he receives a telegram from Stalin in which the latter thanks Silin for his patriotic solicitude. Silin is overwhelmed when he realizes whom the telegram comes from. It increases his working enthusiasm tenfold. We need not doubt Silin's sense of self-sacrifice. We only deplore the lack of mastery in the presentation of this motive. There are three components to this motive: reaching the decision, actualization, its consequences. A modern writer would most likely concentrate his attention on the reaching of the decision, since at this stage the character's mind and personality stand out in the sharpest relief. The author fails to give any sense of drama to the reaching of the decision. Virtually nothing that communicates human vitality to the reaching of the decision appears in the episode. The latter takes less than four pages scattered throughout the 637 pages of the novel.[8] The author does not take the trouble to represent any inner debate, any hesitations, any soulsearching, any selfish interests to overcome, any significant illumination. Now, without such an incisive representation of the inner life or of the sense of drama of which the reaching of the decison is made, this whole event has no or little aesthetic validity. Silin does consult two of his superiors apropos of his intentions. This, we may presume, represents his coming to the decision. However, if these consultations are meant to be of any aesthetic validity at all, they should somehow reflect Silin's inner drama. Actually, the author hardly takes any trouble to represent this inner drama. Neither does he have the right words for it. A soulless talk about soul cannot possibly compel emotional identification with the soul in question. For example, the author might have represented Silin's consultation with his wife since Silin himself states that he wants to speak with her first about his donation. Such a scene would offer a good deal ot dramatic substance: it could show how emotions, thoughts, doubts, changing moods, flights of fancy interact between husband and wife and how they both together reach the noble resolve to give what they have for their country in danger. However, his wife is mentioned perfunctorily. Silin expresses his wish to speak with his wife only as a pretext for declaring that he wants to donate his savings for the purchase of a tank. To be sure, he consults his superiors about his donation. These consultations, however do not go beyond performing the function of a sort of tribune from which to declare the event of the donation. They provide the minimal motivation for the author simply to advertize Silin's patriotism. Little else matters in this whole context and episode.[9] Azhaev does not validly motivate Silin's behavior. And because of this poor artistry of the episode the mature critical reader is unable to suspend his disbelief in regard to Silin's patriotic gesture. Therefore he cannot recognize its human value. The episode does not exceed the value of a crude attempt at propaganda. This characterizes the whole work and all the other works of the vintage.

It would be out of proportion even to undertake a comparative study of the above-mentioned works of the Stalin-prize vintage and the novels of Kaverin on the same level of valuation. This discussion is not intended in these terms. It rather provides a peculiar point of reference which helps us understand certain dimensions of Kaverin's works.

5

At a certain, undifferentiated, scale of observation, Kaverin's novels may seem to offer something similar to the above-mentioned novels. They represent the most dedicated and "life-asserting" segment of Soviet society. These people develop through the most formative and dynamic periods of their lives. They mostly come from humble social backgrounds, which enhances their social and political virtues. They do their utmost to develop their talents, they struggle hard to succeed in life, and they mostly do succeed. Therefore, they have stored up a lifetime of optimism and dedication to the system to which they owe so much. In overcoming obstacles they demonstrate their vitality and strength. In one way or another they all grow to become thoughtful individuals dedicated to the welfare of Soviet society. In their thoughts and deeds they all assert a high political motivation and loyalty to their country, both at peace and at war.

However, on a closer look, Kaverin's protagonists manifest properties less conventional than those expected in the positive heroes of Socialist Realism. Quite unlike Raxmetov, Nechaev, Pavel Vlasov, Pavel Korchagin and others, Kaverin's young protagonists are in no way communist conspirators or "professional revolutionaries." Partly, their age, that is, the age Kaverin chooses to give them, severs them from that heroic generation. His protagonists belong to the generation of the Soviet men and women that in 1917 were, on the one hand, not old enough to judge of the events and to participate in them actively, and, on the other hand, young enough to identify spontaneously with the Soviet order. Nonetheless, they are not active, hard-driving members of the Communist Party, and, what is even more significant, they predominantly are not even members of the Party. In *Fulfillment of Desires*, for example, Nevorozhin somewhat cynically remarks in his conversation with Trubachevskij that the latter already has made one mistake that will prevent him from making headway in life and in his profession: Trubachevskij is not a member of the Communist Party or of the Young Communist League. Sanja Grigor'ev is admitted to the Party but his affiliation does not inject anything new or significant into his personality or life. As regards Tat'jana Vlasenkova's position toward the Party, the author made a significant change from one edition to another: in the 1956 edition of the novel *Open Book* Tat'jana becomes a member of the Communist Party (Book I, p. 540), whereas in its 1965 edition Kaverin eliminates this motive altogether so that in this last edition of the novel Tat'jana Vlasenkova is never admitted to the Communist Party. Neither are the two brothers L'vov. They are, of course, all dedicated to their country, their profession and their friends as may be expected of people with normal sense of values.

Kaverin's young protagonists are individualists. Kaverin hardly allows their public concerns to dominate their private, individual selves. To some extent even, the conflicts of the novels derive from the conflicts between their private selves and public pressures. Kaverin's novels deal with the motive of the formation of youth, it seems, primarily in terms of personal self-fulfillment. In the deepest, the artistically most convincing young people in Kaverin's novels battle throughout their novelistic careers over personal issues, which may or may not have implications beyond their private biographies. Trubachevskij of *Fulfillment of Desires* pursues the mirage of personal glory through scholarship. It is this mirage of personal glory that causes his catastrophe. His vainglory makes him mistake his somewhat unearned mastery in literature for mastery in life, and his bookish vision of life for life itself. His uneven triumph in his little personal school of bookish pursuits turns out not to be valid enough to spare him the bitter lesson from the school of life. Trubachevskij wants to become the master too soon. He does not labor enough through the hard stage of apprenticeship. His trouble is an exclusively self-centered grief, in a sense even a piece of self-pity, which has barely anything to do with his attitudes toward commonweal. This thoroughly individualistic, personal issue of Trubachevskij stands out all the more conspicuously when the author hints toward the end of the novel that his hapless young student enters upon the road of his regeneration when, leaving his self-admiration and self-pity behind, he sets on his journey to Dneprostroj, to participate, along with thousands of other builders, in socialist construction.

Likewise, Sanja Grigor'ev of *Two Captains* actualizes a certain dream of polar discovery which will prove the validity of the accusation he has levelled at his enemy and will justify him in the eyes of the girl he loves. Captain Tatarinov's destiny has become so much a matter of personal honor, personal intellectual issue and, in a sense, of personal ambition that this novel emphasizes the sense of individual human destiny at the expense of the great, national, history. Therefore, for example, even the Great Patriotic War is for Sanja "another life" (drugaja zhizn'), different from his own life, about which he would not perhaps have written, as he says, if it had not unexpectedly furnished the solution to his personal lifelong issue.[10]

It has been outlined above how much of personal issues the whole life of Tat'jana Vlasenkova involves. All her life has centered on the L'vov family, emotionally, intellectually and family-wise: she owes her basic education and her subsequent scientific outlook to the uncle, to whom she also is grateful in a personal way for his kindness in her childhood; with the older nephew her unfulfilled dream of love has remained forever; for the younger nephew she bears her conjugal devotion; she is not even spared minor annoyances in her life with her mother-in-law. Her grim resolve to carry through her scientific project and research even at the cost of a Pyrrhic victory proves how much she values her professional pride and her sense of achievement. For the sake of the integrity of the latter she suffers an abominable personal injustice. The older L'vov brother, Dmitri, is a brilliant but impulsive intellectual, a kind of romantic scientist, self-centered to the point of not noticing or deplorably misjudging the thoughts and feelings of people around him. It is this egocentrism, or rather its fallacies that prevent him from taking a part, commensurate to his superior talent and energy, in the development of biological science. Dmitri is the only one in the novel who keeps a diary. This occupation perhaps points to his somewhat hurried self-communion and his need for introspective withdrawal. In contrast, his younger brother Andrej writes a book in which he describes his experiences of an epidemiologist during the war and which he intends for the information of the public. And the very fact that Tat'jana is in love with the ego-centric Dmitri rather than her more communicative husband may also support the assumption that personal and private issues prevail over the public in this novel.

The heart of the problem seems to lie in this issue of personal self-fulfillment. The classical *Bildungsroman* pursues an aim internal to the subject of its representation. So do to great extent Kaverin's novels and insomuch they belong to this genre. However, this is not much to say because any valid representation of a human character pursues such an internal aim, or at least it starts from such an internal point of departure. This "innerness" matters in a special way. Sanja Grigor'ev, the brothers L'vov, Tat'jana Vlasenkova or even Kartashixin seem to be intended to treasure some inalienable parcel in their selves, some intrinsically individual problem immune against another's interference, either well-wishing or malicious. For example, Tat'jana Vlasenkova's repressed love for Dmitri emotionally conflicts with her loyalty to her husband; likewise, there is a constant nagging tension in her commiserating attachment to her good-for-nothing father. Dmitri L'vov's passion for Glafira has made a dent in his personality and fate that all his intelligence, willpower and energy do not succeed in eliminating. Sanja Grigor'ev struggles all his life to overcome the sense of inferiority or inadequacy which perhaps originated from his unhappy childhood doubly humiliated by his speech difficulty. Even Kartashixin, the well-nigh exemplary young communist, never learns to reconcile his contradictory feelings toward the children of professor Bauer: his love for Masha, his wife, and his invincible antipathy toward her brother. These features of idiosyncracy are inalienable parcels of their individuality because they do not yield to the formative impact of the life of school or to pedagogic transformation in the spirit of Socialist Realism without destroying the artistic integrity of their identities. For example, Tat'jana Vlasenkova, instead of becoming a microbiologist, might have turned into a physicist or archeologist, and might have lived through many more and diverse circumstances, and would still have remained Tat'jana Vlasenkova, would still have preserved the same identity, as long as she remained in love with an older brother and loyally married to the younger, and, possibly, as long as she kept her commiserating affection for her good-for-nothing father. As it has been mentioned above, this Tat'jana's good-for-nothing father cost Kaverin a reprimand on the part of a critic. The latter must have resented just this kind of individualistic twist that is immune to pedagogic transformation. If the author had chosen to deprive Tat'jana of this inalienable parcel of her personality then she would not longer have been Tat'jana Vlasenkova, she would have become essentially another, less complex, character. All this means that in some specific respect the behavior of Kaverin's characters will always respond to some inner motivation and will never take its cue from external sources, such as morality of the group or public indoctrination. And thus far at least they are hard-nosed individualists. And insomuch also does their substance remain alien from the one the positive heroes of Socialist Realism are made of. The permeability that is total with the positive heroes of Socialist Realism affects Kaverin's major protagonists considerably less. In some respects, they remain irreducible to the morality of the group, or life of school, or public indoctrination. Therefore, Kaverin's major protagonists may, at some point of their biographies, swerve from line, that is, from the Party line or the prevailing imperative because they turn out to be following some imperative coming from their innermost selves, the inalienable parcel of their individuality. It is this inability to surrender the deepest of their identities that predetermines their ultimate ostracism.

In the light of the previous discussion it may be inferred that Kaverin has intended his characters to be "round." He also tries to represent them in the round. This means that his major protagonists are above-the-average normal individuals who lead active lives, think a great deal about their lives and the latter's meaning, engage vigorously in their pursuits and see to the welfare of their families. It does not prevent them from dedicating themselves to the welfare of their socialist society, although in this regard the author does not seem to lay any special emphasis on the conventional ideological motives of Socialist Realism.

6

The protagonists of Kaverin's novels do not always stand at the highest level of artistic validity. The author does not always let them become vividly compelling figures. They do not always grow to be characters sustained by their own dramatic substance emancipated from the narrative word mass of the author. Why should it be so? Why should not the creator of Arximedov have repeated his feat in his novels? Even Kaverin does not seem to escape a certain much used phraseology which, unfortunately, for a mature independent reader announces the author's retreat from creative novelty to less valuable novelistic routine. Then the sense of predictability comes to replace the sense of inevitability. It is a retreat from the representation of spontaneous feelings and thoughts conveyed by unconventional characters to something opposite. It is a process whereby the creative word petrifies into a chain of stereotypes extolling civic virtures, patriotism and predictable attitudes. Here, Socialist Realism catches up with Kaverin's pen.

I wonder whether such a retreat is not occuring in *Two Captains* as the narrative moves into Book Two of the novel. It is a sort of surrender to the ever increasing pressure of the norms of behavior. As long as Sanja Grigor'ev is a little boy, a school-boy, even an aviation trainee, the author may attribute a wide range of spontaneous feelings and thoughts to him. And this is where the novel is at its best. However, once Sanja becomes a Soviet Air Force Captain, especially at time of war, the author's range of options of characterization narrows down significantly. At this point the author will not find it easy to avoid the pedagogic pressure of Socialist Realism. At the beginning of the novel, as Sanja Grigor'ev and Pet'ka Skovorodnikov get ready to run away from their homes, they deem it necessary to swear an oath to each other, the "bloody oath of friendship." Just as Huck Finn and Tom Sawyer, they seal their covenant by signing it with their own blood. It is far more literate and literary than what horror-stricken Tom is able to scrawl with his red keel in the old tannery, so much so that we cannot help suspecting the author of complaisantly editing the boys' oath himself. It ends in a maxim-like sentence already referred to above: "To struggle and to quest, to find out and not to surrender." Obviously, the author injects a pedagogic purpose into this sentence, and the boys throughout their subsequent lives actualize its challenge. However, within the context of this initial boyhood situation, the oath fulfills a compelling aesthetic function. It characterizes both boys in a key somewhat similar to the one in which Tom Sawyer and Huckleberry Finn are by their own oath. It shows their adventuresome and romanesque imagination and their boyish naiveté. The latter elicits an irresistible humorous effect. Curiously enough, this humorous effect somewhat veils the truly desperate determination of the boys and their integrity of which they are not yet even aware. Here then, the pedagogic purpose blends marvelously with the aesthetic.

In Book Two, when the war starts, Sanja departs immediately to join his Air Force unit, without even having time to bid farewell to his wife. He leaves her a little note, with only eight words, ending in another sentence: "Pomni, ty verish'," (Remember, you have faith). What "the bloody oath of friendship" is for the first part of the novel, this sentence may be for the second. And we may legitimately wonder whether this sentence does not emphasize pedagogic appeal at the expense of aesthetic validity. It sounds more like a seemly textbook mot concocted at leisure rather than what a loving husband would hastily jot down to his wife before that late June day 1941 suddenly wrings him out of his happy family life and sends him to war. From this point on, characters have a tendency to speak as if in a somewhat prescribed phraseology, which makes them look somewhat like prescribed characters with prescribed attitudes. This cannot fail to weaken them as compelling figures of narrative fiction because the author's discourse tends to interfere between them and the reader, and thereby it dissolves their own artistic substance. In other words, the author is speaking, and not his characters. In another context and for another purpose, Sanja Grigor'ev says somewhat jokingly in this second part of the novel: "[...] there is in the world such a book — *The Disciplinary Regulations*, the reading of which does not dispose to similar flights," (i.e., an AWOL airplane trip).[11] Things happen as if the whole drift of this Book Two also suffers from some such disciplinary regulations. The representation of situations, emotions, speeches, gestures, attitudes tends to become somewhat ritualistic and hieratic. This literary manner may of course reflect the mood of the whole nation at war. This ritualization of the phraseology of representation — stereotype would be a less gracious term — surfaces when it comes to depicting the deeds and circumstances of military valor. Does this tendency toward ritualistic and hieratic phraseology really add to the aesthetic validity of the representation of gallantry? Probably not. Somehow, living human reality, man's throbbing heart and conscience fade out of this phraseology. The latter rather becomes a solemn discourse of an author more concerned with the conventional decorum and traditional gallantry of warfare. The purpose of its representation, in the last analysis, is primarily pedagogic. In a sense then, the most of Book Two of this novel willy-nilly conveys a pedagogic purpose, and not infrequently at the expense of the originality and vividness of representation. The sense of personal drama weakens.

It should probably be conceded that Kaverin's protagonists suffer from two kinds of limitation or incompleteness. One kind of limitation consists in the fact that the censorship of Socialist Realism (or self-censorship imposed by the latter) obligates the writer to elaborate a one-sided representation of personality, namely, that side of personality whose magnification benefits the political doctrine. The above-mentioned novels of Stalin-prize vintage are the extreme examples of this one-sidedness. The effect of persuasion comes first. Poetic truth is, so to speak, optional. In this respect it may make sense to postulate that modern literature, prose or verse, came to existence when the art of unconstrained representation of reality asserted its autonomy from the discredited ancient rhetoric. Socialist Realism then is a kind of archaic phenomenon in the literary evolution: a pseudo-rhetoric reflecting a political dogma and lacking the cultural greatness of the classical rhetoric. As such, it has Soviet literature reflect the dogma in the form of an obligatory stereotype. Only if this condition is met, or at least not contradicted, is Soviet literature allowed to reflect the poetically transmuted empirical reality. This dogmatic limitation exerts its crippling aesthetic effect on the literature of Socialist Realism. If the above-mentioned Stalin-prize novels are (or, possibly, were) the leading examples of Socialist Realism (and why they should not be so, since they are all recipients of the highest literary award?), then we cannot avoid concluding that the works of Socialist Realism tend to lose the wealth of its representational possibilities. They do not know how to convey certain states of mind and emotions adequately. For example, the narrative prose of Socialist Realism wields the language of love and erotic experience with distressing ineptness. Even Kaverin's treatment of this area of emotional experience leaves something to be desired. Because of this limitation imposed by censorship (or self-censorship) Kaverin cannot save his protagonists from its crippling aesthetic effects. This he partially acknowledged in his autobiography:

But *Open Book* was being written so slowly and with such a hardship not only because I had to read books on microbiology or painstakingly to study the "historical background." For the space of almost ten years I had to struggle for this book mainly with some critics, who now blamed me for occupying myself too much with the theme of love, as if in the Soviet land people ceased falling in love, pining, reading and reciting verses, musing on true or imaginary love; and now tried to persuade me to part with my "not fully valuable" heroes and to start occupying myself with the ones positive absolutely in all respects. It was very hard to step over the persistent striving to direct my novel along another path, which did not interest me in the least, and, in essence, was far from the task that stood in front of me. [...] 12

Dmitri L'vov's gunshot nearly kills Tat'jana Vlasenkova at the beginning of her course. This same shot brings to life some of the dormant properties of her character. Tat'jana is a woman of integral and unsplintered passion and moral rectitude, as these properties apply to women. The author may have named her after Pushkin's Tat'jana for this very purpose. The author endows her also with some of those features that in literature we attach to the personality of the conquistador: a certain liking for the extraordinary, the romanesque, the quasi-unreachable. I should observe that all major figures of Kaverin's narrative fiction are of this kind but he does not quite succeed in creating such a figure in its most compelling form. It would be easy to build up a psychoanalytical interpretation of Dmitri's gunshot as the surrogate of the anticipated sexual comsummation that remains forever in Tat'jana's dream and is never fulfilled in actuality. In any case, this gunshot draws her, an innocent bystander, into a lifelong game whose rules condemn her to staying only a helpful best friend where she would like to be more. To some extent she remains a victim of this game. Kaverin has her first try to embark on the career of a movie actress. The choice is certainly not accidental. This career might well have been the one that answered best to Tat'jana's temperament and deepest aspirations. It would give her a life of excitement, a possibility to lead a life of great passions, to fulfill magnificent destinies, to experience beauty and at the same time to let others experience those same passions, magnificent destinies and beauty. It would enable her to tour the world, to encounter romanesque events, constantly to feel the throbbing pulse of life. Just observe with what self-oblivious ecstasy Tat'jana, already a solid biology student, is reading the passionate love letters of O.P. Krechetova, the famous actress of another generation. As Tat'jana is walking along the streets of Leningrad, absorbed in the reading of the volume, she visualizes a beautiful lady on the seashore in the Crimea, or in Paris, or in a church in Petersburg, all to her desperate noble love. Lifted over into another world, Tat'jana does not notice the traffic in the streets, narrowly escapes several accidents, does not recognize her friends she meets, so much she is wrapped up in the beautiful, albeit sad, romance of the famous actress. At this point, isn't Tat'jana unconsciously visualizing her own unfulfilled dream? For the same reason she falls in love with Dmitri. In him she sees, and rightly so, the full-blooded and full-bodied life after which she herself unconsciously aspires. Dmitri, the grand seigneur, naturally does what he wants, serenely mindless of consequences. He gives himself up unsparingly to whatever arouses his intellectual curiosity or appeals to his chivalrous emotions. His intellectual and emotional generosity costs him a good deal of frustrations and reverses. However, his is the domain in which, as Kaverin says,[13] the generous win and the miserly lose. Perhaps Dmitri must pay this price for his scientific vision. No wonder then that Dmitri's image may well be the one that is engraved in the deepest recesses of Tat'jana's heart. For the same reason too, Tat'jana is attracted by Glafira. Glafira has the glamorous genteelness and the devil-may-care kind of abandon that so attracts Dmitri. And surely, deep in her heart, Tat'jana too wishes to have this asset because it too is the manifestation of full-blooded and full-bodied life. It is of course an irony of life and the wisdom of the novel that Glafira squanders her treasure that Tat'jana would have known how to use for good purpose if she, Tat'jana, had had it. But she doesn't. The same gunshot that brings to life some of the springs of her soul cripples her hope for what A. Grin called "the resplendent world" (blistajushchij mir) which in her eyes Dmitri embodies. After all, the shot that shakes her to awareness Dmitri fires for the sake of another girl, Glafira. Her expectation of the "resplendent world" comes to a very early end when she fails her tests to become a movie actress. She has to choose another career. She ends by devoting herself to microbiology, a career poles apart from her early dream.

It may well be that this displacement from the "resplendent world" to "toil and sweat" reflects a certain overall philosophical pressure of Socialist Realism. In any case, such a displacement need not mean that the "resplendent world" is better than "toil and sweat" and *vice versa*. The novel need not become the worse only because of such a displacement. It would again be easy to impose onto the story stuff the pictures of the two extreme points measuring the displacement from the "resplendent world" to "toil and sweat:" on the one hand, the beautiful actress, her noble love, the romantic Crimean seashore, and, on the other hand, an undistinguished State grain farm doctor smelling of mold. If such really were the alternative, Socialist Realism would probably prefer "toil and sweat" to the "resplendent world" and would applaud this displacement. We all know however that there is as much hardship and frustration in the "resplendent world" as there may be in "toil and sweat." However, this hardly is the issue.

The issue lies in the fact that such a displacement seems to change the tone or the pungency of representation. The overall effect of socialist-realism censorship or, possibly, self-censorship, has resulted in the undesirable taming or domesticating, if not shallowing, of the moral and psychological problems and conflicts Kaverin's protagonists live through. Take, for example, the case of Tat'jana Vlasenkova. We certainly would not expect her to turn into another magnificent Anna Karenina, or any of Chekhov's less magnificent adulterous Annas. In a sense, Tat'jana's predicament turns out to be even more complicated than the one Anna Karenina or the Chekhovian adulterous Annas entangled themselves in. For these women their overwhelming passions or trivial liaisons offered the only escape that they could think of from their oppressively drab existence in which they were entrapped. Tat'jana cannot plead this excuse. Indeed, an Anna Karenina is impossible under Socialist Realism. Neither can Tat'jana yield to the devil-may-care kind of desperation that it probably takes to lapse into adultery or any similar course. Tat'jana has too much moral rectitude, she thinks too much to step out of conventional morality. So, what is there left for the author to represent, given her character and her situation? I believe that on this essential point the novel betrays weakness. The author does not seem validly to represent the enormously complex skein of repressed emotions Tat'jana experiences toward Dmitri, of devoted affection, love and respect she bears Andrej (since Tat'jana does love her husband), of the constant tension that cannot fail to arise from her being simultaneously a scientist, a wife, a mother, and, still perhaps, someone who, amid her test tubes, mold and vibrions (that she also loves and understands), subconsciously senses the vanished "resplendent world" of the beautiful actress. Doesn't it take only one social appointment with her former school-mate Vladimir Lukashevich, who has always been in love with her, a concert, beautiful music, for the "resplendent world" to emerge somewhere in her consciousness? This shortcoming appears all the more painful when we think of how in few words and few scenes Kaverin represents with compelling force the tragic love of Èsfir' in *Artist Unknown*.

The reason of this shortcoming lies at the door of those critics Kaverin hints at in his autobiography. At a certain level of complexity the author obviously cannot represent human emotions and thoughts if censorship denies him the right to tell *everything* with whatever means of representation he needs. For this reason, most of the emotional developments that the author attributes to the heroine tend to become censoredly declarative rather than fully lived through. That which is dramatic, if not traumatic, emotional experience for a woman keeps washing out into timid, almost hothouse, domestic disputations between spouses to whom either the censor or the author denies the intelligence to think certain issues to their bitter end. And to make this emotional mediocrity even more anemic, it all ends in some trivially virtuous remarks, such as "of nights one should sleep, and not quarrel with one's husband."[14] Hence this lack of validity, this sense of experience not lived through. We might have expected some storm to burst out to bring her emotional self really to life, to set it in some motion so as to allow her some emotional self-fulfillment or, perhaps, self-destruction. As a matter of fact, a storm does strike but from another quarter. Andrej's arrest offers an emotional upheaval that powerfully affects Tat'jana. It is perhaps this catastrophe that saves Tat'jana and Andrej's marriage. This reversal gives the novel a significantly new direction and dimension.

Another kind of incompleteness which affects Kaverin's protagonists pertains to the consecutive stages the *Bildungsroman* subject develops through in the course of his life. It has been mentioned above that the *Bildungsroman* subject lives through different stages of formation, namely, through years of apprenticeship, of travel and ultimately becomes a master which means that he reaches maturity and wisdom. It would be quite hard to deny that the *Bildungsroman* has borrowed the terms that medieval guilds used in governing their crafts and trades. Just as the member of a medieval craft after years of apprenticeship and journeying must prove his manual dexterity and artistic skill by producing his masterpiece if he wants to become a master in his craft, the *Bildungsroman* subject must show the excellence of his mind and soul by making a masterpiece of his own personality and life, if, in his own realm and his own community of the faithful, he wishes to be recognized as a master. Wilhelm Meister is entering into such a community of the faithful when his seniors deem his personality and life grown up to it. So the *Bildungsroman* has turned its subject's personality itself into the product of his striving and endeavor. It has elevated his very life to the level of a work of art, or rather of craft, in the artistic sense of this word.

Now, don't we find in Kaverin's works a similar sense of hierarchy of craftsmanship, of its gradual maturing? Kaverin's very first book bears the title *Masters and Apprentices*. In this book the young writer records his vision of the way of life proper to the members of ancient, predominantly German, guilds. I find something significant in the fact that the young Kaverin, in this very first book of his, views life in terms of some gradual ascent in the ladder of craftsmanship. It does not change the substance of the argument that in this case the vision was playful. Kaverin himself grew in his early writer's days in the intellectual atmosphere of the Russian Formalists for whom literature was fundamentally a *craft*, a skill which the aspirant writer had to acquire by learning, through apprenticeship. This view of literature, that is, of creative writing, does not essentially differ from the traditional view of medieval crafts and trades as crystallized in the concept of the guild.[15] When Kaverin's tragic hero Arximedov appeals for honesty in labor he draws his examples of honest craftsmanship from the trade practices of the medieval guilds. In his *Skandalist* Kaverin satirizes the older Russian philological school for not achieving anything outstanding in its lifelong craft; that is why, Kaverin intimates, this older generation of philologists experience such a sense of frustration when they look back on their own lifetime. Here too Kaverin views people in relation to the object of their lifelong craft.

What becomes then the main object for the striving of Kaverin's protagonists? Perhaps something akin to the object of striving to which the *Bildungsroman* subject devotes himself: the formation, the perfection of the very personality and life of the protagonist. One of Kaverin's very first attempts to depict the formation of a youthful personality is a short novel having for its title *The Rough Draft of Man* (Chernovik cheloveka). The very title here conveys the idea that the author creates the first rough form of a desirable personality, activity and life. And the subsequent titles of novels still seem to intimate the same drift of the author's thought. *Fulfullment of Desires* reminds one of the reaching of the aim of one's striving. *Two*

Captains project the younger Captain against the background of the older so that the younger strives in some respect to equal and to excel the older. *Open Book*, in the literal sense, signifies the available source of the enrichment of man's mind, and, in the figurative sense, it may symbolize man's command over the mysteries locked in his own nature, in the nature around him and in the cosmos. All these titles seem to convey some sense of continuity along the path toward a more sophisticated form and a higher approximation of the personality, activity and life to aspire to.

Let it be recalled that the central concept of the *Bildungsroman* suggests the vision of man integrally developing his positive potentialities with a view to enrich his personality so as to approach, and perhaps to attain, the ideal of harmoniously developed personality, the universality of the Renaissance man. At this point, the *Bildungsroman* subject becomes the master, and his formation and education comes to its completion.

In their more modest ways, Kaverin's protagonists also aspire after similar all-around culture and universal experience. For example, Sanja Grigor'ev, and arctic and war pilot, turns out to be dabbling in sculpture in his spare time. He blames his wife for not improving her command of foreign languages. Both his old teacher and his wife have noticed that Sanja, in his soul, will always remain a youth athirst for new sights and discoveries, for new knowledge and learning. As if his beloved arctic aviation were for him a means to rise higher the more to see and the greater knowledge to absorb from a bird's eye view. And his interest in geography goes far beyond what may be required of a professional pilot. Neither does Tat'jana Vlasenkova wish to immure herself within the walls of a microbiological laboratory at the end of her medical studies, as she has been expected and even urged to do. Just as a young *Bildungsroman* subject would do, she sets out on a journey in order to gain experience and to try out her professional abilities out in practical life — at a State grain farm in Southern Russia. Significantly, to the part of the novel where Tat'jana goes out into the world the author gives the title "Quest" (Poiski). As for *Fulfillment of Desires*, it depicts the "malformation" of a young man bedazzled by the glitter of his philological research. This state dulls him to all other multifarious impressions of the world, or distorts them. Only when disaster strikes does Trubachevskij "open" his personality to restore the balance. Quite characteristically for the *Bildungsroman*, he goes on a journey in order to straighten out his apprenticeship misdirected through his philological temptation. This becomes apparent during his train ride to Dneprostroj when he meets young engineers and workers bound for the same site. Trubachevskij lets himself be exposed to those vital interests and aspirations that animate Soviet people. And he himself suddenly discovers his own interest for these great issues of the day without, however, giving up that which will forever remain his main interest: Russian literature, in its proper and vital perspective. He has entered upon the road toward maturity.

However, as artistically valid figures of narrative prose fiction, Kaverin's protagonists live an incomplete destiny. As it may be described in the phraseology of the *Bildungsroman*, Kaverin's protagonists travel, completing their apprenticeship, but they do not reach the ultimate stage of their development. They do not make the other shore. In a tender conversation with Sanja his wife says that he is a traveler by vocation and by passion, the one who loves to fly over oceans: "[...] Will you not abandon me when you have flown over the ocean?" "No. But they will order me *back from half-way*," [The italics are mine. H.O.] Sanja answers.[15a] Here Sanja unwittingly refers to this incompleteness of his destiny. Similarly, the most substantial part of *Fulfillment of Desires* is the story of a failure. *Open Book* ends in utter despair. Kaverin's protagonists do not quite have the chance to attain the ultimate inner harmony and illumination. They do not gain the higher sense of wisdom and the philosophical equanimity coming from a self-fulfilling worldview. They fail of becoming masters. Why this failure, this incomplete destiny?

The classical *Bildungsroman* pursues an aim *internal* to its subjects. This means that in the *Bildungsroman* the purpose of representing the development of man's personality prevails over any other. This purpose need not be topical or tendentious. The author tries to show how the protagonist enriches his inner life and his personality. He does so usually at the expense of his external action. There is usually a sort of passivity about such a protagonist, a sort of reluctance at being aggressive.

Things are different in the Soviet version of the *Bildungsroman*, inasmuch as it follows the tenets of Socialist Realism. It pursues an aim *external* to the subject of its representation. For the sake of pedagogic purpose the doctrine encourages the Soviet author to emphasize the protagonist's effective action on his environment. That is to say, the Soviet *Bildungsroman* becomes the story of the formation and education of the *specialist*. A critic could hardly object to this development because modern narrative prose in general represents some form of specialization in its protagonists. To great extent Tat'jana Vlasenkova's biography is such a story of the formation and education of the specialist. For the same pedagogic purpose the Soviet *Bildungsroman* emphasizes the protagonist's unanimity in their political attitudes. It is at the same time conformity to the line drawn by the powers that be. Mental specialization may impoverish man's personality and render it shallow. This liability is universal. The second point of emphasis specifically affects the subjects of the Soviet *Bildungsroman*. An author who is pressed to represent public unanimity and mental conformity will find it difficult to represent the protagonists' spontaneous inner thoughts. He may even never represent what the protagonist really thinks in his innermost mind. Which is to say that the author may choose never to disclose the protagonist's true identity. Such a truncated representation of personality cannot be good art.

This is the difficulty Kaverin faces in his novels, namely, in *Open Book*. How to make the development of the protagonist's personality complete? Tat'jana Vlasenkova's ultimate despair at the end of her novelistic biography can hardly be described as the stage at which her mind reconciles with the world and she attains inner illumination. There would be no artistic impossibility for the author to describe her despair, to show her innermost thoughts, however bitter and accusatory, to show how she lives through her despair, and at length emerges from it, strengthened or crushed. This very process I would define as the reaching of the stage of the ultimate worldly wisdom, truth and maturity, in sum, the becoming of the master.

Socialist-realism censorship would most likely not allow the author to search deeper into her mind; or rather, it would not let him convey the explicit artistic representation of this innermost turmoil in any detail. The doctrine of Socialist Realism would not allow this fulfillment of destiny and the self-fulfillment of the protagonist to be represented because in order to achieve this stage the protagonist would have to call into question the very foundations on which the doctrine rests. Therefore, for the sake of the doctrine, it still is preferable for the censor not to allow the author to let his protagonist grow to his full artistic and moral stature.

This artistic incompleteness that affects Kaverin's above-mentioned major characters marks a definite cultural period. It is of course the Stalinist period when the pressure of Socialist Realism was at its highest. The period involves a whole generation, the one that I. Èrenburg describes in these words:

I have said that the metal of Kuznetsk helped our country stand firm in the years of the fascist invasion. And the other metal — the human? The builders of Kuznetsk, just as all their coevals, lived not an easy life. Some perished young — some in 1937, some at the front. Others began stooping prematurely, they fell silent — really, there were too many unexpected turns, too many things one had to get accustomed to, to adapt oneself to . . . Now, those heroes of *The Second Day*[16] that have survived are some fifty odds years now. This generation had little time for meditation. Its morning was romantic and cruel — collectivization, dekulakization, scaffoldings and constructions. The subsequent events everyone remembers. Of the people born on the eve of the First World War there was required so much courage that there would be enough of it for several generations, a courage not only in work or fighting, but in silence, in perplexity, in anxiety. I saw these people being given wings in 1932. Then wings went out of season. The wings of the First Five-Year Plan came by inheritance to the children together with the giant factories, paid for dearly.[17]

From its formal inception in 1932 the doctrine of Socialist Realism pressed Soviet writers to represent man's personality as the subject of industrial manpower and political unanimity. Kaverin did not avoid this pressure, and on many points conformed to it. This pressure has survived Stalin's rule. However, in his works written after 1953 Kaverin offers a renewed vision of man, the one that he expressed at least as far back as his *Artist Unknown* of 1931. It is the vision of man's personality itself as an intrinsic human value.

CHAPTER FOUR

TRAGIC EXPERIENCE

1

The concept of the tragic is very complex. Within the framework of this discussion I need not attempt to formulate any exhaustive definition of this concept. For my purpose, I only need to elaborate on those aspects of the concept that may bear on Kaverin's works of narrative fiction. The concept of the tragic postulates man at his best and his noblest in the most universal sense of these words. He is in full possession of his empirical state and transcends this empirical state. The tragic hero dares to act to the limits of his power, and to press his quest to the very end, disregarding the consequences. This is what S. Butcher must have meant when in his discussion of Aristotle's theory of the tragedy he commented that the tragedy represents "idealized"[1] persons, that is, I would add, man's humanity cleansed of anything superficial, factitious or conventional. For the tragic hero to reveal these essential qualities, he must encounter some catastrophic event, some ultimate conflict, or he must live through some agonizing experience. It is the characteristic of the tragic hero to choose not to avoid the supreme test of his personality.

One such tragic conflict is the one in which it becomes very problematic to pinpoint moral fault, although the conflict still involves tragic guilt.[2] Such a conflict reaches its highest pitch when the parties at conflict both enforce to the bitter end their best understanding of their respective codes of justice. Both are right. Both act in good faith and with honor. Both observe some code of justice which a thoughtful independent spectator does find cogent and conclusive. We can find such an archetypal tragic conflict in Sophocles' *Antigone*. Antigone defies Creon's decree out of her religious devotion to her duty toward her dead sibling. Now, Thebes has had more than her share of calamities and catastrophes. Who would blame Creon for trying meticulously to avoid anything that might attract affliction upon his State? His decree forbidding the burial of Polyneices reflects this extreme precaution to protect Thebes. Creon and Antigone are both doing the right thing. They are both fulfilling their respective duties. How is it that so much suffering comes from man's highest integrity and his being so much devoted to his noblest duties? The question raises a doubt about human justice. This is the way in which Hegel interpreted the tragic conflict: it is not one between good and evil, but rather between the two attitudes that both have some good.

However, there is no reason to deny the tragic dimension to the conflict felt in terms of iniquity. The great iniquitous trials of history — religious, political or intellectual – are of this nature, for example those of John Hus (c. 1370-1450) and Joan of Arc (1412-1431). However, it seems that even this moral contrast may depend on temporal perspective. At the time of the conflict, that is, of the trial, both parties may feel right. Many honest beliefs contend against one another, many vested interests may be involved, many misunderstandings afloat, many passions colliding. And in this imbroglio of life only one lonely man sees clearly and understands the issue. And the measure of his tragic greatness is that he succeeds in changing the tide through his sheer willpower, courage and intuition. And he does so at the cost of his own life if need be. Only later does it become clear that the tragic hero was right and the others were wrong, or at least that he was more right than the others. In this respect Walter Kerr is quite right in pointing out the evolutionary meaning of the tragedy, or tragic experience.[3] Nor is there any reason to deny a tragic dimension to those who at some point of their lives rose higher than it may be permissible for the human condition to do. They too, of course, have to pay the highest price for their tragic greatness. The Chorus in *Antigone* defined this price: "Never does greatness come to mortals free from a curse,".[4]

There is a good psychological reason for which a catastrophic end "fits" the tragic hero better. A good man who meets a grievously catastrophic end because of some tragic guilt but not because of a moral fault appeals to the spectator's or the reader's sense of "pity" and "fear" more than any other kind of hero. The proper effect of the tragedy is this specific overwhelming emotional impact on the spectator who cannot avoid identifying with the hero and suffering along with him; who experiences an admiring terror in the presence of so much suffering so courageously endured. This is what creates an ennobling effect and emotional elevation about the tragic hero, no matter what the outcome of the conflict. And in this regard, a modern tragic hero such as Solzhenitsyn* or Martin Luther King bear the same kind of hallmark as the great tragic figures of antiquity or of classical European literature. The difference is that the latter have been purified and ennobled by centuries of representational tradition, whereas the former, contemporary to us, have not yet undergone this process.

Now, there is another category of representation that does not answer the traditional definitions of the tragedy or the tragic hero, but still stands in a special relation to the tragic representation. When discussing the plot of *Artist Unknown* I pointed out that the sense of the tragic attached to Arximedov's destiny results to some extent from the particular effect of Kaverin's narrative skill. Toward the end of the story Zhaba reports to the narrator about the incidents he witnessed. Arximedov, the heroic knight, is girding for his ultimate fight. Then we see him engaged in his last philosophical dialogue with Shpektorov. It is a lofty dialogue. Shpektorov does not spare his words to emphasize Arximedov's defeat. Arximedov proclaims that his cause is good. The impression is that, although completely undone, Arximedov still will not concede his defeat because the cause he is fighting for is righteous. It turns out,

---

This was written before Solzhenitsyn's exile from the Soviet Union.

however, that these incidents never occurred. The actual reality is depressingly down-to-earth. Zhaba, the "fibber", has invented the incidents, because he feels that they should have occurred. And this is the gist of the matter. In modern criticism we speak of "tragic farce." Eixenbaum and Chizhevskij detect tragic overtones in the experience of the sub-human Akakij Akakievich. And what about Woyzeck or Willy Loman?[5] All these and others are rather passive victims of suffering, "anti-heroes." They unquestionably stand poles apart from one like Oedipus who seeks the ultimate truth, cost what it may, or like Antigone who actualizes her convictions and beliefs, cost what it may. The "anti-heroes" do not particularly worry about the ultimate truth; neither do they have any particular convictions, not to speak of actualizing these convictions to the bitter end. And still, it would be hard to deny a kind of tragic effect elicited by these pathetic heroes. I believe that this tragic effect comes from the fact that a certain sordid reality represented in a certain way reminds one with an enormous emotional impact of its opposite, of the opportunity lost, of that which should have been instead of that which actually is. It is at best grotesque to fall in love with an overcoat and then to die of grief when this overcoat is gone. However, to a worldwise reader this inept development will convey a special message. It will remind him vaguely of something different but similar, perhaps, of Tristan's love for Isolde, or Romeo's for Juliet. Only in this case does a term such as "tragic farce" make any sense. In this kind of representation, tragic virtue does not reside in the character as such. It is rather a matter of the spectator's or the reader's response to the representation of the character. And tragic sense can in this case appear only if the given representation generates an emotional association with some other representation which is tragic.

2

From the time of his creative maturity, i.e., from about the time of *Skandalist* (1928), most of Kaverin's works contain, or have their actions centered on, catastrophic events. The latter vary in the degree of gravity. However, most of them seem serious enough for us to discuss them in the light of the above-mentioned three categories of the tragic experience.

It may seem somewhat perverse to search for any serious message in "Inspector General" (1926) and "Short Summer Night" (1927). The anti-heroic characters and grotesque situations of the narrative material stand well outside the field of tragic vision. The bookkeeper Chuchugin, madman as he is, worries whether the Association of the Blind (among all mortals!) are not engaged in a fraudulent bookkeeping and cracks down on the blind with all the bureaucratic ferocity of a petty clerk suddenly elevated to high position. He perceives people only in terms of their ranks and judges them accordingly. He does not perceive that all these people may have souls and that something may be going on in these souls and that this is the most important manifestation of humanity. Zezjulin, the cashier, sees the cause of his special prestige among his peers in the fact that he owns a fancy waistcoat he has ordered from abroad. And his ambitious plans for his future are all akin to his fancy waistcoat in which he takes such pride. All in all, both sorry heroes are the very embodiment of what is superficial, factitious and conventional about man. The very antithesis of what the tragic hero is. These two stories may to some extent illustrate the notion of the tragic farce to which I have just referred above.

Only at the ultimate reversals of the plot do Chuchugin and Zezjulin gain the true vision of their condition. For that fraction of time their vision may have become tragic. In a moment of sanity, Chuchugin realizes that his transformation into a finance inspector was a mad dream. There is nothing insane about his pain at the awareness of his mental disease. Likewise, Zezjulin, just before hurling himself to his death from a bridge, sees the image of his mother, and visualizes his whole short life in its true light: a miserable failure without anything redeeming in it, except, perhaps, the becoming aware of it. For a second before oblivion, both men realize in their twisted ways how unstable personality is, and how radically insecure man and his life are. And this is the tragic vision of life.

3

In *Skandalist, ili vechera na Vasil'evskom ostrove* (The trouble-maker, or evenings on the Vasil'evskij island, 1928) Kaverin represents the *byt*, i.e., the daily life and ways of the Leningrad University professors and students in philology, litterateurs and critics, toward the mid-twenties.[6] It is actually a picture of crisis. The older, pre-revolutionary generation of professors and scholars try to preserve as much of the *status quo ante* as possible. They exude, as it were, a sense of failure and intellectual sterility. As of the mid-twenties, they have drifted away from the mainstream of life. The younger generation of philologists, namely, the brilliant school of formalist critics, are already somewhat losing their creative drive and start repeating themselves. Their brilliance proves to be somewhat superficial and threatens to lead them into "dismissing the contemporary epoch by joking about it."[7] This malaise results from the fact that the formalists confront their own no less painful, dilemma. It is the dilemma of intellectual integrity and political expediency. Few are those who can resist the pressure of this political expediency of the time. They do so at an increasingly heavy price of worldly isolation and ostracism. However, in this novel, this dilemma does not gain much dramatic momentum. It will reach high points in Kaverin's later works.

In terms of artistic representation, it is the older generation that stands at the center of the dramatic conflict. It is symbolized in the person of an old philologist, professor Lozhkin. The author chooses to represent Lozhkin at his old age, from a point when Lozhkin undertakes an agonizing re-appraisal of his life and career. What has gone wrong with it? In a conversation with another professor, a bizarre non-conformist Dragomanov, Lozhkin refers to a very small error hidden in the conditions of a problem. However, by the time its solution has been completed, the initial small error has gained "astronomical dimensions."[8] This is a symbolic way for

Lozhkin to speak of his own initial error which has brought about his sense of failure in life. What is this error? Has it been his commitment to philology? If so, it would in no way be a small error. This would mean that there was something wrong in the way in which Lozhkin — and possibly his colleagues — dedicated himself to philology. It is unlikely that the author calls into question the intrinsic value of the humanities. He most likely does not, because the most vital — even if artistically not the most significant — character of the story is a student in the humanities, Nagin by name. It is on Nagin that the author seems to pin his hopes for the future of the humanities. Kaverin's underlying understanding of the humanities is comprehensive: it is a cultural view of humankind, "cultural view" in the sense of its ethical, historical and aesthetic view. Only under such an aspect does the life of humankind appear in its plenitude. Ever since *Skandalist*, Kaverin's works have conveyed the author's concern for the relevance and justification of the humanities, of which literature and fine arts matter most for Kaverin.

So, Lozhkin's "initial small error" lies in his forgetting this essential nature of the humanities. Literature is one of the expressions of this bountiful life of humankind. Erudition is only one of the means that help us know, understand and appreciate literature. Nonetheless, it still remains only a means, only an item of auxiliary discipline toward internal culture. Now, during his scholarly career, without quite noticing it, Lozhkin has substituted the means for the ends. Somehow, he has not gone beyond petty erudition. His incessant work at "The Tale of the Babylonian Kingdom" best symbolizes Lozhkin's failure in life. His scholarship has become a soulless routine in which thought has dried up into a pile of rustling paper; it has become a drudgery over self-contained obscure points of erudition. His "initial small error" and its disastrous consequences come into the open by the mid-twenties, when the new mental climate brings about a show-down. Lozhkin withdraws from life. The author symbolizes this withdrawal by having Lozhkin suffer from agoraphobia. In his alienation from the world Lozhkin walks in the footsteps of the Chekhovian "man in a shell." Not unlike the latter, Lozhkin has cocooned himself into a sterile dried-up shell which closes off his awareness to the wholesome life that the world offers. It dissolves his living link with his fellowmen, and smothers his interest in them, their lives and the world. Thus, Lozhkin becomes "obsolete," as the young technological intelligentsia comes to the fore.

Lozhkin's life has failed. The final scene of the first chapter shows Lozhkin at the moment of his pathetic coming to the awareness of this failure. Absorbed in his analysis of "The Tale of the Babylonian Kingdom," he misses the closing hour of his university building. All gates being locked, he has to spend the night inside. Strolling all over the building, he enters an empty lecture room, steps up to the chair, takes his seat and faces the imaginary audience with a throbbing heart, as if during an actual lecture. And then he realizes, at this imaginary lecture, that he has nothing to say, no message to convey. So he acknowledges his spiritual coming to nought and himself drifting toward intellectual petrification. Himself one of them, Lozhkin comes to visualize those of his academe in a most unflattering light:

"[...] it seemed to him that all this sedate army of readers — this bow-legged insane old man hung with a multitude of decorations, badges and medals, and the cachectic youth with an academic pince-nez, and other library patrons — without noticing it themselves, are sitting and reading stark naked, with that which they had on when their mothers gave birth to them,"[9].

Removed from their habitual context and thus rendered absurd, all these professorial figures lapse into irreality. Real remain only their dullness, invidious malevolence toward one another, and lack of imagination.

In the above-mentioned nocturnal scene inside the university building, as Lozhkin is gazing at the plaque commemorating Gogol's lectures in that very room, he says, as if addressing Gogol himself: "I don't surrender,".[10] Lozhkin does not concede his defeat. Most of his colleagues let themselves go, poor in creative drive, yielding to the ease of unthinking academic routine, too inept for stimulating teaching, gently dozing on their not quite deserved and somewhat faded laurels. Quite on the contrary, Lozhkin attempts to reverse the tide. And in this pathetic attempt lies the dramatic interest of the story. Already lonely and alienated among his colleagues, Lozhkin embarks on something resembling a revolt against his peers. Not in vain does one of his colleagues seem to detect a "renegade" in him. His heretical behavior imparts to Lozhkin something in the order of tragic dimension.

Lozhkin's "mutiny," long in brewing, erupts at a point when one Leman, an obituary-writing enthusiast, approaches him. This Leman, a bizarre non-descript fixture of academe, has devoted himself to compiling obituaries. His necrological technique is peculiar: he writes his obituaries about people while they are still alive. This method, he unobjectionably claims, enables him to interview the prospective deceased in depth, and thus secure reliable first-hand necrological information from the prospective deceased themselves. He also encourages the prospective deceased to write their obituaries themselves whereas he himself then only puts them on file until needed. Leman is a grotesque reminder of death. His perpetual presence at the university, as well as his pre-edited obituary leaflets floating around, impart a sense of precariousness, the sense of insecurity experienced by living people treated as if already deceased. This is what sets off Lozhkin's revolt. Not only does he refuse to be buried prematurely, but he makes up his mind to start a new life uncontaminated by his previous errors. His "gray academic goatee," a symbol of his academic conformism and intellectual sterility; his wife Mal'vina whose whole meaning of life consists in concealing her former trade of a midwife and who, despite this trade, causes Lozhkin's human sterility; his apartment which chains him down to his "arm-chair existence" (kabinetnoe sushchestvovanie); all these and other attributes and shackles of his "old" life Lozhkin undertakes consistently to discard. His "mutiny" reaches its decisive point when Lozhkin leaves his home and wife and vanishes.

As he visits his boyhood friend Neigauzen in a provincial town, and, as later, quite unexpectedly, he ends up stranded at his long-forgotten brother's place, Lozhkin gains freedom from all, or almost all that he has come to loathe in his professional course of life. Lozhkin's flight from his "arm-chair existence" and the shackles of academic and social conformism somewhat grotesquely duplicates Tolstoy's flight toward the simplification of the unshackled life of simple people. It turns out, however, that Lozhkin does not know what to do with his newly gained freedom. He does not even know how to cross an ice-covered street; for some reason he turns up ineptly on the seafront at the flood time, vacantly roaming about at the only time when the likes of him should not be there. Lozhkin's sense of survival has catastrophically declined in the new environment. Both literally and symbolically, Lozhkin has taken his "Babylonian Kingdom" along: the old habits, too deeply rooted in his nature, do not leave their hold over him in what has been to be his "new" life.

Lozhkin's "mutiny" has failed. He has not succeeded in regaining a "second youth" or starting a new and more meaningful life. And still, the "mutiny" has not altogether been in vain. He returns to his volumes inwardly liberated, somewhat at peace with himself, healed from the myopia of his previous life although what has now been left for him to see is of little comfort: old age, loneliness (his wife suddenly died from the stress caused by his disappearance), weariedness of life, and a sense of irrelevance of his erudite's drudgery. As the course of time implacably presses him to leave the limelight of life, he learns the art — and the courage — of withdrawing with grace and some dignity, even if back to his "Babylonian Kingdom." So this professional figure, a figure of satirical derision at the beginning, toward the end of the story gains a sympathetic human dimension whose drama of old age acquires universal significance.

While preparing his "mutiny" Lozhkin comes to see one of his junior colleagues Dragomanov. This Dragomanov lives like a bohemian and tramp, and consorts with quite undesirable companions.[11] He does so, partly, in order to show how little he cares for the academic establishment. He is a brilliant linguist and a much greater scholar than Lozhkin. As he converses with his very academic interlocutor, Dragomanov remembers the time when he was still a freshman student, whereas Lozhkin was already an established professor, "God's deputy on earth" in the eyes of the intimidated freshman. He used to meet Lozhkin as the latter would walk out of the University gate. Lozhkin used to wear a majestic top-hat, a light coat with silk lapels, and a gold pince-nez glittering in the sun. Dragomanov used to bow timedly. Lozhkin would slightly raise his top-hat in a polite and cold manner. "A complete, perfect system was pacing along at that time on earth, wearing a mirror-like top-hat, a light coat with silk lapels," the narrator comments.[12] This is where the tragic experience lies. Or something akin to it. Would that "complete, perfect system" have foreseen that in less than a quarter of a century it would end up in an ignominious intellectual and personal decrepitude?

All in all, *Skandalist* skirts the tragic when the novel shows the characters rather unforeseeably facing the punishing consequences of what they always have believed complacently to be the right thing to do. All the major characters find themselves in the presence of some form of failure. However, only Lozhkin's suffering approximates anything like tragic suffering. Only he recognizes the nature of his failure and is not afraid to face it and take it for what it is. There is no redemption to his failure and Lozhkin understands it too well to rationalize it away. The other losers have not yet reached this point of finality.

4

The conflict that Kaverin represents in his *Artist Unknown* (1931) develops over the dilemma of cultural lag and technological progress. The time of the conflict is the late twenties and the early thirties. The conflict arises in connection with the industrialization of the Soviet Union.

Shpektorov views the problem in an abstractly imperative perspective, and in terms of an inevitable choice — to win or to lose. To win for Shpektorov means to erect factories, to lay out roads, to build power-dams, in a word, to create the technological foundations of socialism.

Shpektorov is still one of those "leather jackets" who through their indefatigable toil and brutal dedication have made the Revolution come about. He is a man who has given faith to a certain fundamental design of things (and here it should perhaps be emphasized that *things* are involved in this design in preference to people). It happens to be the Marxist design of things as it is understood by the revolutionaries at the dawn of Soviet history. What fascinates Shpektorov in this design is its intellectual clarity whereby everything finds its definitive and simple explanation. Shpektorov's own mind craves for clarity and purpose.[13] He carries this dedication to clarity to extreme lengths:

Clarity — this is what was for him the most important. He loved clarity and did not at all feel embarrassed to resort to his revolver for help in order at once to elucidate some affair which has become hopelessly entangled.[14]

The design in question is extremely consonant with his own mind for which, as the narrator says, there is "no essential difference between human thinking and the burning of an ordinary electric bulb.[15]   And here are the two premises that make it possible for energetic and dedicated men like Shpektorov to undertake the task of translating into empirical reality the simple and clear design of things whereby all mankind, or at least Russia, will forever gain happiness. Namely, the following: 1) a clear and simple design of things; one should keep it so; 2) the kind of philosophy that Shpektorov entertains, to the effect that there is no essential difference between complex psychic and emotional phenomena and any known material process of the physical world.

The first premise supplies an infallible and all-justifying program of action, a blueprint good for all times. The second premise postulates that nothing in the nature of man is incompatible with the nature of the blueprint. It offers a mechanical picture of man and human personality: man is a sum of physiological functions, a well assembled machine, analyzable and observable through and through, and therefore devoid of any innerness. Biological and physical causes adequately explain man and his personality. In terms of this second premise man is "human material," fundamentally not different from any other material that Shpektorov and like-minded men use in their task.

Thanks to these propositions, the revolutionaries need not have scruples about the inviolability of this human material: it is totally disposable, expendable and, as it were, renewable. No unforeseeable response need be expected from it. Therefore it will not elude control. Only on these conditions can the revolutionaries plan integrally, and make the grand design an empirical reality. Only the grand design itself, the aim, puts limits to their freedom of action. And this aim certainly justified any means. The only morality that they recognize is, as Shpektorov says, "the morality of the creation of a world."[16] Governmental agencies administer this human material ad lib, mold it and mobilize it according to the needs dictated by the grand design. We should then expect a sense of impersonality in Shpektorov's attitude toward people: they are very much statistical units abstractly considered. A detail at the very beginning of the novel points to such an attitude. Shpektorov and Arximedov, on their way home, come across the motley populace of Leningrad: a thief, floor-polishers, questionable females, some hypocrite in a cab — a picture of human shabbiness. They are engaged in a philosophical discussion. Arximedov, in Dostoyevskian fashion, lays the responsibility for those sorry figures with Shpektorov. Shpektorov responds: "You think, apparently, that I am in charge of the administrative department of the Gubispolkom?"[17] To the personal way in which Arximedov views a problem of morality Shpektorov responds in an exactly opposite way. An issue of morality becomes for him a matter of impersonal bureaucratic management from which live man's personal presence tends to vanish.

And this is the way it should be if Shpektorov and like-minded men want the grand design to succeed. They have to reduce any individual complexity or deviation back to the original abstract simplicity of the design. They must at all cost keep the design in its pristine clarity. If things start losing this intended clarity and simplicity, they must be forced back into it. Otherwise, the grand design itself may collapse. The grand design can function only on the assumption that man's psychic complexities are reducible to physical and physiological laws. Only on these conditions can it control these complexities, just as it controls physical phenomena. This corresponds perfectly to Shpektorov's own view of the world and history. As the narrator says, even the furniture in Shpektorov's room mirrors his philosophical denial of accidental unplanned happenings. He has dedicated his life to the pragmatic task of planning and implementing the material foundations of socialism.

The agents and engineers of the grand design had better be superhuman, or possibly, inhuman. It simplifies their task and makes it easier to settle controversial issues. Especially, it keeps them from debilitating emotionalities. The "morality of the creation of a world" practically means to build the industrial and economic foundations of the new socialist system, and to build it fast, disregarding its human cost. Human factor matters only insofar as it affects this economic and industrial growth. It does not matter in itself. Under this grand design people live for the sake of the machines, and not the machines for the sake of people. To be up to this grand design, its agents and engineers must be ruthless toward the "human material" used, including the agents and engineers themselves.

The tragic failure of Shpektorov is to have yielded to the temptation of being human. For this reason, one half of his personality and life discredits the grand design that the other half is so forcefully asserting and carrying out. It is undoubtedly a very big piece of irony that the most accidental, unplanned and irrational happening befalls the one who tries to be the very negation of the accidental, the unplanned, and who tries to impose mathematical rationality upon things. It turns out that in his own life Shpektorov infracts virtually every principle that he asserts philosophically, as a public figure, and in his profession. He derides Arximedov as an archaic sentimentalist. He despises any kind of romantic illusion-mongering. With all these sober attitudes, what does this articulate and positive utilitarian do? Like a sentimental fool, he falls in love with another's wife, desperately, against any good common sense. Although enemy of irrational and ineffectual behavior and of any kind of quixotry, Shpektorov himself becomes something of an irrational and ineffectual Don Quixote. For example, he suddenly comes, together with Èsfir', to see the narrator, and begs him to accompany his mistress Èsfir' to her husband Arximedov, who with his infant has taken up his quarters at a children's theater. Shpektorov begs the narrator to help arrange a reconciliation between his mistress and her husband. Apparently, Shpektorov does not quite dare to carry through this generous duty himself. If abstracted from its earnestness and genuine drama, this episode would read in a key similar to that in which Tolstoy wrote his grotesque parody of the lordly passions experienced and narrated over many a bottle of claret by Captain Ramballe in *War and Peace.*

Reconciled with her husband, Èsfir' stays with him and her infant in the children's theater. The child is actually Shpektorov's. Most likely, Arximedov does not know about it. Shpektorov does, of course. And it is not a cheerful knowledge. A great love blossoms between a man and a woman. A child is born from this love. What more natural and lawful? But in this case nothing can be acknowledged openly, everything happens by stealth, out of sight of others, as if some misdeed is being committed. They both suffer from this degrading ambiguity because neither is a trivial person and because both are straightforward and self-respecting. It leads Èsfir' to a grievous end. She loves Shpektorov as much as she is resolved, out of remorse, not to abandon her husband whom she feels to be an uncommon man. Seeing no way out of the triangle, she commits suicide. The situation inflicts no less pain on Shpektorov. A man of brutal intellectual straightforwardness, averse to procrastination, who makes a point of cutting the gordian knot wherever and whenever it occurs — this man is now reduced to tiptoeing around the "deceived husband." The man who did not hesitate to go to the very bitter end of the revolutionary terror and who would not hesitate to shoot his own brother for lacking the guts to do likewise, now, in order to see and to speak with Èsfir', has to sneak into the children's theater in Arximedov's absence. When the narrator comes to visit Shpektorov at his work in Southern Russia he finds him a rather different man. Shpektorov's levity hides a very tired man. His mordancy, a habitual sign of his own sense of superiority, now seems to betray a deep inner dissatisfaction with himself. Even his work above and beyond the call of duty seems intended more to counteract his own letdown than to respond to the call of duty.

After Èsfir''s suicide, Shpektorov compels Arximedov to give up the child. He adopts his own child — another sobering experience for Shpektorov. The narrator, the witness of the whole transaction of adoption, observes noticeable changes in Shpektorov. His temper is not so caustic as it used to be. Things are no longer so self-evident. The night before the adoption procedure, for the first time in his life, Shpektorov suffers from migraine, "old woman's thing," as he comments. He has aged. Fatigue marks his features and bearing.

By contributing to the growth of the material foundations of socialism, Shpektorov intends to improve the quality of life of his countrymen. He has not improved it at all. He has ruined his personal life. He has driven to suicide Èsfir', the woman he loved. He has badly unsettled the life of his own little boy whom he has by Èsfir' and whom Arximedov believes to be his own child. Not to speak of Arximedov himself for whose ill fortune Shpektorov partly also incurs the responsibility. Truly, Shpektorov has inflicted ill fortune on virtually all the persons he has happened to do with. And all this for the sake of increasing the material foundations of socialism. Will it ever redeem the misery that he has brought upon himself and other living people in the process? No amount of technological hardware can redeem this misery. It may well be that Shpektorov runs his graders so long in order to drown out an internal voice of reproach. It does not escape his co-workers. One of them observes that Shpektorov works several times more than he is supposed to "in order not to think too much of his personal affairs."[18] The man has irreparably missed his life on its essential. As in the case of Lozhkin, it may all have been the result of a "small initial error" which Shpektorov overlooked in the "conditions of the problem."

In his *Prologue* (1930), a collection of sketches about his journey to Southern Russia, Kaverin describes how new roads are built and new fields plowed. In one episode, a young tractor operator, in control of his heavy equipment, approaches a cemetery — his next object. It is an old cemetery: weeds have overrun the graves, the wooden crosses have bent and stooped from old age. It turns out that the young tractor operator is a local man and that his father is buried at this cemetery. The young man walks over to his father's grave; for a moment, he looks as if he is agitatedly debating something with someone in his mind; angry, he walks away, blows his nose, and for a while still lingers among those ancient graves. Presently, he climbs on his tractor and the whole outfit rumbles onto the graveyard. It does not take long for the mechanized plows to wipe the ancient cemetery off the face of the earth.

This poetic example subtly illustrates the point of the controversy. The young tractor operator unquestionably shares Shpektorov's dedication to building a new world along the rational, materialistic lines, all according to the grand design. He is about to raze an old cemetery. It stands in the way of a magnificent economic progress. The cemetery gone, vast, economically efficient, crop-yielding fields will enrich socialist society. And still, the young tractor operator for a fraction of time hesitates to pursue this triumphant road toward the grand design. His father's grave is at this cemetery. Perhaps it is to the credit of Kaverin's artistic wisdom and philosophical intuition that in the ensuing internal debate the young tractor operator does not quite succeed in persuading someone of something. Apparently, some deep-seated emotions inhibit him from literally bull-dozing his way toward rationality and economic advantage through the grave of his father.

Some irrational core within man's personality resists control, indoctrination and regimentation. This proposition is the Dostoyevskian side of the controversy. The "human material," so completely adequate for the grand design, turns out to be an abstraction. In concrete life there are persons, and their personalities do not always behave as the grand design postulates them to do. The grand design does not allow for the complexities of man's psychic and emotional life. These complexities obscure the clarity of the grand design and upset its simplicity. Shpektorov has not understood this, or has chosen to ignore it. And life will not fail to take revenge on those who ignore its laws. Shpektorov is certainly not a Hippolytus, but he incurs a faintly similar punishment. The apprentice superman has been meted out more than an ordinary share of humanness. The "leather jacket" of the Revolution, the man who worries more about the prosperity of the machines than about that of people, experiences a lifelong muffled passion for his friend's wife. Used to the language of the machine, he is now painfully learning to speak the language of man. It is a painful apprenticeship. Its consequences are tragic for her, and endlessly painful for him. Used to cutting the gordian knot, the proud man has now passively to suffer human imbroglio. Èsfir' loves him, has a child by him, but she will remain with her husband out of remorse and sense of guilt. Her own sense of integrity does not allow her to hurt her husband Arximedov more than she thinks she already has. All the more so because she feels Arximedov to be an uncommon man, difficult to dismiss lightly. It is for the love of Èsfir' that Shpektorov reconciles himself with all these inconsistencies, quixotic bouts and emotional disarray, all of which is so contrary to his own nature. In that much Shpektorov has betrayed both his own morality and the grand design.

There is something of a tragic irony in the fact that by carrying through his ideological commitment Shpektorov demonstrates Arximedov's thinking. "A box with tools — this is too little to start a new era,"[19] Arximedov says apropos of the role of technology in man's life. For him the "living stock in trade" of socialism matters more than its material infrastructure. Arximedov does not oppose technology and its progress out of principle. He rather fears that the quality of human life, the quality of human relations, man's morality, and his cultural self-fulfillment all fall more and more behind the rapid advance of technology. If it is true that man differs from the other species by the fact that he is a moral being blessed with the unlimited creativity of his mind, then he should not allow himself to be enslaved by the machine. He should not, because if he does, he will ultimately allow himself to be re-shaped after the image of the machine,[20] and thereby debase his essential humanity. The machine and, ultimately, the automated system, as compared with human personality, is an "under-dimensioned" phenomenon. In a mechanical environment, not to speak of the environment of automated systems, man must "under-dimension" himself in order to secure the continuous operation of the machine. This is one of the grave objections that Lewis Mumford puts forward against the "mechanical world picture."[21] To "under-dimension" oneself in this context means to keep reducing the complexity of the thoughts and emotions of the moral being. When Shpektorov says: "But if I had to choose between morality and a pair of pants, I would have chosen a pair of pants,"[22] he performs a piece of such a reductionism. What Arximedov fears is precisely this kind of reductionism. Coupled with technological progress, it harbors a grave danger for society. It is a universal threat.

Arximedov essentially asserts that no amount of technological hardware can improve man's soul and the human quality of life. This is a matter of morality and humaneness, and not of technological hardware. For him, the most urgent task is to regenerate a mentally regimented society and to reclaim it from its narrowly technological bent to a more balanced vision of the world.

His being an artist acquires a special significance for the mission he is undertaking in the story. An artist, namely a painter, at his work may well offer the best example of personal and creative involvement with the object, of solicitous attention to it. The artist lets his whole soul and personality be absorbed by the work he is creating. In this way the artist creates his masterpiece. He must invest all his awareness, all his mental energy into it to produce it. Such an attitude precludes unthinking uncaring routine. The artist's work is a very sophisticated and individualized form of craftsmanship. However, it still remains a form of labor. In Arximedov's scheme of things man should extend this personal and creative attitude to all forms of labor. This is when, as Arximedov says, work become valor, and it is a joy to feel tired after work. This solicitous attention to one's work, the desire to make a work of art out of even a humble job will eliminate "machine-like existence," as Arximedov says. That is, if work — any work — becomes a matter of personal interest and creative endeavor, this attitude will ban mediocrity, sluggishness and boredom from life. The thoroughness of high craftsmanship cannot be achieved without integrity in labor. And integrity in labor is synonymous with professional honesty. Professional honesty becomes the substance of personal dignity. People should be helped to cultivate their personal dignity and honesty in labor.

In Arximedov's vision these ideals were once incarnated in the activity of the medieval guilds. In his opinion, the latter generated professional honesty and dedication in labor. By contrast, he finds them sadly missing in his contemporary society:

In the 15th century not one workshop was allowed to admit an apprentice before he had taken the oath honestly to do his work according to the statutes and the aims of the State. The textile-workers of those times used publicly to burn the cloth into which hair had been mixed. Masters who incorrectly measured out wine were thrown down from roofs into garbage holes. A decree on labor ethics — try to imagine that it will be adopted at the next session of the Central Committee. We would not have enough garbage holes for unscrupulous masters,"[23]

Arximedov says to Shpektorov.

Next, man should extend the same personal and creative involvement and solicitous attention to interpersonal relations, to moral relations between people. The very refining of the quality of human relations should become the masterpiece to achieve. Arximedov strives toward a situation in which personality and interpersonal relations are the aim of man's endeavor, rather than simply a means toward the grand design. He engages in what he believes to be a crusade to make the vulgar and the base more humane. The task that Arximedov undertakes is far more elusive than Shpektorov's.

Those who take part in Don Quixote's late 16th-century setting are up to a certain point willing to play along with him; they are themselves somewhat quixotic. This is what Don Quixote owes his "success" to. Does not even the lion neglect to come out of his cage to combat Don Quixote? Quixotry thrives on such active non-happenings. Our Soviet Don Quixote lives in a very unquixotic world. It puts a brutal end to Arximedov's quixotic career. Then, it steam-rollers the pathetically forlorn man. Arximedov's life ends in a failure, a failure even more radical than that of Shpektorov.

Thus, both men end up in misery once their conflict is over. This kind of conflictual situation has all the potentiality of a tragic conflict. Both opponents are honest men, dedicated to the welfare of their country. The conflict between them is not one between a good man, the "positive hero," and a villain. Both of them are good men. Both of them are right. Both are inspired by unselfish motives. Both pursue an aim ennobled by the highest sense of honor and morality, or dedication to the welfare of one's fellowmen. And still, antagonistic lines of action set them apart. The issues that divide them become extremely problematic. The spectator or the reader cannot easily decide on whose side justice, truth and nobility are, or at least which adversary has more of it. When the drama runs its course, neither is perceptibly rewarded for his merits. Rather, both suffer at the end for their respective *hamartia*.

The drama of the two men originates from what they belive man's nature is and what humanity means. This controversy harks back perceptibly to Turgenev's Bazarov, Chernyshevsky's "new men," and Dostoyevsky's response to the latter. Fascinated by the advances of experimental science, Bazarov could not have helped simplifying man's nature; he reduced total man to a mechanical assemblage of particular physiological functions. Chernyshevsky's "new men" believed that through rational organization and mechanization society will forever gain its fulfillment and happiness. The response of the "man from underground" is well known: man's psychology is too perverse and irrational forever to settle for the "crystal palace." If there is at all any improvement in the life of society, it will come about through man's inner regeneration.

Shpektorov and like-minded men take it for an axiomatic truth that if they want their new socialist system to survive in history, they must build its material infrastructure and consolidate its organization in a catastrophically short time. Otherwise, they would be crushed, as Stalin said in a famous speech.[24] Therefore the builders of socialism must proceed at a frantic pace. The engineers of the grand design must force man, animals, environment, nature, everything, into contributing to the triumph of socialism. They must force the construction, no matter how much human suffering and waste it may cause. It then becomes a matter of expediency — even of necessity — to consider man and his personality as no more than "human material." From a certain detached point of view, one could not deny this morality a sort of epic greatness. It postulates a monolithic mind free from doubt, the integrity of a fervent believer who stops at nothing to further the cause.

Tragic experience awaits Shpektorov when he comes to realize the limitations of his morality. His unfulfilled love for Èsfir' makes him aware of it. Here, his functional and quantitive morality does not work. No amount of roads that Shpektorov will have laid out will redeem the loss of Èsfir' for him. Perhaps a tragic hero need not inevitably end in a catastrophic destruction. W. Kaufmann shows this persuasively apropos of Aeschylus' tragedies.[25] However, for this purpose Shpektorov should have adopted another morality. And he does so: in regard to Èsfir', he suspends his own, and adopts the "morality of solicitous attention and trust,".[26] It is the one advocated by Arximedov, a morality which defends human personality as an aim in itself, and gives the paramount importance to improving and refining the quality of human relations.

A ruthless, unthinkingly functional "leather jacket," like the one described by Pil'njak, would hardly have anything tragic about his character. A tragic dimension appears when a split opens in the mind of such a "leather jacket." When he sees another center of loyalty grow in his soul, a loyalty quite different from and hostile to the one he has professed thus far. A whole lifetime of dedication, self-sacrifice, action, and possibly not quite avowable deeds committed for the sake of the cause suddenly come into question. More than that: the grand design itself comes into question. If it denies man something without which life loses its freshness and joy, if it robs him of an irreplaceable part of his life that he lives only once in the whole duration of cosmos, is then the grand design worth carrying out? Some such thoughts must have flashed across Shpektorov's mind when he brooded over the hopeless imbroglio of his love for Èsfir', or after her suicide. Two different and hostile truths struggle in Shpektorov's mind. This is his tragic experience. His "morality of the creation of a world" becomes most likely diluted.

However, for better or worse, there is still a new world to built. It still has to be built at full speed if it is to survive in history. And Shpektorov will not shrink from this responsibility. "History itself has taken upon itself the toil of drafting these plans, and as for him, he will not permit himself to evade its stern command,"[27], the narrator comments toward the end of the story. Shpektorov will keep shouldering what he believes to be his duty toward the new social system, even if at the price of the nagging misery of his own life.

A certain common destiny links Arximedov and Shpektorov. The latter has to step out of his own morality and embrace that of Arximedov in order to attempt to solve his ultimate problems. Arximedov's morality is absolute in the sense that it ministers to the most fundamental needs of human personality. Shpektorov's morality is relative in the sense that it commands a certain way of life at a certain period of history. This radical opposition is the source of Arximedov's tragic fate. Although his morality is right absolutely, it becomes difficult to apply at the time represented in the novel: the time of a certain acceleration and maximalization of history, when massive efficiency takes precedence over individual justice. Not only is Arximedov's morality difficult to apply, but it simply becomes undesirable in the eyes of the powers that be. For this reason, the enterprise Arximedov undertakes is foredoomed, no matter how noble and how true. And he may have done so in the full knowledge of what to expect: a grotesquely quixotic career and a catastrophe in personal life.

On a somewhat similar topic, I. Èrenburg wrote a novel under the title *Den' vtoroj* (The second day). As a piece of narrative fiction, this novel is only a little better than mediocre. However, the underlying idea conveyed in the very title of the novel is significant. The title refers to the second day of the Creation according to the Book of Genesis. It still is only the second day of the creation of the world, when the vault of heaven has only separated from the water underneath. History has not yet begun. It still will take four more days for man – and perhaps civilization – to appear. Èrenburg's idea seems to be that it would be erroneous to expect the good fortune of the sixth day on the second day of the creation of the socialist world. Arximedov suffers the tragic worldly fate of all the prophets: that of being far ahead of his time.

Arximedov is not only a social and moral reformer ahead of his time. His vision is prophetic in the literal sense of the word. He has developed a new way of seeing things, i.e., he perceives new principles of art, of pictorial representation. The prophetic vision of the social reformer and that of the artist are intimately connected. His destiny as an artist is no less tragic than his destiny as a moral and social reformer. The artist in Arximedov remains subdued throughout the story. Nonetheless, only the artist, or rather his artistic message, anonymously survives the disintegration of Arximedov's personality and life. In this respect, his tragic destiny is somewhat redeemed. The commentator speaks of this artistic message in these words:

. . . Only he could succeed in this who with all the freedom of the talent of genius stepped beyond the caution and the dishonesty of the contemporary painting, which has alienated itself so much from people. The blending of the sublime with trifles, of commonplace details with a deep feeling of time – this one cannot learn from either the living masters or the dead. Only the new vision, boldly resting on that which all others consider accidental or hackneyed, could dare such a return to the childlike nature of things. Along with the unconscious strength of representation, here one can see intelligence and memory – a terrifying memory, based, perhaps, on the clear ideas of what is rushing past the eyes of a person falling down from the fifth floor. One had to hurt oneself to death to paint this thing . . .[28]

5

Kaverin's latest novel *Pered zerkalom* (In front of the mirror; book edition 1972) articulates unmistakably with *Artist Unknown*. It appears from this novel that Kaverin is taking as vital an interest in the problems of cultural lag and art as he did forty years earlier in *Artist Unknown*. *In Front of the Mirror* dramatizes the same fundamental issues that *Artist Unknown* does. I namely have in mind the motive of the civilizing effect of aesthetic awareness. In regard of this motive Kaverin steps in his latest novel beyond what he signifies in *Artist Unknown*.

In Front of the Mirror, an epistolary novel, tells the story of a Russian woman Elizaveta Turaeva, who devotes herself to painting. She happens to leave Russia during the Civil War, and pursues her artistic vocation in France. She bears a lifelong love to a friend of her adolescence Konstantin Karnovskij, a mathematics student who later becomes one of the leading Russian authorities in certain branches of mathematics. They correspond for over two decades, from their early student years in Russia to their years of professional maturity in the late twenties and the early thirties. Their love for each other grows as their separation becomes more and more unavoidable. Her return to Russia does not materilize, and it becomes more and more difficult for him to come to see her in Paris.

Konstantin Karnovskij comes from a lowly poor merchant family. His father died early. From his early youth Konstantin has to work in order to pay his own studies and to support his siblings and his mother. He embarks on the career of a teacher. He becomes a successful tutor, with the prospect of becoming a member of the faculty staff at the local university. All in all, Konstantin looks toward achieving an honest but rather undistinguished career in a drab provincial environment. The Revolution and the ensuing new social system immensely improve and widen his professional prospects.

Karnovskij's personality is akin to that of Shpektorov. He believes in mathematics as a means whereby to save mankind from the power of blind contingency. This indicates the same kind of abstract, impersonal and "organizational" attitude toward people and life as Shpektorov believed to be ideal in his own activity. Karnovskij never was a "leather jacket" of the Revolution. However, he responds enthusiastically to the admirable opportunities that the new socialist system offers. His personality fits the function of the "builder:" he is extremely purposeful, hard-driving, he plans his time and occupations in detail and adheres to his plans inflexibly, and works with utmost dedication. And the Soviet Government assigns him the task that he loves. So we would expect Karnovskij to become another Shpektorov, even a more efficient one because of his apparent imperviousness to emotional entanglements with women. Still, Karnovskij grows into a very different man. His "technocratic" soul changes because of his encounter with art. He owes this transformation to his lifelong friend and love, Elizaveta Turaeva, the painter.

Elizaveta is the daughter of an army officer. She reminds one a little of the youngest sister from Chekhov's *Three Sisters*. Unlike Irene, however, Elizaveta is endowed with a strong sense of independence. She nurses vigorous ambitions and puts them into effect without procrastination. Her first ambition — perhaps under Karnovskij's influence — is to become a mathematician. In 1913, after finishing secondary school, she goes to Petersburg with a view to enrolling for whatever mathematics courses there are available for women. However, this erstwhile ambition does not last too long. Her interest in mathematics yields its place to what will become Elizaveta's true vocation, namely, painting. Meanwhile, her relations with

Karnovskij fluctuate from tender friendship to aggressive passion. At the high point of the latter, Elizaveta backs out of their prospective marriage. She is repelled by his family and his drab environment. Moreover, she fears for her independence. Their relations break off at that point. Subsequently they take quite a different course. Since she attained some proficiency in painting, she has strongly desired to go to Paris where she expects further opportunities for improving her art. The chance circumstances of her life during the turmoil of the Civil War and the foreign intervention take her over to Istanbul. Eventually she succeeds to come to Paris. Elizaveta has not left Russia as a political emigree. However, since she left Russia, she has lived through all the tribulations that a refugee in an alien environment is exposed to. The vital part of Turaeva's life unfolds in Paris, in an emigré environment. Now, in describing the lives of the Russian exiles Soviet writers usually resort to a certain hostile stereotype with a view to discredit the exiles' lives. Kaverin's narrative is not of this kind. It is true to life. I believe that the last four chapters in which the author narrates Turaeva's life in Paris are the most interesting in the whole novel.

In these chapters Kaverin dramatizes Turaeva's quest for the identity of her art. This is where Karnovskij's and Turaeva's paths cross again, and merge in their joint quest for creative originality and meaningful life. Along this path, Karnovskij has dealt with scientific truth, which is truth in terms of the general, the abstract, and law. He utilizes this scientific truth through its technological application for society's benefit, namely, by usefully transforming man's environment. To succeed in this endeavor, Karnovskij needs, speaking crudely, only a well-equipped laboratory and competent manpower. In that much he follows in Shpektorov's footsteps. And, unavoidably, he experiences the same ultimate nagging frustration. It turns out that this is just not enough for man as a moral being at a certain stage of mental development and maturity. "No longer did Konstantin Pavlovich hope that he would succeed with the help of mathematics in delivering mankind from the power of blind chance,"[29] the narrator comments about this inevitable point of frustration in Karnovskij's intellectual development. Whereas Shpektorov's development ends at a similar point, in a spiritual crisis and frustration, Karnovskij has a chance to step beyond it.

In the person of Turaeva, Karnovskij finds that which Spektorov did not want to or was not able to discover in both Arximedov and Èsfir'. Turaeva enables Karnovskij to discover the sense of artistic truth, that is, truth in terms of the concrete, the individual, the unique, and the beautiful. Since art at its best means to translate individual experience in terms of universal validity, it requires the "honest eye," as Zhaba said in *Artist Unknown*, that is, the highest degree of independence in the artist. This commitment may, of course, condemn him to less than comfortable life. It requires of the artist to think in solitude, to control his emotions rather than let his emotions control him. It requires a certain disinterested contemplation and observation. And this kind of disinterestedness helps one understand oneself better. It refines and softens the subject's selfish or brutal impulses. In one of the very last comments that the author makes about Turaeva's painting, he shows her painting the portrait of a fisherman, the village fool. In order to paint the portrait well, Turaeva makes an effort to identify emotionally with him. What she then sees is a gentle, almost saintly wise man who does not wish harm to anyone. And this is the figure that will appear on the canvas. Thus, her aesthetic vision penetrates to the very depth of her object, and discovers its inner goodness. It could have been the inner evil in another case. However, with her own temperament, Turaeva would hardly undertake such a portrait. She is blessed with the art of feeling, appreciating and representing the hidden beauty of her object. It is a very humane talent because it generates a naturally sympathetic attitude toward others, and washes out callousness. Thanks to this artistic incisiveness, she develops her capacity to judge everyone on his intrinsic human value, on his individual merit, as it were. It saves her from any kind of narrow morality, professional, political or other. She cannot uphold it because any narrow morality may falsely simplify reality. And the artist cannot afford to deal with such a falsely simplified reality, if he does not want to become a hack. This acceptance of complex reality has its own liabilities. Turaeva does not find it particularly shocking to be married to one man, to live with another, and forever to love the third.

Above all, her art is a continuous revolt, a permanent asking of unsettling questions. And this revolt cannot be solved by firing squads. Neither can these questions be answered with the help of well-equipped laboratories. Nor can all this creative anxiety be removed and settled by another's authoritative statement. Each time we deal with individual mysteries which can be solved only individually and at the depth of an individual mind. In that much a work of art also is an individual mystery which each generation tries to solve in its own way, by appealing to its imagination. Good art cannot survive on other terms. With all these considerations in mind, we may wonder why does it happen that Turaeva, an outstanding Russian cultural figure, is trying to translate her artistic aspirations into reality in an alien environment? Her struggle for her artistic integrity is not an easy one. It is all the more to her credit that she does achieve her high purpose in her medium of art. The question is why does not the author have Turaeva make her way on her own native soil?

Karnovskij learns a great lesson from this encounter with art in the person of Turaeva. He realizes that it is in the sense of the uniqueness of every object and person that the renewal of life lies. And it does renew Karnovskij's life. Without this awareness of the uniqueness of each personality, it becomes impossible to take a vital and serious interest in people. If all are interchangeable, people become depersonalized units of an abstract machinery in which only mass and motion count. Both Shpektorov and Karnovskij had lived in this dehumanized Galilean world. They both had enough vitality to experience distaste for it.

But only Karnovskij makes it to the other world, the world of colors, sounds and odors. This sense of the uniqueness of things, that is, taste for life, he learns from the aesthetic vision of the world. He owes it to Turaeva. Now, Turaeva herself is unique for him because he loves her. As he experiences things, love for her and the sense of the beauty of the world go together.

6

Since his mature works, i.e., since *Skandalist* (1828) and *Artist Unknown* (1931), man's integrity has remained one of the main issues in Kaverin's works. It appears in different situations and in regard to different objects − namely, in regard to man's professional work, his intellectual attitudes and his moral judgment. It takes tragic overtones.

Kaverin's three novels − *Fulfillment of Desires*, *Two Captains*, *Open Book* − and his post-Stalin works "A Piece of Glass" and *Double Portrait* are different views of the drama of scientific and intellectual integrity. This is the problem that keeps recurring in these works, as this problem arises in the fluctuating Soviet medium.

In *Fulfillment of Desires* this problem reveals its most poignant facet in the character of the young philologist and historian Trubachevskij. It turns out that one can entertain a great deal of professional ambition justified by talent, give all one's energy and enthusiasm to one's discipline, and still fail. It turns out that Trubachevskij's intellectual glamor ruins his scholarly debut because he does not know where to stop, and because he goes beyond the limits of what he should have undertaken at the given time of his career. He does not listen to his mentor's advice:

Either to pursue scholarship − and then no [writing of] books until the doctoral dissertation, or whatever it is now called in your circles. Or, to turn out booklets − and then, sorry, I don't see in what respect I can help you![30]

Unwittingly, Trubachevskij steps on the path of perverting the purpose of scholarship. Trubachevskij learns the hard way that scholarship can succeed only if pursued with personal integrity. The scholar is not pursuing a narrowly selfish aim through his activity. There is a certain disinterestedness in this scholarly pursuit. As the author interprets it in this novel, the scholar or scientist unselfishly strive toward the kind of truth and discovery that will benefit people and exalt the motherland. Trubachevskij commits an error. Fortunately, he has a chance to redeem himself because he is a young scholar of integrity. Still, the more compelling drama in this novel centers on this innocent perversion of the purpose of scholarship. Kaverin's subsequent novels bring out this problem in a more ominous light.

In *Two Captains*, Sanja Grigor'ev grows to become a positive character welcome to the gallery of his peers of Soviet fiction. In retrospect, Sanja Grigor'ev and his wife appear somewhat melodramatic. The truly tragic figure in the novel is the first Captain. A passionate explorer and geographer, Captain Tatarinov undertakes his voyage in order to contribute, along with other nations, to the knowledge of Arctic regions. Misunderstood and deceived by all, he sails on his voyage, shortly before the First World War. He is well aware that the odds are heavily against the successful completion of his mission. Soon after his departure it becomes clear to him that the expedition is doomed. Still he courageously continues, collecting scientific data, making an important geographic discovery, and fights the catastrophe to the last. This tragic figure, however, stands on the periphery of the novel.

The epic, and partly melodramatic, substance of the novel faintly reflects the tragic glow coming from the distant figure of Captain Tatarinov. This reflected quality of the story undoubtedly bolsters the artistic value of the whole narrative. It is from this tragic figure that the characters in the story draw what dramatic significance they possess. And it is apropos of this near mythic figure of Captain Tatarinov that the struggle for scientific integrity is being waged. In this novel, the perversion of intellectual integrity goes well beyond what Trubachevskij experiences in *Fulfillment of Desires*. The villain — who happens to be a cousin of Captain Tatarinov — tries to discredit the Captain in the eyes of the latter's family, and gain the favor of his surviving wife Mar'ja Vasil'evna. Nikolaj Antonovich gives a false account of the circumstances under which the Captain undertook his voyage. The former's part in the preparation of the voyage was quite negative. However, he depicts it in his account as most solicitous and far-sighted, while hinting falsely at Captain Tatarinov's lack of forethought. And as a finishing touch, Nikolaj Antonovich tries to pervert the meaning of the Captain's mission, and capitalizing on the latter's growing reputation of explorer and geographer, he makes his own career of a scientist and geographer. He does so with complete impunity since the Captain himself is not around, and most likely will never return to expose the former's falsehoods.

Kaverin describes the one who was to become Sanja Grigor'ev as "a youth shaken by the idea of justice".[31]   The mainspring of Sanja Grigor'ev's life is his determination to seek the truth about the fate of Captain Tatarinov, and to restore the justice denied to this noble figure for so long by so many. This struggle for justice and truth is what animates the character of Sanja. Viewed and represented from a certain angle, this is an eminently tragic motive. Namely, when the conflict or the situation raise a doubt about how just gods' or man's justice really is. Or when either adversary champions a just cause so that it becomes problematic to tell who is right and who is wrong. Or when man seeks truth and pursues honesty so relentlessly that it leads to his own self-destruction. None of these applies to the case of Sanja's struggle. The pattern of the conflict is "sentimental," in the sense that the blameless hero ends up by defeating the machinations of the wicked villain, and the latter at long last is meted out just punishment. Here the sentimentalism of the Dickensian type blends with the optimism of Socialist Realism. Kaverin's narrative skill and incisiveness saves this peculiar blend from triviality. All in all, the universal idea of justice dominates the theme of the defense of the fatherland and dedication to socialism. This perhaps is worth noticing in a work written under the pressure of Socialist Realism.

It is logical that the character that stands closest to the tragic figure of Captain Tatarinov absorbs something of his dramatic quality. The only character that can claim some measure of tragic substance within the plot of the novel is Mar'ja Vasil'evna, the Captain's wife. Only she incurs something akin to tragic guilt. Devoted to her husband, then to his memory, she gradually yields to to the influence of Nikolaj Antonovich, and eventually marries the latter. She does not do so out of frivolity, but rather with the noblest considerations in mind. Then comes the tragic recognition: she realizes that Nikolaj Antonovich has been the scoundrel responsible for the death of her husband and that she catastrophically misjudged the character of the one who has claimed so much devotion to the Captain and succeeded in marrying her on the strength of this false claim. Even her suicide that follows the recognition is in the style of a tragic heroine. In Kaverin's novels woman sometimes introduces this tragic dimension. So do Èsfir' of *Artist Unknown*, Mar'ja Vasil'evna of *Two Captains*, and even Glafira of *Open Book*. They commit suicide when they can no longer live with their despair. It could be argued that these women experience only a pathetic fate, rather than the tragic. However, perhaps this division derives from the analysis of the setting rather than from the understanding of the actual emotion.[32]

7

The fate of scientific integrity appears under its most dramatic aspect in the post-Stalin version of the trilogy *Open Book* and in *Double Portrait*, which is a kind of logical ending of the preceding novel. The representation of the obscurantism and the intellectual terror of the Stalinist period is altogether missing in *Fulfillment of Desires* and *Two Captains*. We could hardly expect it to appear in the Soviet Union in Stalin's own lifetime. In this respect *Open Book* and *Double Portrait* differ substantially from the previous two novels. *Open Book* breaks down into two psychologically dissimilar halves. The first half, including Part I and Chapter I of Part 2, is akin to Soviet "production novel." The second half, i.e., remaining chapters of Part 2, and Part 3 of the trilogy, dramatizes the enormous damage that Stalinism inflicted on Russian science and scientific integrity. This damning material reaches its greatest strength toward the end of the novel.

The immense transformations that started in Russia since the later twenties have been attributed to Stalin's vision and willpower. It was still Stalin who led the country through the ghastly war against the Nazi Germany. Thus, for three decades Stalin had been plying his unprecedented power through internal turmoils and external wars toward his grand design. This enormous impact of Stalin has been achieved with total disregard for the nature of the means used as long as they served the purpose. Seen from this angle, Stalin was a supreme opportunist and schemer expert in plotting conspiracies, playing off one enemy against another, disposing of both and than falsely claiming the credit for their achievements. All this looks more like the mobsters' power struggle than the procedure proper to the head of a civilized government. In spite of his seminary background, Stalin was hardly an intellectual, one of the intelligentsia, in the sense in which Lenin and Trotsky were. He may have wished to be one, or at least to appear like one. It is this aspiration of Stalin to pursue scholarly activity that Solzhenitsyn bitterly parodies in a chapter of *The First Circle*.[33] Deep in his heart Stalin may have harbored a dislike for true intellectuals, a dislike combined with envy. From this point of view, Stalinism is a "Salierism" of the worst and the most vulgar kind. I have in mind the kind of conflict that Pushkin represented in his "little tragedy" *Mozart and Salieri*. That is, one's envy of the creative genius of another, one's indignation at Fate's injustice in the dispensation of genius and talent, and one's desire also to possess them, one's desire at least to appear as a scientist or artist and to reap the wordly benefits of it. This skein of thoughts and emotions probably was a part of what motivated Stalin to act. He must have suffered from some form of paranoia — an abnormal suspiciousness along with megalomania, although this exaltation of Stalin was necessary component of his system of government irrespective of Stalin's personal attitude. His enormous and uncontrolled power enabled him successfully to steer through crises, turmoils and wars. The abnormalities of his personality wrapped his government in an atmosphere of mass schizophrenia, generated wholesale butcheries and unleased a physical and spiritual terror unprecedented in history.

Stalinism naturally breeds lesser stalins, a species psychologically akin to their progenitor. They imitate the methods of the progenitor, without, however, matching his redeeming greatness and crookedly grand vision. The lesser stalins reflect the "Salierism" of the progenitor and translate it into trivial human reality. What helps them all in this task is their excellence in the art of conspiracy toward seizing coercive power, the art of character assassination and not only character assassination. The lesser stalins apply the progenitor's underhanded methods to secure for themselves worldly prosperity and influence. Stalin does not mind their underhanded quest for personal prosperity as long as they remain subservient. Solzhenitsyn points out this tacit agreement between the two parties in the chapter of *The First Circle* where he describes the relations between Stalin and Abakumov.[34] The only thing that the progenitor does not tolerate is intellectual independence. Under penalty of severe reprisals, these lesser stalins, fourth-rate scientists or no scientists at all, make themselves be treated and spoken of as the leading and the most authoritative scientists extant. It is of course all a grim farce in which the actors borrow their garbs from the wardrobe of "The Emperor's New Clothes." In the Epilogue to the trilogy, Kaverin refers to it in these words:

> The sham, made-up science needed a sham animation — and wide discussions were organized in order to show to the world the brilliancy of creative work, the clash of opinions. But under this artificial light there became visible only the shabby scenery of ready-made shows, prompted thoughts.[35]

Stalin's intellectual and physical terror keeps the show on. And the actors reap the worldly benefits of this fraud.

This is the background against which the ultimate drama of Tat'jana Vlasenkova is unfolding. In this broader historical context her destiny as a scientist is a tragic experience. It symbolizes the desperate impasse in which the best of the Russian scientific community were placed during the worst period of Stalinism.

Arximedov of *Artist Unknown* dedicated himself to narrowing the gap between man's culture and humaneness and man's exclusive drive for scientific and narrowly technological development. His tragedy came from this struggle. However, the conflict that set him apart from Shpektorov was a philosophical duel between two gentlemen unselfishly dedicated to their country. Arximedov did not call into question the honesty of Shpektorov's exclusive interest in technology. Compared with this situation, Tat'jana Vlasenkova's is far more desperate. She cannot even afford to worry about the cultural gap. She struggles for nothing less than the very integrity and survival of Russian science and scientific quest. It only happens to be biology, but it could be any other discipline. As she is represented in the novel, she is pioneering a new trend in microbiological thinking. It will become the theory and the practice of anti-biotics. Unfortunately for her and the Russian scientific thought this scientific revolution coincides with the worst period of Stalinist intellectual obscurantism and terror.

Her adversary is Valentin Sergeevich Kramov, a senior biologist who has behind him a rather distinguished scientific career. Several decades before he introduced a concept new for Russian biology. In the novel it is called "physico-chemical theory of immunity." By the time when Tat'jana Vlasenkova comes to her scientific maturity, this theory has become of questionable scientific value. Thus, two different scientific theories come to confront each other: one less and less productive scientifically, the other still in its infancy but rich in tremendous potentialities which Tat'jana Vlasenkova senses intuitively. These are undoubtedly the ingredients of the drama that science has permanently gone through in its development.

The hostility that Kramov bears against Vlasenkova reminds one, albeit somewhat remotely, of the enmity that Pushkin's Salieri experiences toward Mozart. Salieri poisons Mozart for what he believes to be a noble cause: to correct the injustice of fate which, in contempt of all devoted and hard-working musicians, bestows the crown of genius on Mozart; the latter does not deserve it because of the levity with which he treats his own genius. Kaverin's Kramov, to be sure, is not akin to Pushkin's Salieri. His attitude toward science in no way resembles the selfless, ecstatic devotion of Salieri to music. Nor does Kramov possess the philosophical sublimity of Salieri who commits a crime for the sake of art and justice, only to start to realize after committing the crime that by doing so he has only proved his being alien to art and has mistaken an artist's prejudice for art's wisdom. However, there are some similarities and points of contact. In spite of other emotions and philosophical attitudes which in some sense extenuate his guilt and redeem it from utter vulgarity, Salieri kills Mozart out of envy and out of fear that Mozart's music will eclipse his own musical achievement. These are the same reasons for which Kramov tries to ruin Vlasenkova's scientific career. Undoubtedly, Kramov belongs to an entirely different cosmos of representation: the cosmos of narrative prose bent on reproducing in some detail ugly deeds and despicable characters that are not imaginary. The two are artistically incommensurable. Nonetheless, the archetypal analogy of the situations is compelling enough. For this reason, perhaps, Kaverin has Kolomnin, one of Vlasenkova's colleagues, paraphrase the first two lines from *Mozart and Salieri*.[36] Likewise, in "A Piece of Glass" a young scientist refers to a similar conflict as "Salierism."[37] However, Salieri's romantic aura and philosophical garb would not at all fit Kramov. Compared with Salieri, Kramov is a vulgar figure.

In the gallery of Kaverin's villains, Kramov should probably hold the foremost place. He is a man of considerable intellectual capacity. He must be in his late fifties or early sixties. He is full of zest for life, hale enough to marry a much younger and attractive woman, the former wife of Dmitri L'vov. His urge for action and leadership, his thirst for honors and prestige run high. Amidst this good fortune, there is lurking one ominous "but." His intellectual capacity, that is, his scientific potential, starts declining. This is all the more ominous for him because younger outstanding scientists, such as Tat'jana Vlasenkova, are reaching their own scientific maturity, and start taking a hard look at Kramov's actual scientific achievement. This is where the dramatic interest of this character lies. Is this situation not somewhat similar to Salieri's tragic predicament? A master lawfully enjoying his hard-earned prosperity suddenly faces the eclipse of his prominence because of the emergence of an immeasurably superior genius. Salieri's concern is not crassly vulgar. He defends the right to recognition and respect due to the honest achievements of lesser masters. Even his fear of being superseded is of a philosophical nature: Salieri does understand Mozart's genius; what worries him is the fact that in his own judgment he is being superseded by Mozart. It is a sort of philosophical envy rationalized in beautiful Romantic phrases. He does not seem to worry so much about his worldly position. Kramov's attitude is quite sordid compared with Salieri's. He also envies the creative drive of the younger scientists that he himself no longer has. However what he fears most of all is the possibility of the loss of his worldly position. If his intellectual vitality declines, how should his worldly prosperity survive? How to reconcile these incompatible propositions? One way would be the way of wise resignation. Salieri, too, had this opportunity. He could have treated Mozart as his spiritual brother. This is the way in which Mozart treated him. Mozart considered both himself and Salieri as "sons of harmony," both loving music above everything else. As "sons of harmony" bound to each other by their common all-absorbing love for music, they may have overcome divisive selfish ambitions. They may have created their respective shares of harmony and still wished each other well. These were Mozart's feelings because he loved music more than he loved himself. Salieri misunderstood and misjudged. It turned out at the crucial moment that he loved himself more than he loved music. Therefore he could not have avoided choosing the destructive way.[38]

Kramov, too, misunderstands and misjudges. He may vaguely feel that Vlasenkova's "mold" is endangering the primacy of his own theory. And for this reason he may underhandedly be opposing her work. However, he most likely does not quite bother to familiarize himself with Vlasenkova's ideas. His misjudgment is the measure of his declining intellectual perceptiveness. In a sense, the relation between Kramov and Vlasenkova parallels that between Salieri and Mozart. Kramov's mind is not seminal. He has not created the "physico-chemical theory of immunity." Kaverin has him adopt it from the microbiologist Bordet. Kramov has only re-worked and presumably developed Bordet's theory in a new direction. Kramov's derivative intelligence contrasts with the originative power of Vlasenkova's mind. It turns out that at the crucial moment, just as in the case of Salieri, Kramov's personal primacy is for him more important than the progress of Russian biology. Kramov also has to choose the destructive way. If he cannot afford to generate creative thought, then, at least, he will display the *appearance* of creative thought and force it upon others. Even Vlasenkova becomes at first a victim of this biological formalism. Kramov suggests that Vlasenkova conduct a series of experiments. They look intriguing and consume a good deal of time but lead to no new discovery. Woe be to those who perceive or uncover the fraud! From now on, Kramov has no other choice than to destroy them, lest he should forfeit his worldly well-being. And so Kramov plays his game with the doggedness of a gambler who has everything to lose if he fails to keep all his power. Under the pretense of planning theoretical research he has his own name and his loopholed theory incessantly advertised. This also helps him eliminate from his empire those who are not willing to take their cue from him. For this sordid reason he has a brilliant student's dissertation turned down, although outwardly he sympathizes with him. Kramov carries out his plans with supreme self-control and sophisticated duplicity so as always to appear on the side of justice. Far from being a petty swindler, Kramov plays his fraudulent game on a big scale and at a high level. His confederates and devotees sit in Government offices, they staff universities and research institutes. All together, they noisily lay claim to spearheading biological science. By means of this fraudulent claim they seize governmental agencies on which scientific work depends and thus take control over scientists and their work. This control depends little on the actual achievements of their scientific research. It depends far more on their administrative manipulation and scheming. They owe their careers and their worldly prosperity to this kind of organizational conspiracy. For the latter to succeed best, the men of "the Kramov school," and especially the chief himself, have thrown their scientific integrity to the winds. In this way, they build, consolidate and police a phantasmagoric empire of pseudo-science and pseudo-intellectual activity, carefully wrapping the dead dogma in the garb of creative living thought. This false pretense of intellectual creativity is vital for them all: should they fail to convince others — and perhaps themselves — to accept this pretense at its face value, they might be swept away from their positions of authority and affluence. Undoubtedly, the hideous picture that Kaverin draws has historical relevance. In the excerpt about the made-up science quoted above[39] the author adds: "Of course, it was the victory of Kramov — the victory whose terrible significance he, perhaps, himself had not foreseen." Kaverin has Vlasenkova commit these thoughts to her diary sometime between the end of the war and prior to Stalin's death in 1953. It obviously refers to the state of Soviet science from the latter part of the thirties to the end of Stalin's personal grip over the intellectual life of the country.

In a sense, Kramov is caught at his own game. In order to safeguard the primacy of his position he resorts to an elaborate scientific obscurantism. For this purpose he needs plausible accomplices and confederates. His course forces him into a collusion with the lesser stalins, the opportunistic brethren who ride the muddy wave of political expediency. For them any field is a convenient medium to arrive at positions of influence and affluence. The scientific field is no exception. In his drive to preserve his own primacy Kramov cannot avoid allying himself with these politically appointed, fourth-rate, pseudo-scientists. As the champions of Kramov's theory, they become, so to speak, his power-base. In his turn, Kramov with his name and his theory endows them with the appearance of scientific respectability. With such people in charge of the advancement of Russian science, no wonder that its quality has deteriorated. Kramov must hardly have intended things to follow this course.

However, once Kramov has chosen to ally himself with the lesser stalins, he cannot avoid becoming prisoner of his champions and their methods. Kramov cannot help changing. One such change Kaverin emphasizes in the 1965 version of the trilogy. In the latter, the author gives explicit indications of what people thought and felt during this period of anonymous denunciations, distrust and treason among friends, schizophrenic vigilantism, wiretapping,[40] secret police terror, arbitrary night arrests, group show trials, wholesale executions and deportations, witchhunts after the "enemies of the people," and other ill-famed phenomena of "ezhovshchina." In the 1956 edition of the trilogy the atmosphere of the purges of the latter thirties hardly finds any expression. In the 1965 version Kramov is given a dimension which logically grows from his alliance with his Stalinist champions and which is hardly referred to in the previous edition. Kramov's scientific discourses take on political overtones, the kind of overtones that marked the criminations dispensed by Stalinist prosecutors at the time. When accused of incompetence by other scientists at a meeting, he interlards his response with ominous hints at the political disloyalty of these honest scientists, including Vlasenkova. At the time, this may have been enough for these scientists to be arrested and put to death or be deported. Vlasenkova notices that Kramov acts like a gambler at the peril of losing much and betting on a sure card. At this point, Kramov is trading the rest of his scientific integrity and decency for this sure card. He is using it in order to re-impose through political intimidation his scientific authority on those scientists who question his scientific leadership.

From now on, to keep power Kramov and his Stalinist champions will not hesitate to resort to any character assassination, any slander, any anonymous denunciation which would send an innocent person to death or concentration camp. At their last interview, his little well-groomed face, his tightly set lips and his little hands with weak fingers remind Tat'jana of an evil dwarf with the "half-closed eyes of an assassin,".[41] The whole tragic ambivalence of this man hides in this scene. This last interview between Vlasenkova and Kramov occurs shortly after the suicide of Kramov's wife. The suicide has cruelly shocked him, to the point that he is taken severely ill. Tat'jana realizes that Kramov is genuinely grieved by his wife's death and feels responsible for her suicide. Apparently, there are some decent feelings left in him. Which will not prevent him from trying to ruin Vlasenkova's life and career, should he find it expedient for his interests. Kramov is a much worse man than he needs or perhaps even cares to be. Once he was a brilliant and true scientist. As such he enjoyed the respect of the best in the profession. He may have had the temperament of a clever politician who plays his game according to certain rules of civilized, albeit ruthless, intellect. He has preserved certain old-fashioned habits of doing things with a certain decorum excluding brutality, crudeness and ill manners. And now, this once genteel man consorts with potential murders and anonymous informers in the garb of scientists. What is even worse, he is one of them.

At this stage, Kramov grows into a symbolic figure. The unenviable figure of the scientist and man of intellect who has betrayed those of his colleagues who defend the free pursuit of truth. For the sake of worldly fleshpots and creature comforts Kramov has allied with those who want to corrupt scientific quest into an intellectual fraud which they also use for their own sordid selfish aims. The logic of his course compels him to identify more and more with Stalinism. And inasmuch as Stalinism is the negation of the free quest for truth, this once brilliant scholar is now drawn more and more into the fiendish enterprise of destroying this free quest for truth.

In another medium and on another level, Kramov is re-enacting the tragedy of Pushkin's Salieri. Winner as he seems to be, he does not escape the punishment of the traitors. The punishment of having missed the true vocation of his life that would have brought him true greatness and lasting recognition. The punishment of having ever to pretend, ever to wear a mask that obliterates his real face. Kaverin has Vlasenkova refer to this deceit in her diary in the Epilogue of the trilogy:

In the post-war years we came to a standstill confronting a strange task — to demonstrate that our medical science is developing with an extraordinary speed or, at least, faster than the science of other countries or the whole world. To us, and to no one else, belonged all the medical discoveries of the 19th century and the 20th — this was asserted in books and articles, in movies and theaters. And no one noticed that while defending an invented sham primacy we were losing the real primacy, the one obtained in agonizing work and quest.[42]

On the surface, Kramov enjoys all the prosperity and creature comforts he may have wished. But in a deeper sense, this too is illusory. Perhaps he is not subtle enough to understand it but he must vaguely feel it. Before her suicide Glafira, Kramov's wife, confides to Tat'jana that Kramov, in spite of his apparent influence, bows to the will of his Stalinist henchmen who may betray their figurehead whenever their own sense of expediency so decides. Feared and unloved by everyone including his wife, he is condemned to ever growing loneliness. And that perhaps is the worst punishment of all. Why has Kramov ultimately born so much enmity against Tat'jana Vlasenkova? Perhaps because her very person and work keep reminding him of his own betrayal of true science, of the great vocation that he has not had the wisdom and the courage to carry out.

It is Vlasenkova's destiny, within the framework of the trilogy, to open a breach in this intricate structure of vested interests which tie up in a common conspiracy all those who "feel insecure in laboratories, but, to make up for it, feel self-assured in committee meetings and in ministries,",[43] as Vlasenkova observes. In her struggle, Vlasenkova holds powerful weapons: bold creative thought and dedication to discovery. As far as these weapons can reach, she prevails over her enemies. But Tat'jana Vlasenkova's struggle turns out to be not only a matter of scientific activity. Actually, it is only remotely scientific. It is not a purely intellectual clash between different scientific attitudes, as, for example, the controversy between modern cosmologists over the different theories of the creation of the universe. As things appear in the novel, she is drawn into a conflict in which decisive scientific issues are not even settled in laboratory tests or with the help of clinical observations. And it is an altogether different venture for a laboratory-trained scientist, sophisticated but straightforward, to struggle against envy, against calumny and anonymous denunciations, against the deviousness of career-minded civil servants. It turns out to be almost above her strength to break through an elusive conspiracy of malevolence, all the more injurious because anonymous; to overcome amorphous administrative obstacles subtly erected by her powerful enemies and upheld by incompetent or timeserving bureaucrats. In this struggle to defend the integrity of science against these selfish ambitions and political expediency Tat'jana Vlasenkova's destiny takes a tragic dimension.

Vlasenkova gains a truly Pyrrhic victory. With the help of her few devoted friends she manages to set up the production of penicillin. Thus, Russian soldiers wounded at war are treated with the Russian penicillin and restored to life. She proves the therapeutic potency of her drug in spite of the obstinate efforts of her enemies to discredit it. She publicly triumphs over Kramov. She publicly exposes that which Kramov must have been hiding in the deepest of his consciousness, and hiding it even from himself. It is as if she removed his mask and let him see his own face. And it probably does not appear attractive even to him. It is probably ugly enough for him to lose respect for himself. This is probably what motivates him to take his infamous step, which, perhaps, otherwise he would not have taken. Had Tat'jana known the consequences of her savage onslaught, perhaps she would have refrained from it. However, at that point she gives in to her own *hamartia* – her persecuted scientific passion, her feeling, so much frustrated, that her intuition and her biological theory have been right all along, and now it comes out in the open. As a matter of fact, she herself is aware of giving in to her *hamartia* (as it may be felt from the brutally changing point of view: from the first-person to the third-person). However, she certainly is not aware that at that very moment she has sealed the fate of her husband. Is this not again a piece of tragic irony that she should doom her husband and herself at the moment of her highest triumph? Without foreknowledge, of course.

In the last encounter with her, after the arrest of her husband, Kramov appears at his basest. In slightly veiled words to Vlasenkova he offers to help her have her innocent husband freed and rehabilitated if she devotes her scientific authority to Kramov's service. Vlasenkova has the courage not to give up her intellectual integrity, and faces its grievous consequences. Her husband, a dedicated epidemiologist, undergoes an unspeakably iniquitous trial during which the official investigators do not even bother to read the documents proving his innocence. All the lawlessness of the Stalinist period unfolds over these closing pages of the trilogy. It is worth quoting. Tat'jana and her little son are both thinking, in the night, of their husband and father:

I came to my room, and again nocturnal restless thoughts and feelings started in their train. Always the same but still one thing too: pride for my son. And not for my own sake did I suddenly demand – I don't know myself from whom, from fate, from my lot, from good fortune — for the door to fly open and for Andrej to enter, the same as ever, with his raincoat thrown over his shoulders, with a cap on, beneath which one could see his good face with his firm homesick eyes. Or another Andrej, it's all the same — tired, downcast, grown thin — such as he used to return from his trips, when another's dullness and indifference hindered his luminous work. Let him enter, if there is in the world justice and honor and if we brought to mankind this justice and honor that our children trust and without which they cannot live. Let him enter or let me die, because I do not want to live any longer, disappointed of expectations and at a loss and trembling with fear lest baseness may win — baseness and lie.[44]

The novel, that is, its dramatic substance ends at this point of unrelieved despair. The protasis implies a negative. Andrej does not enter. There is something relentless about this movement of the trilogy toward this grievous end. One has a feeling that the whole development from Chapter 2, Part II has been written for the sake of this end. This ultimate despair casts doubts on human justice in general, and its administration in the Soviet Union of Stalin's era in particular. The shadow of fate appears in this tragic lament. Tat'jana's defiance calls to witness some higher force beyond human control.

8

The clash between the fundamental sense of justice toward the individual and the injustice of the impersonal *raison d'Etat* has always been one of the powerful motives of the tragic conflict since at least Sophocles' *Antigone*. Now, does Tat'jana Vlasenkova take part in such a tragic conflict which opposes an individual absolute sense of justice to the no less compelling *raison d'Etat*? This motive acquires its true tragic significance only when both parties have an equally valid case. It is not at all so in this novel. The problem centers on the validity of the *raison d'Etat*. Creon did have a good case to put Antigone to death. So does, for example, Racine's Titus in dismissing Berenice. So does even Bulgakov's Pontius Pilate. As it is represented in this novel, Tat'jana Vlasenkova's experience hardly dramatizes this kind of tragic motive. In this conflict, the State performs a function hardly different from that of an accomplice in the crime. And this is not the *raison d'Etat* in its tragic significance. In this specific sense, Tat'jana Vlasenkova does not participate in a tragic conflict. She is rather the victim of a vicious miscarriage of justice. The whole trilogy ends in a picture of the wholesale miscarriage of justice that engulfed Russia in the latter thirties and through the forties.

This point of view places Tat'jana Vlasenkova in a different perspective. The fact of being a victim usually implies a certain passivity. And passivity is hardly the attribute of a tragic figure. We should not, however, do her injustice. She is an extremely purposeful and hard-driving person. In her student years, she must not have read *Don Quixote* in vain, since in all her subsequent life she has pursued her scientific and other projects with a truly quixotic stubbornness, if not ineptness.[45] As a matter of fact, not unlike a tragic hero, she has caused her own ultimate suffering and misery through too much relentlessness in the pursuit of truth, albeit scientific truth. Even at a particularly despairing time for her, after her husband is arrested, she finds enough energy and drive to go the front-line hospitals in order to demonstrate the therapeutic value of her drug in the most compelling way. Likewise, her husband is a very dynamic man, articulate, first to rush into the breach. So is Kolomnin, the sardonic chemist who during the critical stage of their research remains so maniacally absorbed in his research work that they have virtually to drag him out of the laboratory by force for fear that he should never leave it. All these scientists are by no means apathetic or flabby or spineless. Neither do they seem lacking organizational skill.

And still, as a body of scientists, they somehow have allowed the control of their disciplines to slip out of their own hands. A kind of natural selection in reverse has set in: scientific quest comes to depend more and more on those who are unworthy of managing scientific affairs; hacks and incompetent careerists domineer true scientists. The author has his characters sharply criticize this deplorable situation in the Epilogue of the novel. The scene is set in the L'vovs' residence at the 1956 New Year celebration. Toward the end of this celebration, Tat'jana and her whole family, along with their closest friends engage in a sober discussion of what has gone wrong with Russian science over the past decades. Too many would-be scientists have enjoyed the status without deserving it. They are phony scientists and by their vocation and achievements do not belong to the profession. Now, there is going on a re-evaluation and a re-allocation of manpower. The phony scientists at long last will end up where they always should have belonged. New competent scientists are emerging. They claim their rightful place in the scientific community. For their sake and for the sake of the integrity of Russian science, the true scientists, that is, Tat'jana Vlasenkova and all her colleagues, should now get rid of "Kramovism," i.e., the men of "the Kramov school," their psychology and their mobsters' methods. And these men of "the Kramov school" understand that their time may be waning. And therefore these denizens of ministries and secretariats in scientific garbs feel nervous, although pretending that nothing has changed.

"[...] They are still active, these people, but they already start losing their self-confidence, they feel nervous, they remember every minute that their influence, their position have been stolen from others, hundred times worthier. They still hold on to their chairs tooth and nail, but one beautiful day they will simply melt into thin air, like a mirage, like a dream phantom,"[46]

Dmitri says about them. These people cannot help retreating when facing the spirit of truth and straightforwardness. However, nervous as they may be, they remain active and don't want to recognize their defeat. And whose fault is it? This is the crux of the problem. The fault is the true scientists' themselves, Tat'jana Vlasenkova's and others'. Dmitri acknowledges that much during the discussion:

"[...] But who, if not ourselves, are guilty of the fact that it is too crowded in scientific institutes, that people who have nothing in common with science aspire to an academic degree which doubles the salary; that we don't dare to pick real disciples without looking around for a cue, or without the approval of organizations which, in essence, have nothing to do with medicine. Isn't it, to say the least, a nonsense which hampers the development of science, whereas we are afraid of quarrelling and take this nonsense as something due and in the end we encourage stagnation which binds us ourselves hand and foot,".47

However, things are taking a turn for the better, Tat'jana Vlasenkova believes, the mobsters' way of struggle is gone, never to return. The very year 1956 may be decisive on the way toward a brighter future. This is the substance of this discussion which sums up the fate of Russian science during the previous decades and anticipates a hopeful future, i.e., a chance for the scientist to pursue his quest freely, without the chilling surveillance of security agencies or fear of arbitrary arrests and deportations. These bitter-sweet opinions appear in the Epilogue of the 1956 edition. It would have been surprising if the author himself had not shared these opinions of his characters. The reader may wonder in what respect it may be significant that the whole above-mentioned scene of discussion is altogether missing in the 1965 version of the Epilogue.

One of Tat'jana Vlasenkova's young colleagues describes the opportunistic pseudo-scientists as *lishnie ljudi*, – superfluous people, i.e., superfluous in the business of scientific quest. He obviously re-interprets an old Russian term of Russian socio-intellectual history. The term was coined by Turgenev who applied it to the ineffectual Russian liberal intelligentsia of the 1840ies nurtured on German Romantic philosophy. The term has had a remarkable fortune in Russian socio-intellectual thinking. Obviously, Russian critical thinking must have found something fundamentally, if now clearly, relevant in this term, if the term was applied to such a variety of characters as Onegin, Pechorin, Rudin, Chulkaturin.48 What serves as the common denominator to which the term reduces all this wide range of dissimilar characters is their corrosively analytical introspection and a certain ineffectuality in external action, a kind of hamletism. When the young biologist brands the champions of Kramov as "superfluous people," he obviously gives the term a derogatory meaning. In this context, the term may conceal an ironic relevance unsuspected by the young biologist. Perhaps this term "superfluous people" with its traditional implication of corrosive introspection and ineffectuality may in a certain sense also apply to this young biologist himself, to Tat'jana Vlasenkova and her colleagues and friends? It may apply to them in the sense of their inability of organizing a concerted, open and far-reaching action against the screaming injustices of the government. Did not the historical "superfluous people" of Turgenev's time also suffer from the same shortcoming? This young biologist is now himself an influential scientific figure. He complains about the oppressive conditions under which they have to conduct their scientifc work:

"And may I work at least three years without thinking that I am guilty toward someone? — Viktor [the young biologist in question. H.O.] asks plaintively. "I feel like working quietly, cheerfully, without stumbling over trifles. I am dying to do so!"

he exclaims. This lamentation is quite in the key in which the flabby intellectuals in Chekhov's plays complain about their fate. Now, if anyone at all should act and defend the Russian scientific community against intellectual oppression, he should be the one. Instead, he "skulit," that is, whimpers, as another colleague blames him: "Well, work. Instead, you are whimpering [A ty skulish']."[49] This is the congenital sound of the historical "superfluous man." We are undoubtedly overstating our case here. Tat'jana Vlasenkova and her colleagues are in no way akin to the spineless hamletic types of Turgenev. At the same time, however, it is legitimate to ask whether some tenuous and deeply buried psychological constant does not somehow connect the two.

Tragic reality postulates man striving to reach his full human stature, and more. Which means that the tragic hero acts in full freedom, that is, he takes his decision independently of what others may advise and irrespective of what prophecy may predict. Viewed from this angle, tragic experience is, to quote from W. Kerr, "an investigation of the possibilities of human *freedom*."[50]

Tragic urgency compels the tragic hero to attack the essence of the problem. The conventions of tragic representation will hardly allow him the opportunity for anything else. Therefore, his conflictual situation favors straightforward contest and lack of equivocation. It is not so much a matter of moral scruple as it is that of the most intense means toward self-fulfillment. It would be wrong indiscriminately to apply the principles of classical tragedy to evaluating the characters of modern narrative prose. However, if the former are objectively valid, they should provide some insight into the character of Tat'jana Vlasenkova from this tragic angle, even if we deal with not quite commensurable phenomena.

Tragic conflict seems naturally to tend toward a head-on clash of willpowers in which they fight out the essence of their conflict through forthright discourses. Tragic characters speak out the blunt truth. They tell each other explicitly what they really mean. Now, in the battle that Tat'jana is waging, she can ill afford straightforwardness and lack of equivocation which seem to mark the tragic hero. The nature of the conflict is determined by her enemies. And Tat'jana and her friends cannot ignore this. They cannot ignore that their fight unfolds in a kingdom of deviousness and duplicity. For example, deviousness and duplicity mark all the actions that Kramov initiates in order to undo Vlasenkova's scientific career. He deals her his blows without appearing to do so, or even under a pretense of friendly service. Tat'jana's outbursts of savagely ironical reproofs do not change the nature of this devious conflict. They do not change Kramov's underhanded line. Somehow, the contest between generous decency and disciplined treachery favors the latter, at least in the short run. What is even worse, the latter corrupts the former. At one point, when Kramov asks her whether she has calculated her strength well, she replies that she has, that she is, after all, his disciple. In the atmosphere of prevailing intellectual terror and deviousness, she cannot help also resorting to dissimulation. Her conflict with Kramov ends in this kind of false appearance. "For the first time in my life I lied with clear conscience because only thus was it possible to vanquish another lie against which there was no other weapon,"[50a] Tat'jana Vlasenkova says about this interview. It looks as if the worst enemies were the best friends, although their antagonism is greater than ever. No ultimate collision resolves their conflict. No redeeming catharsis clears the desperately oppressive atmosphere that pervades the end of the dramatic development.

Is lie the only weapon against lie? Has Vlasenkova not misjudged? Perhaps at that sensitive moment, when Kramov shows a spark of human decency in mourning his wife, Tat'jana has missed a chance. Perhaps to act with rectitude, to speak the ultimate serene truth — the weapon of the tragic hero — at that point would be of greater help for her than her dissimulation. Does not Tat'jana demean herself by stooping to Kramov's own game of duplicity? All the more so because it does not seem to help her in any way. She earns her misery without any redeeming nobility of her suffering. However, Kaverin must have felt any other behavior to be out of character within the given moral atmosphere. This deleterious atmosphere could hardly have generated the tragic serenity, the freedom of Gleb Nerzhin of *The First Circle*.

Another character of Kaverin's fiction does dare to bid the heroic defiance under no less trying conditions. The tale "Sem' par nechistyx" (The seven pairs of the impure ones, 1962) deals with a drama which unfolds aboard a small ship, "Onega" by name, while she is transporting a motley group of convicts. This drama originates from a double miscarriage of justice: a common criminal who gets away with a much smaller punishment than he deserves; an innocent man who does not deserve any punishment at all is sentenced to death. The villain of the story, Alamasov, is much worse a man than the court of justice was able to convict him to be. The court did not even succeed in discovering Alamasov's criminal purpose. Therefore, the inveterate criminal has been administered a substantially milder punishment than he deserved. As a result of this miscarriage of justice in reverse, Alamasov turns up among the convicts transported aboard the "Onega." Owing to his formidable personality, he promptly consolidates his own leading position. As the foreman of the convicts, Alamasov sets methodically about carrying out his long-cherished and long-denied purpose. With the help of other convicts he would hijack the ship and escape from the Soviet Union.

It is the underlying tragic purport of the story that another convict, a victim of a revolting miscarriage of justice, should, at the risk of his own life, stand up to Alamasov. This convict is a former sub-marine captain Verevkin. His superior appointed him unlawfully to command a ship that Verevkin was not qualified to captain. As Verevkin was leaving the harbor, a trawler took great pains maliciously to ram into the side of Verevkin's ship unable to avoid the trawler for lack of maneuvering space. The ship sank instantly and Verevkin did not even have a chance to go to the bottom with her. It turned out that the trawler's captain guilty of sinking

Verevkin's ship was drunk at the time. At the court-martial all factual evidence proved Verevkin clear of any fault. Nonetheless, the military tribunal, which judged him according to war-time laws, although there was no war at the time, sentenced him to death. It is a small consolation that the Supreme Court commuted the initial death penality to a ten-year imprisonment. The fundamental evil of justice subordinated to expediency has remained. The lawlessness of the Stalinist period has thus ruined Verevkin's life. He is an embittered man now, but adversity has not impaired his sense of integrity.

Without undue strain, the rickety "Onega" may symbolize the Russian "ship of the State" of the time. Aboard this veritable floating prison, three different species of men live elbow-to-elbow. First, the law-abiding ones. Second, the outlaws. Literally and figuratively both are in the same boat. The line that separates the law-abiding ones from the outlaws is extremely tenuous and unsteady.[51] This reflects the worst of Stalinist legality: its fluctuations depend almost exclusively on political expediency. To-day one is within the law, tomorrow he is without. Not because he has committed any crime but because it seems politically expedient to have him outlawed. This is how there appears a third category of passengers: the victims of political expediency and formal legality. The law-abiding ones reject them as legal villains, although morally the latter are no criminals at all. Verevkin is such a legally "impure" one, although he psychologically identifies with the law-abiding ones. He is thrown into the world of the outlaws with which he cannot identify, and where he does not belong because he is morally pure. For this very reason the outlaws do not acknowledge him either as one of theirs.

At the time to which the story refers — shortly before the war between Germany and the Soviet Union — the divorce between Stalinist legality and the elementary sense of morality has reached schizophrenic dimensions. Hence a profound malaise that the little antiquated "Onega" reflects as in a microcosm. Things go from bad to worse aboard this ship. A carefree elderly captain and an inexperienced conceited commanding officer form the inarticulate leadership of this floating jail. No one among the crew is aware of the catastrophe shaping up in the bowels of the ship.

Down in the hold, Verevkin does see the catastrophe coming. And herein lies the ultimate tragedy of the situation. The only one both awake to the outlaws' criminal conspiracy and ready to defend law and the law-abiding community has no means to do so because the latter has rejected Verevkin as an outlaw and has withdrawn its trust in this only man at that point that could have saved this suicide-prone law-abiding community. Thus, in his lonely limbo, Verevkin is fighting on two antipodal fronts two losing battles: he has no means to get his warning across to the law-abiding community; he has a slim chance to overpower the outlaws. Something of a jungle rule reigns in the hold of the "Onega." There is only one, brutal, way of frustrating Alamasov's criminal design: to beat him up into submission and thus to wrestle from him his leadership over the convicts. Physically, Verevkin is far outclassed by Alamasov, since his enfeebled frame is no match for Alamasov, a cold-blooded murderer and a bull of an athlete who bosses around a whole gang of submissive convicts. In engaging in a hand-to-hand fight with Alamasov, with the whole gang of convicts behind the latter, Verevkin would be courting a suicide. Still, with quiet, albeit desperate, courage, Verevkin proceeds to do his duty. At the decisive moment Verevkin assaults Alamasov. At this tragic moment of Verevkin's life, Kaverin has another, major, event coincide with this climactic point of Verevkin's personal courage. A German war-plane attacks the "Onega." In the ensuing confusion the situation radically changes. The war, long in brewing, has broken out.

It is a remarkable example of Kaverin's sense of timing. Any criticism of this coincidence as implausible and not true-to-life is irrelevant. Even in empirical reality an out-of-the-ordinary coincidence conveys the impression of something pre-arranged and not resulting from the immediate objective situation. In the fictional reality of literary representation the validity of a coincidence is not a matter of plausibility because the coincidence is by definition invented. In fictional representation the validity of a coincidental event depends on the degree of the psychological power with which the dramatic event attracts another, coincidental, event. It depends on the degree of the compelling force with which the dramatic event demands the coincidence. It depends on whether the character has enough dramatic potency to generate it. Perhaps another way of putting it would be that this validity depends on whether the character has done his or her tragic utmost to deserve this coincidence. The example of Tat'jana Vlasenkova may corroborate this assumption. At the end of the dramatic development, in her despair she asks of fate for Andrej, her husband arrested by the authorities, to come home, to enter at that very moment. He does not. He does not perhaps, because Tat'jana has not done her tragic utmost, especially in her last interview with Kramov. If she had, perhaps the coincidence – Andrej walking in – would have occurred. Compared with her, Verevkin does do his tragic utmost. Stalinist legality cripples his life, innocent as he is, and favors a common criminal. Verevkin still finds enough integrity and courage to stand up and uphold the law of morality and common decency. He anticipates that the criminal will kill him in this fight. And yet, he struggles on to the bitter end, with all conceivable odds against him. Fate has favored the brave, but it is a costly favor.

It takes a national catastrophe to bring Verevkin victorious out of his desperate venture. The latter generates the convicts' change of mood and expectations in conjunction with this national catastrophe. At this point, all the passengers of the "Onega" break down into two clear-cut categories. First, the morally pure ones, those for whom the fate of the native land is more important than anything else, and who act accordingly. Second, the morally impure ones, that is, those who set the fate of their homeland at naught, and even intend to exploit its disaster for their own selfish purposes. It turns out that aboard the "Onega" such are few. Only the most inveterate criminals make up this group. At this moment of a great national emergency the worst of the formal legality, i.e., Stalinist legality, loses its schizophrenic hold over both the law-abiding ones and the outlaws. Legality is catching up with morality and common human decency which Verevkin has defended at the risk of his own life. As true justice comes into its own, the stigmas of the previous schizophrenic legality tend to fade. This is why it becomes so easy for the commanding officer of the "Onega" to befriend the convict Verevkin. The latter incurred the stigma of a convict only through the effect of schizophrenically unjust legality. Once true justice is restored, Verevkin becomes again what he has always been: a dedicated navy officer well trained in his specialty. In his case, the line dividing the alleged outlaw from the law-abiding has been itself unlawful. And so it turns out to be for many other convicts. They have experienced a fate similar to Verevkin's. Stalinist legality has condemned them arbitrarily or out of political expediency. Once the unjust stigma vanishes, they regain their ordinary state, that of reasonably honest citizens.

The very title of the tale ironically points to this arbitrarily imposed change of state. The "impure ones," i.e., "impure" in terms of Stalinist legality, turn out to be honest people. At the time of crisis, when the established authority comes nearly to shambles, they forget their grudge, reject the tempting way of a mutiny, and, although formally convicts, they choose the way of responsible Soviet people defending their homeland. Only with their help does the ship complete her war mission. Undoubtedly, Kaverin has taken this phrase from Mayakovsky's *Misterija-Buf*. In this political satire the poet uses the phrases "seven pairs of the pure ones" and "seven pairs of the impure ones" with a double irony: the "pure ones" are in reality impure, and the "impure ones" are pure. Is there any implication of this nature in this tale of Kaverin? Perhaps. What is one to think of Verevkin's best friend, who was one of the members of the military tribunal, and who voted for Verevkin's death penalty, although he knew him to be innocent? The best friend did so for fear of jeopardizing his own career and in deference to the mood prevailing in influential quarters. The best friend, the influential quarters, these all are the "pure ones." They hardly are so if we judge from the actual subject matter of this tale. Of course, we have to keep in mind the unsteadiness of the line dividing the "pure ones" from the "impure ones."

Apart from confirmed criminals such as Alamasov, other rank-and-file convicts feel the war to be a new lease on life. They may redeem themselves through exemplary conduct during this national emergency and earn commutation or pardon. This is why Alamasov has lost his authority so fast. Almost no one among the convicts needs him any longer. Now, they look up to Verevkin and take their cue from him. As for the innocent victims of miscarriage of justice, they may hope for prompter rehabilitation. This is what happens to quite a few of them. Among others, Verevkin is rehabilitated, restored in his former rank of a sub-marine captain, and returned to active duty.

Within the framework of this tale, the war is represented as having a cleansing effect on the injustices of Stalinist legality. The great national emergency tends to restore true morality and universal human decency. It even exalts these virtues. The "Onega," the ship where the drama unfolds, may symbolize all of Russia. The drama occurring on board may reflect similar drama affecting all of the country. However, the story still deals with a concrete ship and concrete people. As such, the "Onega" and her passengers represent an infinitely small fraction of Russia during the time of the war. The drama of the miscarriage of justice and its redress is being played on a limited scale and while war conditions prevail. Now, what will happen everywhere else, and subsequently?

Double Portrait (1966) describes the fate of a Russian ichtyologist Ostrogradskij. We may assume that in the person of Ostrogradskij Kaverin draws a composite portrait of the Russian scientist at his best and the latter's encounter with Stalinist obscurantism. The novel actually deals with the last months of Ostrogradskij's life. He returns from the concentration camp in winter 1954. He is actually released before he serves his full term because his health had been undermined by subhuman conditions of life in the camp. His release coincides with the time when the Soviet Government is carrying out the legal rehabilitation of the innocent victims of the stalinist purges. Ostrogradskij happens to be one of them.

Trading on the political course of lawlessness and obscurantism initiated by Stalin, Ostrogradskij's foes, dishonest mediocrities, worked relentlessly toward their own heyday at the cost of his downfall. Their leader Snegirev had a deadly enmity toward Ostrogradskij ever since the latter gave a poor rating to the former's doctoral dissertation and demonstrated Snegirev's scientific ineptitude. Ever since, Snegirev had been nursing his revenge. Because of Ostrogradskij's absolute intellectual superiority, Snegirev was not in a position to humiliate him through scientific confrontation. He could have challenged Ostrogradskij only by having experimental data falsified. He did so but to his own discomfiture. The fraud drove one of his students to suicide. Still, Snegirev had been biding his time. It came, when in 1948 a new political terror and intellectual obscurantism engulfed the Soviet scientific community, especially men in biological sciences. That was the "moment of falsehood" for Snegirev and his confederates. It became at that point possible for them to turn scholarly polemic into a campaign of political vilification against Ostrogradskij. Through fraudulent experiments conducted in secrecy Snegirev falsely proved that Ostrogradskij's scientific activity had all been a disguised sabotage. Thus, on fantastically trumped-up charges an innocent and dedicated scientist was arrested and condemned to concentration camp, and his valuable scientific achievements discredited. Ostrogradskij fell a victim, among the first, to the Stalinist obscurantism of the late forties. Under the protection of their political patrons of the day, Snegrirev and his clique seized positions of administrative power in their scientific discipline. They defended their fleshpots with their own attempts at scientific activity, naturally meager because of their creative ineptness.

Released from the camp, destitute, Ostrogradskij returned, still illegally, to Moscow early in 1954 and started painfully readjusting to civilian life. His wife and little daughter had died during his imprisonment. For six months Ostrogradskij was knocking about Moscow in a humiliating search for shelter and subsistence. However, these months were also the bright months of hopes for actual rehabilitation, when he met his old dedicated friends and new ones, when he saw himself resuming his scientific work and even finding the devotion of a loving woman. What is more, during these months true scientists seemed at last to come into their own, whereas the rule of pseudo-scientists seemed to start crumbling. With the help of the former, Ostrogradskij was stepping into a new stage in his life: that of complete rehabilitation, effective reinstatement to his rightful scientist's status, and a new upsurge of creative activity supported by a loving woman. However, the weight of the past evil crippled the redress. At this happy turn, Ostrogradskij died suddenly, if not unexpectedly, of the heart disease contracted in the concentration camp.

All three works — *Open Book*, "The Seven Pairs of the Impure Ones," and *Double Portrait* — dramatize the miscarriage of justice that Stalinist legality inflicted on Soviet people, and the victims happen to be the best of them. Viewed from our vantage, *Double Portrait* logically and symbolically terminates the story told in *Open Book*. To be sure, *Open Book* has an Epilogue appended, in which the author succinctly refers to the events subsequent to Stalin's demise. Kaverin must have written this Epilogue with a topical purpose because the events narrated in the Epilogue come to an end on the first day of the year 1956, the very same year when the book appeared in print. This Epilogue may reflect the euphoria that Soviet liberal intelligentsia seems to have experienced for a few years after the death of Stalin. The year 1956 was perhaps in this respect the most significant. In this Epilogue, the author sketches a hopeful picture. Vlasenkova's husband returns from the concentration camp, and, fully rehabilitated, succeeds in re-entering the mainstream of contemporary life. This return should symbolize the redress of past injustices. Moreover, it opens a gate to a better future, which for Vlasenkova and her friends always means unhampered intellectual life and freedom from political terrorism. Now, from our vantage, this Epilogue is more of a polemical attitude, albeit vital. It does not quite belong to the tragic substance of the novel. *Double Portrait* appeared in 1966, then followed by a slightly revised (and more interesting) edition of 1967. It is my thesis that *Double Portrait* offers the philosophical ending of *Open Book* which the topical Epilogue of the latter displaced in 1956.

In epic poetry, there is a recurrent motive of the return of the hero. The foremost example may be the return of Odysseus. The epic poet has the hero return because without his return, justice in Ithaca would never have been restored. The hero punishes the villains and rewards the virtuous. The return of the hero in Kaverin's narrative symbolizes a similar process. The return of the hero as referred to in the Epilogue of *Open Book* symbolizes such a restoration of justice. The meaning of this Epilogue significantly disagrees with that of the dramatic substance of the novel. It may be the perspective of the year 1956. In his 1966 work, that is *Double Portrait*, the perspective significantly differs from that of the 1956 Epilogue. The 1966 perspective fits better the perspective of the dramatic development of *Open Book*, i.e., *Open Book* without its Epilogue. In *Double Portrait* the hero returns, to be sure, but he does not survive too long the crippling effects of his life in the concentration camp. He dies before being rehabilitated and re-instated in his former scientific status, before having a chance to translate into reality his brilliant scientific theories. Should it mean that as of the year 1966 the author came to reconsider his hopeful anticipations of 1956? That the nation-wide miscarriage of justice was not removed, and justice, fundamentally, not restored? That intellectual freedom ended quite short of what Tat'jana Vlasenkova and her friends had hoped for?

At this point we can discern another tragic overtone in Kaverin's work. The best people have displayed so much dedication, quiet courage, accepted so much self-sacrifice, lived through so much suffering and paranoiac persecution, carried on so much work toward humanizing this injustice. And the result is disappointing. It is true that a dent has been made in the commanding position of the politically appointed hacks. One of these opportunistic appointees Kuljabko is dismissed (*Double Portrait*). However, as Snegirev, his partner, says "[. . .] in the place of Kuljabko there will be another Kuljabko!"[52] Snegirev, Krupenin and other mediocrities have all criminally conspired against Ostrogradskij in order to oust him out of his scientific position and to take it over for their own benefit. And now that Ostrogradskij is being rehabilitated, and the villainy of Snegirev *et al* made clear, should the latter not be meted out the just punishment for their evil doings? Far from that. In spite of minor annoyances, these villains all remain retrenched in their influential functions, reluctantly willing to patronize their former victim whose boots they are not fit to polish. "At Vorkuta or at Magadan [locations of the Siberian concentration camps. H.O.] – or wherever he was – they must have taught him something,"[53] Snegirev comments about Ostrogradskij, and his thoughts about this great scientist now being rehabilitated do not go too much beyond this comment. In his own reflection, the author states that Ostrogradskij's fate is a "common story" (obyknovennaja istorija), and because of this commonness it is hard to convey the whole monstrosity of this commonness (vsju chudovishchnost' ètoj obyknovennosti). Unfortunately, scientists themselves, beginning with Ostrogradskij himself, take these monstrosities somewhat fatalistically, as if they were some unavoidable flaws of existence. True scientists' voices are still weak and timid in asserting their rights and their creative independence.

Kaverin chooses to depict the fate of the scientist at a particular point of Soviet history. He represents the scientist as an idealistic researcher absorbed in the task of unlocking the mysteries of nature. Kaverin's scientist puts a certain poetic sense into the objects of his intellectual pursuit. Least of all does he aspire to personal enrichment or promotion. Not that he despises the betterment of his station and circumstances. He somehow happens not to worry about it. I believe that this attractive representation of the scientist is artistically valid in Kaverin's works. Kaverin's scientist is somewhat like a poet.[54] He is something of a dreamer. A substantial part of his life goes on in the world of abstract data and concepts. He is one of those to whom the young scientist of "A Piece of Glass" applies Khlebnikov's term "izobretateli" (inventors).

To this true type of scientist is opposed the one that the same young scientist, still using Khlebnikov's term, calls "priobretateli" (the acquisitive ones). This is the scientist that betrays his original vocation; the pseudo-scientist who cannot hope for too much headway in the profession; the pseudo-scientist who has nothing to do with science. Now, this second type of "scientist" certainly cannot hold a candle to the true type of scientist when it comes to investigating and explaining the phenomena of nature, conducting and interpreting laboratory experiments, intuitively grasping the relations between apparently alien phenomena. However, and, as it were, to make up for this incompetence, he learns the art of using social influences, of defeating an adversary through timely conspiracies. He becomes an expert in manipulating the levers of the power struggle between individuals and groups. Now, this is the kind of skill that the true scientist with his contemplative temperament usually cannot match. As such, this activity has nothing to do with scientific research and discovery. But it gives the hack scientist an unexpected edge over the true scientist. This rather dubious art enables its expert administratively to control the scientific activity of the true scientist, that is, to control the true scientist himself. Now, the reverse is not true. This need not mean, of course, that every mediocre scientist or pseudo-scientist unavoidably becomes such an expert of underhanded power struggle. It is a matter of his moral awareness. This perverse dialectic is neutralized in a normal atmosphere, that is, in an atmosphere of open public information, unconstrained press and unhindered scientific discussion.

However, it all changes in the atmosphere of Stalinist thought-control, paranoiac distrust and fear, and secrecy. The gate is wide-open to conspiracies, anonymous denunciations, and the hushing-up of the true information under the pretense of secrecy allegedly necessary for State security. It was this paranoiac secrecy that was the main cause of intellectual stagnation during the post-war years, Kaverin complains in the Epilogue of *Open Book*: "[...] none of us had the right to share our discoveries even with the laboratory of our neighbor."[55] This is when the unscrupulous hacks have the best chance to assert their role:

Oh, this sham secret, this twilight in which we hardly discerned one another. Even still now – I am writing this in the year 1956 – have we not gotten rid of the ignorant nonsense, the mysterious rubbish around which barbed-wire fences were erected and which after a working day were kept in sealed safes! How many crafty people, who had nothing to do with science, received high titles under the cover of this artificial secret, without which for some reason it was impossible either to work or to live.[56]

And the tragedy of the true scientist living and working in this atmosphere is that because of his temperament and fundamental decency he turns out to be practically defenseless against this rule. Now, in this case, the miscarriage of justice is not the tragic injustice of the *raison d'Etat*. In the case of Kaverin's scientist, the motivation is nothing short of criminal or it originates from a criminally paranoiac source. The powers that be are neither just or right, whereas the scientist is. However, he still lives through a tragic experience, albeit not like Antigone's.

As the scientist appears in Part III of *Open Book* and *Double Portrait*, he is trapped in a tragic dilemma. He may give in to the dominant order of things, join the establishment, partake of the fleshpots along with the hack scientists, in a word, submit to Stalinist thought-control. And the latter must have sunk deep, and overwhelmed the best and the strongest minds. Kaverin may be acknowledging this overwhelming effect in an unmistakably authorial comment at the end of *Double Portrait*. The author has just read a book written by a young biologist about Stalinist obscurantism in science, and he states in this connection:

Reading Lepestkov [the name of the young biologist in question. H.O.], I kept thinking of the fact that all things are correlated, all things are irremovably connected.

I too was deceived, and guilty without guilt,[57] and obstinately kept working, stumbling at every step, and entangling myself in contradictions, trying to prove to myself that lie was truth. I too felt miserable, trying to forget oppressive dreams in which I had to reconcile myself to senselessness, had to use guile, and to dissemble.

But this is already quite another book which I will some day write.[58]

At the end of this road, the scientist destroys his integrity of the scientist, that is, he destroys himself as a scientist. And if so, what is left of him? That is the way that a Snegirev, a Krupenin, the unscrupulous hacks, have chosen. And they get on in their small world. Or, the scientist may value his integrity as a scientist above everything else. That sets him at odds with the powers that be, the snegirevs and others. And they will most likely destroy him, rob him of his scientific achievements and fraudulently claim the credit for them. As it appears in Kaverin's novels, the scientist does not even have the ultimate relief to tell his persecutor the truth, that he, the persecutor is wrong and why, and that he, the scientist, is right and why. The scientist's situation is that of the tragic hero who faces grief and destruction whichever way he turns.

9

As it is discussed in this chapter, the "tragic experience" in Kaverin's works results from the particular combinations of the concept of the "tragic guilt" and that of the "moral fault." Within the context of this discussion, tragic guilt means the hero's determination to translate into reality his ideals of right and justice in contempt or in defiance, if need be, of any actual human reality. The conflict of the tragic guilt involves an antagonism between different views of right and justice. In such a conflict none of the adversaries is the "villain." Each of them is right in his own way in the judgment of an independent observer. The adversaries fight against one another in the name of what they believe to be an unselfish ideal. *Artist Unknown* still remains the most valid representation of this kind of tragic conflict. Both heroes of this novel suffer because of their tragic guilt. Their tragic guilt relates to their understanding of socialism and their approach toward socialist construction. Certain other works of Kaverin, namely, *Skandalist*, *Fulfillment of Desires* and *Two Captains*, offer a weakened version of this fundamental tragic guilt.

In his later works, namely those which deal with Stalinism in retrospect, the concept of moral fault supersedes that of tragic guilt. The hero becomes the object of a moral fault external to him, that is, he becomes the victim of the immoral legality of Stalinism. The final version of *Open Book*, *Double Portrait*, and "The Seven Pairs of the Impure Ones" are such. What creates the tragic overtone in these works is the perversity and the immutability of the relation between the immoral legality of Stalinism and the integrity of the victim: the former destroys the latter against all sense of justice, decency and honor.

In his last novel *In Front of the Mirror* Kaverin tries to deal with the basic situation of *Artist Unknown* by solving its tragic contradictions. Karnovskij, the Shpektorov of *In Front of the Mirror*, overcomes his tragic guilt of the exclusive dedication to the mechanical world picture[59] by opening his soul to the organic world picture. Elizaveta Turaeva, the artist, succeeds. Instead of being destroyed by her art as Arximedov was by his, she grows along with her art. Here the tragic dimension consists in the fact that it is impossible for both Turaeva and Karnovskij, through no fault of theirs, to achieve their common fulfillment on their native soil.

From as far back as *Two Captains*, the idea of justice or of the redress of injustices has inspired the works of Kaverin. In his later works this inspiration, because of the reality represented, has shaped the author's aesthetic perception into a tragically colored vision of life.

CONCLUSION

In this limited study of Kaverin's works I have tried to show some of the features of his prose that reveal the originality of his narrative art.

Kaverin may have been right in lending only a slight retrospective attention to his first story "The Eleventh Axiom" and in dismissing his early experimental fantastic tales. However, they may have been the early indication, if not the cause, of Kaverin's treatment of time and space in his narrative.

Lobachevsky's revolutionary concepts of space inspired Kaverin to produce his very first piece of creative writing. And this fact in itself was pregnant. "The Eleventh Axiom," judging from Kaverin's words, challenged the conventional notions of time and space. So did his early fantastic tales. There was nothing particularly inventive about this challenge. However, the youthful author's approach toward representation and his treatment of narrative material acquired a special significance within a certain historical context.

Immature and imitative as these juvenilia may have been (this does not weaken the argument), they challenged certain traditional characteristics of Russian prose fiction. Russian prose fiction is deeply rooted in "chronologism." It seems to lack a certain objective flexibility. These features undoubtedly contributed to the earnestness of the Russian classical prose, namely, that of the 19th century.

It has turned out, however, that later in our own century Russian literature — just as any other major literature — has come to face a world transformed by modern theories of space and time, and by modern psychoanalytic concepts. These innovative intellectual attitudes toward the world and humankind have further unshackled the categories of mind. They have expanded the freedom of mind and made any intellectual dogmatism more difficult. Literature could not have avoided the impact of these new forms of awareness. And it seems that Soviet literature has come to face this modern world with somewhat antiquated means of artistic representation because it has not assimilated the dynamic ethos of the modern man's awareness.

My assumption is that the ultimate purpose of Kaverin's early experimentation was to challenge the "chronologism" of the traditional Russian prose and its lack of objective flexibility, that is, to bring the spirit of Lobachevsky from the domain of abstract thought to that of artistic perception in literature and that of the very texture of literature. All in all, this attempt failed. One is tempted to theorize that this early unfulfillment of aspiration has reverberated throughout his subsequent works, and has done so for similar reasons.

Russian prose usually dramatizes the development of individual mind and character. Conflicts and interactions serve rather the purpose of individual characterization. This assumption seems especially relevant when the apparent strength of the character conflicts with the relative insignificance of the action. No one will deny Pechorin a kind of overpowering personality. If "character" were to serve "action," the latter should, so to speak, burst at the seams with dynamism. It hardly does. Whatever actions there appear in *A Hero of Our Time*, they are mostly pseudo-dramatic by-products of Pechorin's lyrical protest. Only in "The Fatalist" does the action rise to the level of genuine dramatic confrontation. The very fact that *A Hero of Our Time* breaks up into loosely connected travelogue accounts, diary items and confession stories demonstrates that the "unity of character" prevails over the "unity of action," which is to say that the purpose of characterization dominates the purpose of building a well-articulated plot sweeping the characters to a single dramatic end.

Any kind of representation of action pre-supposes the presence of a challenge and a more or less active response to it. In Russian narrative prose, plot mostly takes the form of a response to a challenge in terms of personal self-fulfillment. For example, the plots of Tolstoy's works are of this nature. The challenge that Pierre tries to meet is to find the moral truth. This is his most deeply rooted characteristic. Whatever incident he lives through either brings him nearer to or away from the moral truth Pierre is seeking. The purpose of each incident is to characterize Pierre. The duel, for example, characterizes Pierre in one way, and Doloxov in another. But it does not matter so much by itself. Its significance differs vitally from the duel of Pushkin's story. In the latter, it of course also characterizes both Silvio and the count. However, what probably matters even more is the *event* of the duel as such: its initial frivolity, its gradual approach and its ultimate catastrophic advent. In Pushkin's story the movement of the plot or the "unity of action" overshadows the "unity of character." Pushkin represents man organizing his energy an intelligence and converting them into purposeful incidents as if contingencies of history did not, or should not, exist. In the matter of plot, Pushkin's prose is somewhat "un-Russian" in its dynamism. Tolstoy may be parodying this concept of plot in *War and Peace*. The biggest game of them all is going on with drums beating. And what are the two antagonists doing? One is not doing anything, except, perhaps, sleeping at crucial councils of war, or chewing roast chickens at decisive battles, or writing letters to Madame de Staël and reading French novels at the tragic hours of the war. The other, grotesquely misshapen by the author, boils with illusory activity, beguiling the time with megalomaniac fallacies, with no hold over actual events. And still, the plot worked itself out, antagonists or no antagonists.

These minimal fragments of parody may be pointing out that it is just beyond the possibilities of representation to force the infinite complexity of empirical reality into a fictional construct which through the artifice of the plot tries to duplicate the endless intricacies of the former. For this reason, perhaps, in Russian narrative prose, conflicts emerge more or less at random as the characters' biographies advance in time. The protagonist bends his energies toward settling the conflict that the hazard of his biography brings about at the given moment. Once settled, the conflict of the moment need not necessarily generate any related subsequent conflicts. From this it ensues that the hero does not necessarily confront the same foe, or the same set of foes throughout his narrated biography. Actually, he need not confront any foe whatsoever, since the novel need not have one. Unity of character seems to prevail over unity of action.

It would be a mistake to reduce the whole complexity of Russian narrative prose to the description I have just attempted. However, it would be hard to deny that a significant part of Russian narrative prose answers this description. The latter matters for my present discussion because it helps me bring out Kaverin's own contribution to Russian prose.

In his autobiography Kaverin complains[1] that Soviet critics never ceased taking him to task for being a writer of pattern-plot prose (sjuzhetnyj pisatel'). Kaverin says that he has never understood the reason for this stricture. One of the reasons for it may lie in the fact that an involved plot and out-of-the-ordinary setting may appear frivolous in the mind of the Russian critic. He may believe — after Belinsky — that such a plot does not "reflect" life and therefore it contains some kind of falsehood. Such a plot is nothing but flimsy play. It is not "serious." In the judgment of a Soviet critic it may in addition promote what he beliveves to be the undesirable influence of the Western fiction of adventure, especially the Anglo-Saxon fiction. This influence would be judged undesirable because it is escapist. Was Alexander Grin not ostracized for this very reason?

Perhaps we might venture the assumption that the Russian awareness of literary representation has to a degree inherited what seems to be the Russian medieval view of literature. It is a religiously colored view that there is something suspicious about the make-believe of fiction. The Russian medieval literature avoided dealing with fictional characters and fictional situations. Only historical characters and historical situations enjoyed the privilege of being recorded. Even fantastic and supernatural events were treated in the belief that they had actually happened.[2] The medieval mind must have thought that to represent what did not actually happen was to indulge in falsehood and lie, and to practice deception. And lie and deception emanate from the Evil One, and therefore vitiate the occupation that gives rise to this lie and deception — the "craft of fiction."[3] It seems to me that even the very notion of fiction as a literary concept is somewhat alien to Russian terminology and that it carries some derogatory overtones.

To this literary awareness the pattern-plot — with its intricate development, incredible reversals, exotic setting, and a certain escapist irrelevance — may seem to be straying away from "serious" narrative prose. The latter "reflects" life through its commitment to "chronologism," sense of history (even if deliberately distorted), and a certain solidity of setting. In this regard, Kaverin's prose has more than once dissatisfied the Soviet critic.

Kaverin has earned his reputation of a writer of pattern-plot prose since his very early works. In the literary polemics of the time pattern-plot prose was opposed to *bytopisanie*. The latter stands for a more or less impressionistic description of everyday life and mores. In a sense, *bytopisanie* is synonymous with chronicle under the aspect of ordinariness and peculiarities of speech. Lev Lunc well-nigh identified the genre of *bytopisanie* with the sloth of Russian life.[4] He looked to pattern-plot prose for the renewal of Russian prose.

Kaverin has not been labelled as a writer of pattern-plot prose without a reason. Pattern-plot becomes the object of Kaverin's creative writing. This means that in his representation Kaverin emphasizes conflictual situations. Adversaries, locked in conflict, ply their intelligence and willpower to defeat one another's purposes or at least to prove their respective points. Thus Kaverin puts the traditional characteristics of Russian narrative prose in a very dynamic narrative structure. The traditional Russian narrative prose likes to represent comprehensive human destinies. So does Kaverin's prose. The comprehensive human destinies or their significant fragments that Kaverin represents unfold in terms of conflicts, contests, or endeavors to achieve identifiable aims. For this reason, changes of situations, i.e., reversals or peripeteias, play a significant part in the dynamic structure. These reversals always throw the action in a new, and perhaps, unexpected direction.

The proper timing underlies these reversals of plot. Kaverin has achieved the true mastery of timing during the years of his creative writing. In his earlier works, such as *The End of the Gang* or *The Nine Tenths of Fate* timing has no inner necessity. In these works simplistic coincidences prop up the plot rather obtrusively. However, in his later, mature works, timing, i.e., reversals, acquire a compelling inner necessity. Tat'jana Vlasenkova returns from her gratifying emotional tryst with Volodja Lukashevich, her boyhood friend and suitor, only to learn about the arrest of her husband. In *Chernovik cheloveka* (The rough draft of man, 1931) Kaverin recounts the destinies of two young men. Kuusinen intends to become a medical doctor. Rovinskij is obliged to embark on a military career because he is expelled from secondary school. However, the Revolution reverses their plans. Rovinskij is the one who becomes a medical doctor and scientist, whereas Kuusinen embraces a military career. But their fates still seem to remain "rough drafts." At the 1934 International Congress of the Physiologists Tat'jana Vlasenkova hears the forward-looking speech of Pavlov in which he delivers the challenging phrase "We are the seekers of truth."[5] In a decade Tat'jana lives to see the tragic reversal of these proud words. I have already discussed the timing in Kaverin's tale "The Seven Pairs of the Impure Ones."

In all these cases the moment of triumph suddenly turns into a disaster, or conversely. The reversal is something more than a mechanistic trick spectacularly to move the plot on. It is rather the result of the deep insight into the fate of the character. The character encounters his or her fate in the most unmitigated form. For this reason, these reversals have a tragic significance, not unlike the encounter with Nemesis in Pushkin's works. The encounter is necessary and well beyond the control of individual person.

More than once does Kaverin in his works revert to the motive of "chuvstvo vozvrashchenija vremeni" (sense of the return of time).[6] These recurrent references to the "sense of the return of time" may be indicative of the author's special kind of awareness of time. It is then tempting to assume that this special awareness of time harks back to Kaverin's interest in Lobachevsky's revolutionary concepts of space, and, by extension, in time, as Kaverin says in his comment about his first tale "The Eleventh Axiom." Kaverin's sense of timing then may originate from this dynamic "manipulative" sense of time. It would be different from the kind of neutral, "non-manipulative" sense of time which prevails in the most part of Russian narrative prose.

In an article on scientists and scientific research as material for imaginative writing,[7] Kaverin suggests that books should be written about the "biographies" of ideas, i.e., history of discoveries. Now, what Kaverin himself does in some of his works is not quite this, but still something that comes close to it. For example, in *Open Book*, at one point of the plot a kind of controversy centers on whether a certain fungus has enough pharmaceutic promise to be studied and developed in the laboratory. At a subsequent point another controversy arises about whether the Soviet Government should rush the development of the native Russian penicillin or purchase the British one. Each consecutive controversy generates its own dramatic tension. The latter is brought about by the conflict that opposes the advocates of the antagonistic terms of the controversy, namely, Tat'jana Vlasenkova and Kramov. Thus, the adversaries locked in conflict with one another actualize the antagonistic potentialities of the controversy. It is the fate of the scientist to actualize such controversies arising apropos of certain issues.

Viewed in these terms, Kaverin's narrative is a discourse on an underlying controversy concerning a process, or an event, or an issue. This is one of the reasons why Kaverin predominantly resorts to the binary plot. The binary plot brings out with the greatest incisiveness the issue or process that generates the controversy. The "anti-narrator" of *Artist Unknown* pictures an ultimate confrontation between Arximedov and Shpektorov as a philosophical dialogue in which two minds are engaged. And this may well be the underlying drift of Kaverin's prose. That is, a discourse on intellectual and philosophical issues whose binary plot results in a philosophical dialogue. For example, the very form of Kaverin's last novel *In Front of the Mirror* emphasizes this sense of dialogue. The novel is cast in the form of an exchange of letters between the main characters. They live very intensely. However, their passionate lives and even their abandons become refined and matured through their representation. The epistolary form gives a kind of mental concentration to the dialogue. Thanks to it, the two characters may choose to convey only their most important thoughts, disregarding the kind of details of setting that an objective third-person narrative has to dwell on for the sake of plausibility. So, this rather old-fashioned narrative form gives to the novel the dimension of a philosophical dialogue.

The binary principle pervades the whole work of Kaverin. It dominates its dramatic structure. The philosophical message of Kaverin's works also assumes a dialectical form. Perhaps, a thesis could be defended that Kaverin's narrative prose in a certain sense relates, first, to the Homeric tradition of the tragic, and, second, to the Platonic tradition of the philosophical dialogue. In the first case, the binary principle I have been discussing corresponds to the sense of an exhilirating but ruthless duel unfolding in the atmosphere of impending catastrophe, which may well be the touchstone of the tragic in Homer as well as the source of the tragedy.[8] In the second case, the binary principle develops the philosophical dialogue about justice, truth and beauty. It makes one think of Plato, the originator of this genre.

2

The dialogue between Shpektorov and Arximedov of *Artist Unknown* represents one of the tragic pages of this message. I have already mentioned that Shpektorov and Arximedov stand in a tragic conflict with each other. The source of this tragic conflict lies in the fact that their priorities as to the building of socialism are in an irreconcilable opposition to each other. Shpektorov sets the building of the material foundations of socialism before everything else. Everything else must totally serve Shpektorov's primary purpose. Art also must remain totally subservient to this primary purpose. This is what Shpektorov must mean when, according to Zhaba's report, he admonishes Arximedov to learn how to paint in order to be able to color the banners of socialism if Arximedov is called upon to do so.

Arximedov starts from the exactly opposite premises. He represents the modernistic trend in art that asserts its existence in Russia during the first decades of this century. In the thinking of these modernistic artist (Tatlin, Evreinov, Khlebnikov)[9] art, instead of "reflecting" life, should assert its supremacy over life; it should dominate life and transform it in its own image. This is undoubtedly the source from which Arximedov draws his philosophy of art and life. At the beginning of the story, while engaged in a discussion with Shpektorov, he notices a socialist emblem hanging on the gate of an apartment house. And this emblem in Arximedov's eyes indicates the plight of socialism in Russia. He draws Shpektorov's attention to this emblem and observes that it is inexpertly made and is in poor taste. This observation describes Arximedov as incisively as Shpektorov betrays his own character in his above-mentioned admonishment to Arximedov. Arximedov approaches reality in aesthetic terms. His program of social regeneration is essentially the expansion of his artist's ethics. Just as his painting absorbs all his solicitous attention, his creative drive and all his craftsmanship in the same way, Arximedov preaches, man should devote all his solicitous attention, his creative drive and all his craftsmanship to human relations. Interpersonal relations become in themselves a form of art, and should be cultivated as such. It involves man's whole personality, especially in terms of its "solicitous attention" toward and "trust" in another personality. This form of art will overcome the cultural lag that Arximedov believes to adversely affect Russian society. Curiously enough, Arximedov does not quite practice what he himself preaches. His ideological opponent Shpektorov in fact, if not in theory, demonstrates more responsiveness to others, namely, to the woman that has caused their human conflict.

This dialectic of ends and means polarizes what they stand for: Shpektorov's pressing drive for building the technological manpower and Arximedov's aspiration for humaneness and civilization. And because of this very polarization, their attitudes foredoom them to grief and destruction. The most significant words in this regard come from Arximedov. In his debates with Shpektorov he observes that "A box with tools — this is too little to start a new era,"[10] and expresses his fear in these words: "I am thinking of morality lagging behind the technics,".[11]

These words may contain in gist the kind of problems Kaverin deals with in his subsequent works. The first proposition states that the "box of tools," that is, from our vantage, indiscriminate technology and the ultimate "megamachine," do "underdimension" man's personality and give a detrimental one-sided twist to a whole civilization; they stamp out some essential dimensions of life. The second proposition may anticipate the advent of a moral being very much "under-dimensioned," that is, with no ethical inhibitions left, and equipped with the most advanced technological means of control and coercion. Pil'njak entitled one of his works *Mashiny i volki* (Machines and wolves). Now, viewing in perspective such works as *The Rough Draft of Man*, *Two Captains*, *The Open Book*, "A Piece of Glass," "The Seven Pairs of the Impure Ones," *Double Portrait*, a careful reader may perceive a slight outline, speaking figuratively, of "wolves" wielding "machines" for their purposes. It is also possible to assume that the early innocuous goblins and monsters re-emerge in Kaverin's mature works infinitely less innocuous, in the shape of timeserving officials or conspiring scientists. However, even so, the author keeps them in the background.

In *Artist Unknown* the quixotic artist is waging a losing battle for the precedence of cultural and humane values over exclusive commitment to technological growth. It had not received substantial artistic treatment in Stalin's lifetime. Censorship must have resisted the frank and extensive treatment of the dialectic between the growth of technology and cultural lag. Moreover, it is perfectly conceivable that, not unlike during the preceding centuries in the Western world, technological progress fully embodied *the* progress in Russia under Stalin's rule. So that in Kaverin's major works of the thirties and the forties this motive survived only in a fragmentary form. During this period the author focuses his creative attention on scientific research.

Kaverin represents man in relation to science. He seems to be attracted primarily toward the aesthetic side of this relation. Scientific research and discovery at its best strikes us by its ingenious elegance, its neatness of design and smoothness of execution, by its incredibly complex processes synthesized into ultimate simplicity. A bold scientific hypothesis transfigures incomprehensible contingency into intelligible and intelligent harmony. Once the scientist succeeds in explaining certain phenomena, we marvel at the bewildering wealth of links, hitherto unsuspected, between them, and a kind of mathematical beauty of these links. The participation in this scientific adventure generates a truly aesthetic pleasure. This, essentially, seems to be Kaverin's attitude toward science in his narrative fiction.

We would not overstate our case in postulating that the locus of many, if not most, works of Kaverin is the level where scientific attitude and aesthetic meet. This means the level of creativity where things are seen with particular insight and illumination. In his most significant works Kaverin depicts these two processes. Science discovers reality and renders it understandable. Art transcends reality through aesthetic medium, namely, it transcends the reality discovered and rendered intelligible by science. For example, in *Artist Unknown*, the narrator comments that Arximedov's art is of the kind that succeeds, brushing aside intermediate stages, in reaching the absolute; that intuitively conveys the future; that can in its own destruction foretell the coming catastrophe.[12] In that far, Kaverin may be interpreting art as an ascent toward the absolute.

Kaverin reverts to the controversy of *Artist Unknown* only in his post-Stalin narrative fiction. What is the fate of man, namely, of the scientist, as the above-mentioned polarization deepens and reaches its rock-bottom during the worst years of Stalinist years? What Arximedov had anticipated with apprehension did materialize. Technical progress is actualized at such a staggering cost of human and cultural values that it is not able to relieve the ultimate sense of frustration (*Open Book*).

In the very last pages of *Double Portrait* the author refers to both Ostrogradskij and Snegirev in a peculiar context of a dialectical unity:

... A double portrait suddenly presented itself to me: Snegirev-Ostrogradskij, and in the background — people infinitely far apart from one another, peering into the future with expectation and hope.[13]

This seems to be a statement about the potentialities in the destinies of the scientist during the Stalinist period. The very term "double portrait" signifies this. These potentialities are actualized in the form of a joint destiny of two kinds of scientists. One does the right thing, that is, he does not surrender his intellectual integrity of a scientist. The other does the wrong thing. For this reason, their fates follow different courses. However, there is a kind of dialectical unity in these courses. They remain joint. They reflect one another. They characterize one another, and explain one another.[14] They symbolize the courage and the weakness, the dedication and the temptations that the scientist simultaneously experiences under Stalinism. Above all, they remind us of how unstable personality may become, and how insecure man and his life are under this pressure of Stalinism.

This issue of the integrity of scientists brings about a generation conflict. Kaverin describes this process in his later works — "A Piece of Glass" (1960), *Double Portrait* (1966), "Slanted Rain" (1962). The young generation, grown up after Stalin's death, is not implicated in the misdeeds of Stalinism. The older generation is. The young generation condemn the "stariki" (the old men) for having traded off their intellectual and moral integrity for security, affluence and influence. By doing so the older generation made themselves accomplices in Stalin's crimes. Only the most heroic, the most dedicated to science, that is, to the integrity of Russian science, did not surrender their intellectual and moral integrity, and courageously faced the consequences of their noble disobedience. The common run of scientists submitted, and willy-nilly compromised with their own sense of integrity for the sake of their survival. "[...] I have three children and only one leg," says in a manner of self-justification a biologist as he betrays his friend and lends his support to an obscurantist campaign. The comment rings too true circumstantially for Kaverin to have invented it.[15] Only the unscrupulous, or even criminal, self-serving careerists throve in this environment of Stalinist obscurantism. It is toward this last category of scientists or pseudo-scientists that the young generation bear a disdainful resentment. In *Double Portrait* the sons grew out of their innocent adolescence only to realize that their fathers are contemptible mediocrities who have reached their positions of influence and affluence through forged denunciation which sent to death far better men and scientists than they could have hoped ever to become. The fathers have tried hard to make themselves and everyone else believe in their own respectability. And now, the retribution has caught up with the fathers and disturbed them where it hurts most. Their own sons can see through their fathers' despicable game. The sons come to despise and reject their own fathers.

Actually, this alienation between fathers and sons need not be so much a matter of generation gap as it is rather a matter of a spontaneous polarization between the "inventors" and the "acquisitive ones."[16] The young generation, with their spontaneous sense of justice and honor reject those whom they believe to be the accomplices in Stalin's crimes and moral turpitude. Thus, a particular generation gap is unmistakably there, but Kaverin represents this conflict rather episodically. Its outcome remains uncertain.

The two young scientists of the tale "A Piece of Glass" (1960) have the most significant views in regard of this "generation gap." For them, the above-mentioned alienation between the "fathers" and the "sons" is, to be sure, a deplorable development, but it is a development which, at that point, is already of secondary importance. Their sense of "generation gap" is different. It harks back to Arximedov's ideas.

In this tale Kaverin describes an episode in the life of a young physiologist Petja Uglov. The reader learns little about Petja beyond a few incidents of this episode. And still, in a few pages, the author succeeds in depicting a certain significant psychology which may be symptomatic of the time and the generation. Petja Uglov arrives at Leningrad in order to acquire a special kind of glass developed by the Glass Institute. He needs this experimental product in order to complete his scientific instrument in his provincial laboratory. His scientific credentials should help him settle the transaction with the Glass Institute in no time. This is what Petja anticipates. However, unexpected obstacles threaten to ruin his theoretical purpose. The glass he has been looking for is also only theoretical. This is what he learns from the Glass Institute Director Kruaze. The latter does not turn down Petja's request because it is perfectly lawful. He even takes interest in Petja's project and adds his well-wishing suggestions. And still, Petja is not getting the glass. Somehow, the Director and the other senior members of the Glass Institute keep referring Petja to one another. Some conflict seems to divide the members of the Institute. None of them wants personally to take the initiative of having the glass produced. Petja's scientific project becomes almost an incidental victim of this conflict. Petja does not quite understand what the matter is, and why no one wants to help him get possession of the glass; all the more so because it is a trifling matter for the Glass Institute but vital for Petja's project.

It starts dawning on Petja, a brilliant young scientist as he is, that a theoretical purpose, easy to implement while still only a project of mind, encounters unanticipated obstacles when it reaches the stage of practical actualization. These obstacles arise not from the difficulties rooted in the nature of the scientific project itself but from the moral atmosphere among those who work on it. Interpersonal conflicts do not yield or submit readily to abstract purposes, no matter how rational. The gaining of support for a theoretical purpose may turn out to be not only a matter of the asking or giving an order; not only a matter of the narrow technical arguement of a specialist. In order to enlist co-operation, Petja may have to exert an utmost effort to understand, to sense or to intuit the working of the finer chords that make up a personality. This he can succeed in doing only if he himself has enough of emotional maturity. At this point, because of his inability to size up other people's less obvious thoughts and feelings, he does not manage to harness the interpersonal conflicts dividing those on whom it depends to help him. Consequently, his own scientific project bogs down.

Thus Petja lives through a minor crisis which enables him to take stock of his own liabilities. Even before, he realized that he understood people — mostly scientists — only in their relation to science. But once he would step out of this rarefied atmosphere of science and intellectual speculation, he felt estranged because he did not understand and experience living emotions as people understand and experience them and live by in everyday common life. What Kaverin seems to intimate here is that this young post-Stalin generation, technologically oriented and in many respects outstanding, should have a chance to learn the art of human relations; to its acquired art of intellectual speculation, which is an abstraction of life, it should add the art of life itself, that is the art of living humanely and gracefully. And Petja takes a step in this direction during his stay in Leningrad.

In the person of Kruaze Petja encounters a man for whom good manners and social decorum have become like a second nature. Reviewing his experience, Petja and his friend Val'ka sense that in at least one respect this circumstance is not trivial. Kruaze has evolved a certain external social polish, the understanding of how to conduct himself in any given situation. Both boys perceive the paramount importance of this social polish: it presupposes the sense of inner self-control and a well-trained taste. Kruaze has attained the art of disciplining himself into constantly assuming courteous and humane form in his behavior with others. And this does matter. Perhaps somewhat unwittingly for the boys themselves, their casual inferences predicate a whole style of life, perhaps even the quality of a whole civilization. At one of the twists of their freewheeling conversation Val'ka refers to Chekhov. And appealing to Chekhov, the boys, perhaps somewhat unwittingly, advance a Chekhovian, far-reaching, challenge. It resounds in Doctor Astrov's memorable phrase: "Everything ought to be beautiful about a human being: face, clothes, soul, and thoughts . . .".[17] Both boys seem to have speculated far enough to give the first rough form to this challenge. However, as of this point, they have not measured up to it. The challenge does not admit of man's being an oustanding scientist in one's narrow speciality and, at the same time, a sloppy vulgarian or muddlehead in everything else. And Petja's life somewhat suffers from such a discrepancy. Neither does his friend Val'ka outdistance him markedly in this course. He remarks upon this count:

"Neither of us knows how to enter a house, how to exit, how to express a greeting civilly, or how to keep up a conversation. [...] For everything we have enough time, whereas for courtesy we don't,".[18]

Here, things are clearly stated. Val'ka, more mature than Petja, feels the need for a new dimension or quality of life that he must believe to have so far been missing.

It is quite obvious that the style of life that Val'ka advocates stands poles apart from the one extolled in the literature of the preceding decades. For him, classical figures and ways glorified in the early Soviet literature must undoubtedly have become a matter of hoary legends. How much would Val'ka empathize with Gleb Chumalov, the iron-fisted proletarian, more devoted to cement than to people? Or with Pavel Korchagin, the visceral hater of bourgeois, let alone aristocractic, amenities? Or with Chapaev, the quasi-neolithic slab of mankind and an intrepid fighter bursting from the soil of the wind-swept steppe? Or even with his own historical elder brother, the technocrat Shpektorov who claims that for him a pair of pants is more important than morality? Not much, probably. And conversely, those heroic figures of another age, men dedicated to "unfeeling, proud machines," would feel ill at ease if exposed to the way of life for which the two boys are groping.

Both young scientists start feeling that in order to live a fuller and more meaningful life they should step beyond technological functionalism; that powerplants, factories, space rockets, experiments in physiology and other paraphernalia of science and technology are rather means toward an end whose full measure turns out to be a certain imponderable human quality of interpersonal relations. Ultimately, the boys obscurely feel, only this imponderable human quality of interpersonal relations is what makes life worth living, and what gives man his deepest sense of self-fulfillment. It amounts to a more cultured and more genteel way of life, free from rudeness and vulgarity, in which social graces, delicacy of manners, amenity, courtesy, and simply good manners would preside over people's behavior to one another; a life which would foster "the art of human relations, love, the capacity for valuing the beautiful, the ability to be enraptured," as Kaverin says.[19] In this respect art assumes a greater significance in Kaverin's works than it may appear at first sight. As Kaverin lets it appear subtly throughout his works – especially *Artist Unknown* (1931) and *In Front of the Mirror* (1972) – the most important mission of art lies in its civilizing influence. This fulfillment of Doctor Astrov's dream would thus overcome the cultural lag which Petja and Val'ka – and possibly their generation – believe themselves to experience.

Viewed from a different angle, the two young Soviet specialists debate the virtues of generalism and agree on its desirability, and even move in this direction. Thus, Kaverin may have drawn a somewhat impressionistic picture of the incipient rebellion in which more thoughtful scientists engage against the philosophy and the way of life that scientific and technological specialization has so far brought about.

Petja and Val'ka's rambling inferences belie, three decades later, the somber prophecies of Olesha's grotesque hero Ivan Babichev. The "old feelings glorified by the poets" have not withered away under the new order of the "New Man." The "old feelings" have affected the "New Man" as well. Their inferences acquire a significance all the more vital because the two boys reasoned them out from their own experiences, of which Petja's happens to stand at the center of the episode.

As the two young scientists pick their way through drizzle and fog along the avenues of Leningrad, engaged in small talk, it dawns on them that "the art of knowing how to behave" (umenie vesti sebja), at its best, arises from a lengthy civilizing process which means inner discipline and self-control among other things. And they feel that, should they try to improve the quality of the life of their time and environment, they would have to master this art, the "art of knowing how to behave." Significantly enough, Kaverin has his two young technocrats revert to the ancient concepts of the *Bildungsroman*. It takes Petja a near theft to attain his aim. Had he had a better understanding of people's thoughts and emotions, and had he known how to be more sympathetically responsive to them, he would not have needed to place himself in such an extreme situation. It is intimated that personality as a subject of civilization is the least painful means of action in society. This precisely was the dream of Arximedov. Will the young Soviet scientists and technocrats take up the forlorn mission of the quixotic artist of *Artist Unknown*? Will they shift their emphasis from manpower to humaneness?

History never duplicates itself in particular. However, it may be assumed that the fundamental motivation for human behavior is universal. If so, it is tempting to postulate a broad historical parallelism. The rebellion against the narrowness of theological dogma generated the Renaissance man. Would a similar spirit and man emerge once the shackles of mental specialization fall? It would be unwise to expect an explicit answer in a work of belles-lettres. However, if we allow of certain symbolism in the tale, the answer seems curiously ambivalent.

The piece of glass symbolizes the very heart of Petja's scientific quest at the time. The inert object of the beginning becomes, in the process of Petja's endeavors, a part of Petja's life, cheered with its warmth and, as it were, a live depository of Petja's emotions and hopes. In this symbolization, scientific specialty turns into a part of personality rather than the latter becoming a part of the former. Specialty does not enslave personality; it leaves the latter free and open to other enriching experiences. This is, no doubt, what Kaverin hopes for his two young scientists.

However, things may follow a different course. Apparently, Leningrad offers the best stocks whereon to work up revolutions. In a sense, Leningrad occasioned Petja's change of heart. And here is the intriguing circumstance: Petja did not even see Leningrad. The whole landscape, structures and monuments floated by, wrapped up in fog, invisible, tantalizing, dreamlike. So this source of Petja's new awareness almost was not there. Kaverin chose to leave to Leningrad a modicum of the phantasmagoric quality that the Petersburg of Gogol and Dostoyevsky displayed. It may, of course, have been a matter of poetic accident. Or, also, a purposeful hint at the insubstántial origin of Petja's own little revolution, soon to be buried and forgotten underneath the heaps of cigarette-butts (in the tale, Kaverin insists on these cigarette-butts) and specialists' books strewn around the barn-like room of the morose bachelor bent, as the modern saying goes, on knowing more and more about less and less. Kaverin's poetic vision does not quite exclude this melancholy outcome either.

3

This brings us to considering another issue, perhaps the most important in Kaverin's mature narrative prose. It is the fate of the Russian intelligentsia. In *Skandalist* (1928) there is a curious character named Xaldej Xaldeich. He is a poor devil, an obscure clerk about whom people hardly know anything. His duty is to count the types of the printed material sent to his desk. He can see these types floating before his eyes everywhere, even at the bottom of his soup plate. People have hardly ever seen him uttering a word. He mostly mumbles, hums, and giggles foolishly. It is irresistible to interpret this character as a modern version of Akakij Akakievich.

Now, this Xaldej Xaldeich turns out to be the brother of Lozhkin, the professor.[20] The two brothers fell out twenty-five years ago and have broken off any kind of relations since. Now, twenty-five years later, it turns out that Lozhkin has ended in an intellectual and spiritual impasse. The awareness of his moral bankruptcy makes Lozhkin commit various grotesque actions. His misadventures bring him at last to his long-forgotten brother. As the two brothers meet, they both realize — after reciprocal recriminations and a tearful reconciliation — that they both in their own ways have failed in their lives. At this point, Lozhkin symbolizes the tragic failure of a whole generation of the Russian liberal arts intelligentsia, the one that, as the author says, was "begotten" by the prerevolutionary Russia, "nurtured" by the pre-World War I years, the War and, possibly, the pre-bolshevik revolution, and "attempting to live" in the Soviet Union.

In a wider sense, Lozhkin may be symbolizing even a more far-reaching failure than the one just referred to. Namely, the failure of the Russian intelligentsia that "came out of Gogol's *Overcoat*." This intelligentsia has come upon its undoing and now it abjectly withdraws to where it came from: underneath Akakij Akakievich's overcoat. This famous coat may be aptly symbolized by Xaldej Xaldeich's own clothes that Xaldej Xaldeich — Kaverin's modern version of Akakij Akakievich — has his stray brother the professor put on after the latter nearly drowns in a Petersburg flood. Perhaps even Lozhkin's eternal companion "The Tale of the Babylonian Kingdom" symbolically characterizes those for whom Lozhkin stands: not unlike the builders of the Tower of Babel they displayed a sterile cosmopolitanism and a thoughtless arrogance.

In the same novel Kaverin depicts the demoralization of another intelligentsia, much closer to the author. The fate of the Russian Formalists is in certain respects even more catastrophic than that of the intelligentsia that Lozhkin symbolizes. Would Dragomanov, the brilliant linguist, the intellectual successor of Shaxmatov and Baudouin de Courtenay (as one of the establishment conceded), foresee at the beginning of the Formalist movement that by the mid-twenties he would have only enough courage left to lapse into an intellectual limbo? Would Nekrylov himself, the leader of Formalist criticism, foresee that his fierce intellectual non-conformism would already by the mid-twenties be a thing of the past; and that he himself would be embarking on a course not quite in tune with his intellectual integrity?

What may make matters even worse is the fact that the new technological intelligentsia is displaying no less blindness to its own fate than the old humanist intelligentsia or the contemporary one. It is tragically ironic that this technological intelligentsia is committing the same kind of mistake toward technology and science as the old humanist intelligentsia committed toward the humanities: the mistake of narrow mental specialization. Will the instant relevance of the technological intelligentsia make them happier than the instant irrelevance made the humanist intelligentsia? After all, it is this enthusiastic technological youth of *Skandalist* that ends in the tragic impasse of Tat'jana Vlasenkova and her friends some two decades later.

All in all, the fate of the Russian intelligentsia as depicted in Kaverin's narrative prose does not seem to be too re-assuring. In certain regards it is tragic. This intelligentsia seems to be one-sided. Its lack of vision dooms it to a certain mental narrowness. External circumstances, political climate, non-intellectual pressures prevent it from achieving a complete and uninhibited development.

Now, a segment of this intelligentsia is truly heroic, motivated by the noblest purposes and extraordinary vision. This segment includes those scientists, artists and men of letters who are spearheading creative thought in their respective fields, i.e., those who cannot avoid being spiritually independent. They are the ones who face a tragic fate in the atmosphere of Stalinist obscurantism. Their achievements, marked with intellectual independence and creative integrity, undergo destruction, mutilation and persecution. Undoubtedly, Kaverin himself is one of these heroic figures.

Although Kaverin's narrative is usually objective, the presence of the author's incisive personality may be felt in all his representation. It is not an obtrusive presence but rather one that enriches the narrative with Kaverin's wit and wisdom. And still, at times, the authorial figure is emphatically projected and the authorial voice raised. At such a point the objective narrative yields its place to the author's subjective analysis of his own feelings.

These authorial statements may be deceptively short. It is, for example, the case in the last lines of *Double Portrait*.[21] Here, the author's subjective analysis of his own feelings articulates with the message of the plot. Kaverin's appeal does not have the passionate explicitness of Yu. Daniel's "Iskuplenie" (Redemption). Neither does it have the overpowering breadth of Solzhenitsyn's appeal. But it has no less intelligence, especially literary intelligence. It is an invitation to a collective soul searching. People should openly identify and name the mistakes that caused the horrible excesses of the Stalinist period. This process is akin to the tragic catharsis: the recognition and the discovery of the past mistakes that caused the suffering will cleanse one of the shared tragic guilt. Otherwise, this tragic guilt will never fade.

FOOTNOTES

INTRODUCTION

1. Kaverin's original family name is Zil'berg. Actually, he is far better known by his pen-name.
2. I propose this year because it is the earliest date of Kaverin's published work that I have been able to ascertain. The story "Pjatyj strannik" [Fifth wanderer] has the date "October-December 1921" (*vid*. V. Kaverin, *Mastera i podmaster'ja*, M.-P., 1923, p. 177).
3. V. Kaverin, *Sobranie sochinenij*, M., 1963, vol. 1, pp. 5-24.
4. Kaverin completed his studies at the Institute of Oriental Languages in 1923 and graduated from the University in 1924 (both in Leningrad). In 1929 Kaverin successfully defended his dissertation and obtained the rank of "starshij nauchnyj sotrudnik pervogo razrjada" (*vid*. *Pisateli-laureaty Stalinskoj Premii*, M., 1954, pp. 44-49: a concise biography of Kaverin and basic bibliography).
5. Kaverin must mean *Zapiski mechtatelej* which appeared between 1919-1922.
6. The original title of this tale was *Devjat' desjatyx sud'by* (The nine tenths of fate).
7. *Pisateli*. Avtobiografii i portrety sovremennyx russkix prozaikov. Ed. by Vl. Lidin. M., 1926, p. 134.
8. K.A. Timirjazev (1843-1920): an outstanding Russian botanist and physiologist. He supported the Bolshevik Revolution.
9. *vid*. footnote No. 2 of Chapter Two.
10. Cape Flora: of Nortbruk Island, which is one of the islands of Franz Josef land.
11. For his war-time activity Kaverin was awarded the Order of the Red Star, *vid*. *Pisateli-laureaty Stalinskoj Premii*. M., 1954, p. 48.
12. *Two Captains* earned Kaverin a Stalin Prize, which he received in 1946.
13. Gorky's idea is to give a literal dramatization to the figurative meaning of a Russian proverb or saying.
14. *vid*. *Literaturnaja Rossija*, April 2, 1965
15. This letter was also submitted to the Presidia of the Supreme Soviets of the USSR and of the RSFSR.
16. *Novoye Russkoye Slovo*, New York, November 19, 1966..
17. The Russian text of this letter may be found in Aleksandr Solzhenicyn, *Sobranie sochinenij*, vol. 6, "Delo Solzhenicyna," pp. 94-96, "Posev," 1970.
18. *Xronika Tekushchix Sobytij* No. 6, February 1969, p. 11.
19. "A Question of Madness," by Zhores A. Medvedev and Roy A. Medvedev, *The New York Times Magazine*, November 7, 1971, p. 120.
20. *Radio Liberty Dispatch*, June 10, 1970, p. 2.

CHAPTER ONE

1. This must have been in 1918, since Kaverin was born in 1902, April 19.
2. *Sovetskie pisateli.* Avtobiografii v dvux tomax, M., 1959, vol. I, pp. 496-497. V. Borisova dates it as of the year 1920 and states that "The Eleventh Axiom" has never been published, *vid.* her critical essay "Rannee tvorchestvo V. Kaverina," in vol. I of Kaverin's *Sobranie sochinenij*, M., 1963, pp. 461-477.
3. V. Kaverin, "Poiski i reshenija," *Novyj Mir*, No. 11, November 1954, pp. 187-197, the phrase quoted on p. 187.
4. One of the stories of this collection, "Shields and Candles" has been translated into English by Professor Gary Kern in *Russian Literary Triquaterly*, No. 2, 1972, pp. 125-132.
5. V. Kaverin, "Ocherk raboty," *Sobranie sochinenij*, M., 1963, vol, I, p. 5
6. The Russian titles: "Stoljary;" "Shchity (i svechi);" "Inzhener Shvarc;" "Xronika goroda Lejpciga za 18 . . . god;" "Purpurnyj polimpsest [sic];" "Pjatyj strannik."
7. *Sovetskie pisateli.* Avtobiografii v dvux tomax. M., 1959, vol. I, p. 503. Actually Kaverin uses this phrase ("dan' uvlechenija nemeckimi romantikami") apropos of his own "enormous torn cloak" which he wore during his student years.
8. Viktor Shklovskij, *Povesti o proze*. M., 1966 (2 vol.)
9. V. Kaverin, "Gor'kij i molodye," *Znamja*, No. 11, November, 1954, pp. 158-167. The letter in which Gorky berates the young Kaverin because of his *Masters and Apprentices* is on pp. 162-163 of this article. The main points of Gorky's criticism of *Masters and Apprentices*: poor language, no style, groundless exoticism, aimless play of fantasy, no concern for disclosing the nature of social relations.
10. V. Kaverin, "Purpurnyj polimpsest," *Mastera i podmaster'ja*, M., 1923, p. 121
11. "Stoljary," *Mastera i podmaster'ja*, p. 18
12. "Inzhener Shvarc," *Mastera i podmaster'ja*, p. 69
13. This story can readily be interpreted as a political satire. It has not been reprinted.
14. In his novel *Travels with My Aunt* Graham Greene has Aunt Augusta narrate an episode which illuminates this play-within-a-play affair in a curious light. When she was in Tunis a traveling company staged *Hamlet* in Arabic. In the Interlude an attempt was made to actually murder the Player King: real molten lead was poured into his ear. Police arrested not the man who poured the lead but the one who acted Hamlet's uncle. A play within a play becomes something like "reality-within-a-play." The "inner" play becomes "reality," but for Shakespeare-bound police the "outer" play still keeps its rule enforced over the no longer existing "inner" play. The actual murder (or attempt) destroys the make-believe quality of the whole play-within-a-play system.
15. R.J. Nelson, *Play Within a Play*. New Haven, 1958, p. 30.

CHAPTER TWO

1. I mean different critical pronouncements by Eixenbaum, Tynjanov, Zamjatin, Lunc, Shklovskij, even Trotsky, and others. *Vid.*, for example, Kaverin's paper about the development of contemporary prose that he delivered in 1924 in the Institute of the History of the Arts; this paper and the discussion it caused is summarized in "Diskussii o sovremennoj literature," *Russkij sovremennik*, No. 2, 1924, pp. 273-278.
2. In his study on Kaverin, D.G.B. Piper uses the term "pattern-plot" for *sjuzhetnyj* (D.G.B. Piper, *V.A. Kaverin*. Duquesne University Press, 1970, p. 7). It is a convenient term. I will be using it in my discussion.
3. *Vid.* the preceding footnote.
4. Quoted from Hongor Oulanoff, *The Serapion Brothers*. Mouton 1966, pp. 14-15. This debate must have been held toward the end of February 1921: the Serapion Brothers met for the first time on the 1st of February 1921, and met every Saturday.
5. *op. cit.*, p. 27
6. *op. cit.*, p. 11
7. K. Paustovskij, *Sobranie sochinenij*. M., 1968, vol. IV, pp. 65-66
8. A.S. Grin *Sobranie sochinenij*. M., 1965, vol. VI, p. 229

9. *Kratkaja Literaturnaja Enciklopedija*. M., 1964, vol. II, p. 907a
10. Gleb Struve, *Soviet Russian Literature 1917-1920*. Norman 1951, p. 143
11. N. Aseev, "Kljuch sjuzheta," in A.I. Beleckij, N.L. Brodskij, *Novejshaja russkaja literatura*. Ivanovo-Voznesensk, 1927, p. 95
12. A. Slonimskij, "V poiskax sjuzheta," in A.I. Beleckij, N.L. Brodskij, *Novejshaja russkaja literatura*. Ivanovo-Voznesensk, 1927, p. 95
13. Gleb Struve, *Soviet Russian Literature 1917-1920*. Norman 1951, p. 143
14. Herman Ermolaev, *Soviet Literary Theories 1917-1934*. University of California Press, Publications in Modern Philology, vol. 69. Berkeley and Los Angeles 1963, p. 34.
14a. Robert Kiely, *Robert Louis Stevenson*. Harvard University Press, 1964, pp. 81-2.
15. V. Kaverin, "Ocherk raboty," *Sobranie sochinenij*. M., 1963, vol., I, p. 13. *vid*. p. 17 of this study.
16. *Pisateli*. Avtobiografii i portrety. Ed. by Vl. Lidin. M., 1926, p. 134
17. V. Kaverin, "Kutumskie chasovshchiki," in *Bubnovaja mast'*, L., 1927, p. 81.
18. "Stejfors" is the transcription of the Russian spelling.
19. *Russkij sovremennik*, No. 2, 1924, p. 103.
20. V. Kaverin, *Xudozhnik neizvesten*. L., 1931, p. 99
21. "Vorob'inaja noch'": literally, it means "sparrow's night;" in Russian, the expression means: 1) a night with continuous thunderstorm or (summer) lightening; 2) short summer night [*Tolkovyj slovar' russkogo jazyka* by D.N. Ushakov, vol. I, p. 364]
22. *Sovetskie pisateli*. Avtobiografii. M., 1959, vol. I, pp. 501-502.
23. V. Kaverin, *Devjat' desjatyx sud'by* in *Kovsh*. L. 1925, Book III, p. 77
24. *Aristotle's Theory of Poetry and Fine Art*. New York 1951, p. 41
25. Arthur Koestler, "Character and Plot," *Science and Literature*, New York 1970, p. 173
26. *vid*. footnote No. 14a
27. V. Kaverin, "Bochka," in *Sochinenija*. "Priboj," L. 1930, vol. I, p. 348
28. *vid*. pp. 66-68 of this study
29. The 1964 edition of this introductory sequence of *Fulfullment of Desires* is slightly shorter than that of the 1935 version.
30. Kaverin uses this "birth-mystery" motive in *Artist Unknown* and in his tale "Kosoj dozhd'" (Slanting rain) of 1962, but in a different spirit.
31. I am aware that in this context, "documentary" has a meaning different from the one that I give to this word when I use it to describe such works as *Artist Unknown* or *Double Portrait*. In this sense, by "documentary" I mean a certain convention of narrative fiction in which the material is represented as a personal experience of the narrator, the narrative being conducted in the first person.
32. The vital problem in these "documentary" works of Socialist Realism is the problem of the correlation between the actual historical fact and its fictional context. *Vid*. M. Kuznecov, *Sovetskij roman*. Ocherki. M. 1963
33. Ark. El'jashevich, "Geroi istinnye i mnimye," *Zvezda*, No. 2, February 1958, p. 201
34. Raisa Messer, "Bol'shoj schet," *Literaturnyj sovremennik*, No. 11, 1936, p. 150
35. V. Kaverin, *Xudozhnik neizvesten*. L. 1931. p. 50. This short novel has been republished in volume 2 of Kaverin's *Sobranie sochinenij* of 1964. It differs in certain details from the original version.
36. *op. cit.*, p. 50
37. *op. cit.*, p. 89
38. *op. cit.*, p. 123
39. *op. cit.*, p. 135
40. The 1931 book text has "vtoroe," i.e., "second."
41. V. Kaverin, *Xudozhnik neizvesten*. L., 1931, pp. 138-9
42. *op. cit.*, p. 146
43. *op. cit.*, p. 119
44. This statement may need a slight qualification. It may look as if at times Kaverin treats the narrative consistency of his work somewhat casually. This happens in *Artist Unknown* and *Double Portrait*. Both works are a particular combination of the first-person narrative and the third-person. This technique communicates to the narrative the character of a chronicle with the first-person narrator assuming the part of a witness, at least a partial one, of the controversy. Now, at times the first-person narrator assumes the function of the

"omniscient author." This is in a sense also true in Kaverin's latest, epistolary, novel *Pered zerkalom* (In Front of the Mirror; book form 1972). The "editorial fiction" has always been the traditional device in composing this type of novel. Kaverin does not too scrupulously observe the traditional conventions of the epistolary narrative. His commentary – although not too large – goes beyond what an "editor" could have known about his characters. In all these cases, the author must deliberately be choosing not to conform to certain narrative conventions. It hardly weakens the narrative. If anything, these failings communicate a greater sense of drama to the controversy. These interferences of the author have a particularly dramatic effect in *Double Portrait*.

45. V. Kaverin, *Xudozhnik neizvesten*. L. 1931, p. 58
46. *op. cit.*, p. 138.

CHAPTER THREE

1. Susanne Howe, *Wilhelm Meister and his English Kinsmen*. Apprentices to life. New York, 1930, p. 5
2. My main theoretical source of information for this discussion is the article by Christine Touaillon (Christine Touaillon, "Bildungsroman," in *Reallexikon der deutschen Literaturgeschichte*, Berlin 1925-26, vol. I, p. 141; also: *Reallexikon*, vol. I, pp. 174-178, 2nd edition, Berlin 1958). Christine Touaillon divides the life of the *Bildungsroman* subject into three distinct parts: the sheltered younger years; the years of travel; maturity. If *Wilhelm Meister's Apprenticeship* and *Green Henry* are the typical examples of the *Bildungsroman*, it is very questionable whether the first stage – the sheltered younger years – is that "sheltered." To begin with, both protagonists lost one of their parents in their tender age. Wilhelm Meister starts his biography in his early adulthood, that is, the "younger years" are hardly mentioned in the novel. As for Heinrich Lee's childhood and boyhood, it is hardly idyllic. It is rather a frustrating piece of "younger years." It seems to me that the *Bildungsroman* subject starts his trials much earlier in life than Christine Touaillon states.
3. The protagonists of, respectively, Gorky's novel *Mat'* (Mother, 1907) and N. Ostrovskij's novel *Kak zakaljalas' stal'* (How the Steel was Tempered, 1932-34).
4. The criticism lamenting the scantiness of scientific information in *Open Book* belongs to Ark. El'jashevich. Here is the excerpt in question: "[...] I kogda uznaesh', chto V. Kaverin, rabotaja nad romanom, oblozhil sebja mikrobiologicheskimi trudami, stanovitsja obidno za pisatelja, kotoryj poterjal tak mnogo vremeni. Ved' vse, chto on potom vylozhil nam v kachestve 'nauchnyx problem' svoego romana, legko mozhno pocherpnut' iz toshchej broshjurki o penicilline." (Ark. El'jashevich, "Geroi istinnye i mnimye," *Zvezda*, No. 2, February 1958, p. 198). The quotation from Kaverin is from *Sovetskie pisateli*. Avtobiografii. Vol. I, "Gixl," M. 1959, p. 509
5. Abram Tertz, *The Trial Begins and On Socialist Realism*. New York 1965, p. 172
6. Ark. El'jashevich, "Zamysel i ego voploshchenie," *Neva*, No. 4, 1958, p. 214
7. It may have been embarrassing for Kaverin to have been awarded a Stalin Prize for his *Two Captains* along with those other writers.
8. V. Azhaev, *Daleko ot Moskvy*. "Oblastnoe knizhnoe izdatel'stvo," Groznyj 1949
9. It is interesting to compare this episode of the novel with Aldanov's story "Mikrofon" (The Microphone) in which the author works out the same motive, pertaining even to the same point of history (M. Aldanov,"Mikrofon."*Kovcheg*. Sbornik russkoj zarubezhnoj literatury. New York 1942, pp. 25-46). The story is about an electrical engineer who installs a microphone in Winston Churchill's office for the latter to deliver a speech over radio during the darkest moments of the war that Britain was waging against the Hitlerite Germany. Aldanov succeeds in depicting the bundle of emotions that has suddenly taken hold of the mind of this common electrical engineer. The latter now has a chance to observe the Prime Minister as no other man may have had a chance to do. He can compare his indomitable public figure with his private self, at this very fraction of time utterly shattered by the disastrous war news. The engineer's early snobbish dislike for the Prime Minister (whose name the author does not mention once in the story) vanishes as he realizes what burden

this cheerfully grinning gentleman is carrying, what war he is waging, what responsibility he is bearing on his shoulders so lonely at this particular moment. And as he listens to the Prime Minister's speech, a veritable hurricane rises in his soul. It floods his soul with a grim determination. He has already given half of his savings; he must give everything; but it's not enough; he must go himself, and fight this war to death, if need be, and win it because there is just nothing else left. Now, this does not at all mean that a British engineer is intrinsically more devoted than the Russian. It is a matter of artistic representation. Aldanov proves to the mature critical reader, in terms of human emotions, judgments and valuations, what is so precious and noble about this electrical engineer's self-sacrificing gesture. He proves it because he shows in some depth a valid psychological motivation for the man's behavior. Such a masterly short story tells infinitely more about human self-sacrifice and courage than the 637 pages of Azhaev's novel do.

10. V. Kaverin, *Dva Kapitana* in *Sobranie sochinenij*, vol. 3, M., 1964, p. 483
11. *op. cit.*, p. 512
12. *Sovetskie pisateli*. Avtobiografii. M., 1959, vol. I, pp. 509-510
13. V. Kaverin, *Otkrytaja kniga*, M., 1956, Part III, p. 256
14. *op. cit.*, p. 150
15. In 1912 Gumilev founded "Cex poètov" (the Guild of Poets). It may very well be connected with the intellectual atmosphere of Russian Formalism.
15a. *Dva Kapitana* in *Sobranie sochinenij*, vol. 3, M., 1964, p. 413
16. I. Èrenburg, *Den' vtoroj*, a novel written in 1932-33, published in 1934. It is a novel about Socialist contruction.
17. I. Èrenburg, "Ljudi, gody, zhizn'." kniga tret'ja. *Novyj Mir*, No. 11, November, 1961, pp. 157-158.

CHAPTER FOUR

1. Aristotle's *Theory of Poetry and Fine Art*. Translated and with critical notes by S.H. Butcher. New York 1951, p. 369
2. These two terms are borrowed from Walter Kaufmann, *Tragedy and Philosophy*. New York, 1969, p. 244.
3. Walter Kerr, *Tragedy and Comedy*. New York, 1967, p. 131.
4. Walter Kaufman, *Tragedy and Philosophy*. New York, 1969, p. 278
5. I mean, of course, the protagonists of Georg Büchner's (1813-1837) play and Arthur Miller's *Death of a Salesman*, respectively.
6. For the historical context of this novel *vid.* D.G.B. Piper, *V. A. Kaverin*. Duquesne University Press, 1970, namely, Chapter II of this study.
7. V. Kaverin, *Skandalist*. L., 1931, p. 97
8. *op. cit.*, p. 48
9. *op. cit.*, p. 15
10. *op. cit.*, p. 40
11. I believe that the historical Osip Senkovski (1800-1858), the fictional Panaev of *The Great Game* and Dragomanov of *Skandalist* all share some common basic features. In his book, Professor Piper states that the prototype of Dragomanov is the orientalist E.M. Polivanov, p. 75.
12. V. Kaverin, *Skandalist*. L., 1931, p. 47
13. It is worth noting that Shpektorov inherited this attitude of mind from his early, and still grotesque, prototype Korchaga of "Inzhener Shvarc."
14. V. Kaverin, *Xudozhnik neizvesten*. L., 1931, p. 27
15. *op. cit.*, p. 23
16. *op. cit.*, p. 11
17. "Gubispolkom" is an abbreviation for: Provincial executive committee of the Council of the workers', peasants', and Red Army men's representatives.
18. V. Kaverin, *Xudozhnik neizvesten*. L., 1931, p. 74 Kaverin puts these words in the mouth of an Italian engineer who speaks Russian with amusing grammatical mistakes. This

garbeled Russian emphasizes Shpektorov's predicament in a way in which a grammatically correct Russian sentence would not.

19.   *op. cit.*, p. 9
20.   Olesha represented this degradation of essential humanity in *Envy* (1927): Kavalerov envies Andrej Babichev, who envies Volodja Makarov, who envies the machines. "Envy" here moves in the direction of the increasing primitivity of personality, and ends in pure mechanical efficiency.
21.   Lewis Mumford, *The Pentagon of Power*. New York, 1970 p. 183
22.   V. Kaverin, *Xudozhnik neizvesten*. L., 1931, p. 11
23.   *op. cit.*, pp. 9-10
24.   Arthur E. Adams, *Stalin and His Time*. New York 1972, pp. 63-64.
25.   Walter Kaufmann, *Tragedy and Philosophy*. New York 1969, p. 193 ff.
26.   V. Kaverin, *Xudozhnik neizvesten*. L., 1931, p. 59
27.   *op. cit.*, p. 141
28.   *op. cit.*, p. 149
29.   V. Kaverin, *Pered zerkalom*. M., 1972, p. 150
30.   V. Kaverin, *Ispolnenie zhelanij*. Book I, L. 1935, p. 233
31.   V. Kaverin, "Ocherk raboty," *Sobranie sochinenij*. M., 1963, vol. I, p. 14.
32.   Walter Kaufmann thoughtfully questions this theory of the pathetic, *vid.* his *Tragedy and Philosophy*. New York 1969, p. 364
33.   Aleksandr Solzhenicyn, *V Kruge pervom* in *Sobranie sochinenij*. vol. 3, Posev, 1969, the Chapter "Jazyk – orudie proizvodstva," pp. 133-141
34.   *op. cit.*, the Chapter "Vernite nam kazn', Iosif Vissarionovich!" pp. 141-158
35.   V. Kaverin, *Otkrytaja kniga* in *Sobranie sochinenij*. vol. 5, M. 1965, p. 217
36.   *op. cit.*, p. 211
37.   V. Kaverin, "Kusok stekla," in *Sobranie sochinenij*. vol. 6, M. 1966, p. 28
38.   In my discussion of "Salierism" I have used (apart from Gershenzon's article on *Mozart and Salieri*) the material from I.M. Nusinov's short study "Mocart i Sal'eri" in his *Istorija literaturnogo geroja*. M. 1958, pp. 484-548
39.   *vid.* p. 214 of this study
40.   When Tat'jana Vlasenkova and her close friends have a private conversation about the political terror that is engulfing them in the second half of the thirties, they take the trouble to cover the telephone with pillows (*Otkrytaja kniga* in *Sobranie sochinenij*, vol. 4, M. 1965, pp. 446-7; this episode is missing in the 1956 edition of the novel).
41.   V. Kaverin, *Otkrytaja kniga*. M. 1956, Part III, p. 231.
42.   *op. cit.* p. 246
43.   *op. cit.*, p. 128
44.   *op. cit.*, p. 245
45.   Quixotic motive is a recurrent one throughout the works of Kaverin.
46.   V. Kaverin *Otkrytaja kniga*. M. 1956, Part III, p. 260
47.   *op. cit.*, pp. 260-261
48.   Ernest J. Simmons included into this category of characters such a latecomer as Andrej Starcov of Fedin's novel *Goroda i gody* (Cities and years). *Vid.* Ernest J. Simmons, *Russian Fiction and Soviet Ideology*. New York 1958, p. 25. Dobroljubov identified the phenomenon of the "superfluous people" with that of *oblomovshchina*. Isaac Deutscher traces Zhivago's typological genealogy back to Oblomov ("Pasternak and the Calendar of the Revolution," *Partisan Review*, No. 2, Spring 1959, p. 256). Would this imply that Zhivago is another belated "superfluous man"? By tagging all these very different socio-literary figures as "superfluous people" we may be lapsing into facile overgeneralizations.
49.   V. Kaverin, *Otkrytaja kniga* M. 1956, Part III, p. 261.
50.   Walter Kerr, *Tragedy and Comedy*. New York 1967, p. 121
50a. V. Kaverin, *Otkrytaja kniga*. M. 1956, Part III, p. 230
51.   This line reminds one of the equally unsteady line that separates the world of puppets from the world of humans in Kaverin's early story "The Fifth Wanderer."
52.   V. Kaverin, *Dvojnoj portret*. M. 1967, p. 184
53.   *op. cit* , p. 64
54.   This brings him closer to the *Bildungsroman* subject, who is akin to the Renaissance man.

55. V. Kaverin, *Otkrytaja kniga*. M. 1956, Part III, p. 246
56. *op. cit.*, p. 247
57. This Russian saying (*bez viny vinovat*) sums up the essence of the tragic situation or the tragic guilt as it is being discussed in this study.
58. V. Kaverin, *Dvojnoj portret*. M. 1967, pp. 222-3.
59. The concepts of "mechanical world picture" and "organic world picture" belong to Lewis Mumford, *The Pentagon of Power*. New York 1970, pp. 57, 384.

CONCLUSION

1. *Sovetskie pisateli*. Avtobiografii. M. 1959, vol. I, p. 504. *Vid.* also p. 17 of this study.
2 & 3. In this connection, *vid.* D.S. Lixachev, *Chelovek v literature drevnej Rusi*. M. 1958. Especially Chapter VIII: Ot istoricheskogo imeni literaturnogo geroja k vymyshlennomu.
4. L. Lunc, "Pochemu my Serapionovy Brat'ja," *Literaturnye Zapiski*, P. 1922, No. 3, pp. 30-31.
   – – – "Na Zapad," *Beseda* (ed. by Gorky), Berlin 1923, No. 3, pp. 259-274.
5. V. Kaverin *Otkrytaja kniga*. M. 1956, Part I & II, pp. 400-401.
6. "Znaete li vy, chto takoe vozvrashchenie vremeni? Eto, kogda [...]" (*Xudozhnik neizvesten*. L. 1931, p. 116) "Sluchalos' li vam kogda-nibud' ispytyvat' chuvstvo vozvrashchenija vremeni, kogda nachinaet kazat'sja, chto [...]" (*Otkrytaja kniga*. M. 1956, Part I & II, p. 162) "[...] i strannym pokazalos' mne to chuvstvo vozvrashchenija vremeni, kotoroe ja ispytal, kogda [...]" (*Dva Kapitana* in *Sobranie sochinenij*, vol. 3, 1964, p. 510)
7. V. Kaverin, "Neotkrytye dorogi," in the collection *Formuly i obrazy*, M. 1961, pp. 68-78.
8. Walter Kaufmann, *Tragedy and Philosophy*. New York 1969 *Vid.* especially Chapter V: Homer and the Birth of Tragedy.
9. D.G.B. Piper, *V.A. Kaverin*. Duquesne University Press, 1970 *Vid.* especially Chapter I: The Left-Art Movement
10. V. Kaverin, *Xudozhnik neizvesten*. L. 1931, p. 9
11. *op. cit.*, p. 8
12. For possible historical references of this comment *vid.* D.G.B. Piper, *V.A. Kaverin*. Duquesne University Press, 1970, p. 131 ff. I do not always agree with Professor Piper's opinion, *vid.* my review of Professor Piper's book in *Slavic and East European Journal*, Vol. 16, No 2, Summer 1972, pp. 236-238.
13. V. Kaverin, *Dvojnoj portret*. M. 1967, p. 222
14. Here we can see how Kaverin's motives evolve. For example, in his early tale "Bochka" (The cask, 1924) Kaverin uses the motive of the villainous brother trying maliciously to despoil his sibling, the scientist or inventor, of the fruit of his labor. This common adventure-novel motive evolves into a mature vision of the contradictory, dialectical nature of man's personality.
15. V. Kaverin, *Dvojnoj portret*. M. 1967, p. 48
16. *vid.* p. 242 of this study
17. Chekhov, *Plays*. Penguin 1966, p. 210
18. V. Kaverin, "Kusok stekla," *Sobranie sochinenij*. M. 1966, vol. 6, p. 30
19. *op. cit.*, p. 22
20. *vid.* p. 187 of this study.
21. *vid.* p. 244 of this study.

APPENDIX

Synopses of: *Konec xazy* (The end of the gang, 1925)
                   Devjat' desjatyx sud'by (The nine tenths of fate, 1925)
                   Ispolnenie zhelanij (Fulfillment of desires, 1934-36)
                   Dva kapitana (Two captains, 1938-1944)

Konec xazy (The end of the gang, 1925)

A gang of Petrograd robbers planned a daring burglary: to break the safe of the State bank. The leader of the gang, Shmerl the Turkish Drum, as he was nicknamed, wanted the burglary to be a carefully organized and smoothly executed enterprise. For that purpose he and his accomplice Sasha the Lord kidnapped Pineta, a man whom they believed to be a steel specialist thoroughly acquainted with the construction of bank safes. Pineta would, according to their plans, make all the technical contrivances necessary to crack the safe. They committed a blunder in kidnapping Pineta: he was but the namesake and nephew of the true steel specialist. The gang also lured away a girl stenographer, Molotova. They presumably needed her for secretarial work. It turns out that Shmerl the Turkish Drum was in love with her. One of the gang, Frolov, with whom she had fallen in love, betrayed her and helped Shmerl the Turkish Drum abduct her. The gang kept both Pineta and Molotova captive in their den. Before her treacherous abduction Molotova wrote a letter to her former boy-friend Sergej Travin, in which she let him know that she was breaking off her relations with him. Travin, a political prisoner, after reading the letter, escaped from his jail and came to Petrograd in order both to revenge himself on Frolov and to meet Molotova. He challenged Frolov to a duel and killed him. Two letters put Travin on the trail of Molotova. He found one in Frolov's pocket-book. The landlady of the house in which Molotova lived showed him the other: the letter was addressed to Molotova and contained an offer of secretarial employment. The same man, namely Shmerl the Turkish Drum, wrote both letters. Travin came to the right conclusion that the Turkish Drum and his gang had abducted Molotova. Travin finally succeeded in finding a trace of her. While haunting different joints he met a prostitute Sushka who was connected with the gang of the Turkish Drum. Sushka agreed to help Travin in coming to the rescue of Molotova. Sushka, Travin and Sushka's friend who stayed at the robbers' den planned Molotova's escape. While the gang went on a spree on the eve of the safe-breaking, Sushka's lover Pjatak, one of the gang, got an inkling that Sushka was being won over by another man. He shadowed Sushka and Travin while they were heading for the gang's den to carry out their plan of rescuing Molotova. Pjatak realized that Sushka had betrayed the gang and himself. He decided to kill her. There occurred a fateful confusion: as Molotova was leaving the robbers' den, Pjatak, mistaking her for Sushka, stabbed her in the back. Travin, carrying lifeless Molotova, reported to the police and disclosed all that he knew about the gang of the Turkish Drum. Travin was arrested: the police found out that he was a runaway prisoner. On the faith of his testimony the police raided the robbers' den. The whole gang fell into the hands of the police.

[Note: in editions subsequent to the first, 1925, edition, Kaverin made some slight changes of the text. E.g., in the 1930 version, Travin's name is changed to Veselago. The girl stenographer Molotova becomes Molostvova in the 1963 edition. In the 1925 version Pineta begs for cigarettes and the robber describes his gang as "organizers;" in the 1930 edition, Pineta asks for a Havana cigar; in the 1963 text the robber describes his gang as "anarchists and syndicators." Some meaning might, of course, be ascribed to these and similar modifications. However, they barely affect the substance of the plot and the drift of the tale.]

Devjat' desjatyx sud'by (The nine tenths of fate, 1925)

In 1915, a young ensign Shaxov went to war, leaving Galja, the girl that he loved, in Petrograd. On the German front he took part in illegal anti-governmental activity, equivalent to treason and punishable by death under war-time regulations. Military authorities discovered his subversive occupations and court-martialed him. He was sentenced to death. Caving in under the stress of the circumstances, Shaxov betrayed one of his fellow revolutionaries, and thus saved his own life at the price of the latter's death penalty. This disgrace was the "one tenth" of his fate that would mar the remaining "nine tenths." Relentlessly guilt-ridden, Shaxov exiled himself to Siberia, not even answering Galja's letters, for fear of exposing her to his disgrace (of which no one actually knew). Only two years later, in October 1917, he departed for Petrograd, still yearning to see Galja. He did not find her at home. His arrival at Petrograd coincided with the Bolshevik uprising and take-over. He joined the Bolsheviks and gallantly participated in the assault on and the capture of the Winter Palace. While searching through the attic of the palace, he engaged in a gun fight with an anti-Bolshevik officer in hiding. Shaxov shot the ensign in the dark and then identified the motionless body: the ensign was none other than Galja. He carried her to her home, risking not a little along the streets of Petrograd already torn by civil war. So they met, as unwitting enemies. It turned out that in her enthusiasm to support and defend the Provisional Government, Galja had disguised herself as an ensign. Even when she recovered from the worst of her wound, Shaxov found her alienated. Another man seemed to enter her life. Shaxov had gone on fighting in the ranks of the Bolshevik troops until he was taken prisoner by the counterrevolutionary forces. He was sentenced to death. Pending his imminent execution, he managed to have a letter smuggled out which his friends conveyed to Galja. She sensed from this ultimate message how much Shaxov loved her, and how much it matterd for her too. In order somehow to save his life she left Petrograd for the war zone where she believed him to be held captive. Meanwhile, a successful Red offensive drove the counterrevolutionary forces out of Gatchina, their head-quarters, and liberated Shaxov. He joined the troops again and during an action with counterrevolutionaries met Galja hiding in a shelter, now a different woman. The violence and the magnitude of the events swept away all petty grievances and misunderstandings that had kept them apart. His life was straightening out at last: his union in love with Galja and his dedication to the Revolution were opening out to his life a boundless vista. At this point of rising happiness, the damning "one tenth" of his fate came to catch up with Shaxov. A witness of Shaxov's infamy made an unexpected appearance and, in a manner of blackmail, reminded him of how he, Shaxov, in 1915 denounced and doomed to death his fellow revolutionary in order to save his own life. The witness was the clerk of the court-martial in Warsaw that sentenced Shaxov to death. He had even preserved the official record of the case. Shaxov again came up against the unsurmountable obstacle that had been denying him a new lease on life, that "one tenth" of his fate. The blackmailer seemingly pressed Shaxov to engage in some illicit traffic or even to spy on Bolsheviks' activities in the former's behalf. In his letdown, Shaxov failed to conceal incriminating evidence from his best comrade-in-arms. The latter, prompted by his revolutionary vigilance, had Shaxov arrested and brought before revolutionary tribunal. No one doubted, including Shaxov himself, that he would undergo the capital punishment. The ultimate reversal came at this hopeless instant. A respected Bolshevik leader rose from the floor in Shaxov's defense. He turned out to be the very man whom Shaxov supposedly betrayed. He had escaped before his execution and now pleaded for Shaxov's acquittal in view of all the suffering that Shaxov had since lived through. Shaxov was acquitted and at last freed from the nightmare of his guilt. Henceforth he started, together with Galja, a new life of dedication to the Revolution.

Ispolnenie zhelanij (Fulfillment of desires, 1934-36)

The story narrated in Kaverin's first major novel, *Ispolnenie zhelanij*, covers, including the Epilogue, over nine years, from April 1927 to winter 1936. It centers on the destinies of two young students, Trubachevskij and Kartashixin, at the University of Leningrad during the crucial period of their developments: on the threshold of the First Five-Year Plan, in the years 1927, 28 and 1929, when the two boys are reaching their adulthood and each of them is taking his first steps on the path of his calling. Their careers develop quite differently. Still, Trubachevskij and Kartashixin are devoted and steadfast friends. They make their headways side by side, occasionally comparing notes, encountering similar difficulties and temptations, and helping each other in need. In an Epilogue, the author summarily mentions how the two men have fared during the subsequent seven years.

Trubachevskij comes from a family of musicians. His father is a mediocre clarinetist. His mother was an outstanding violinist. She had divorced her hapless husband and had gone abroad where she had died. Trubachevskij is extrovert, in his character a youthful enthusiasm for history bubbles side by side with his worldly aspiration for celebrity; his intense intellectual curiosity feeds on his love for literature; he is not immune to flattery; on him a beautiful woman can exert an infinite fascination.

As the story opens, Trubachevskij is a second-year student in literature and history. He has just found a remunerated part-time employment: he will be assisting professor Bauer, a distinguished historian and literary scholar, in the study of the rare manuscripts that the latter owns and keeps in his archives. Trubachevskij devotes himself with fervor to this occupation, and takes a legitimate pride in this early honor. This research for professor Bauer absorbs Trubachevskij more than his formal course work at the University. It brings him his most gratifying moments and, subsequently, his bitterest reverses. Actually, the whole dramatic development of the novel derives from his association with Bauer's work and family. As he pursues his research work for Bauer, Trubachevskij makes friends with the latter's energetic daughter Masha; he comes to know better his good-for-nothing of a son Dmitri and the latter's bohemian or even dubious friends. Of greatest consequence, however, turns out to be his becoming conversant with Pushkin manuscripts stored in Bauer's archives.

Among other documents, Trubachevskij comes across one that Pushkin wrote in cipher for fear of censorship. No one has ever been able to decode it. Despite Bauer's advice to the contrary, Trubachevskij undertakes to solve the mystery of this manuscript. The mysterious Pushkin text haunts his wake and sleep. As it were, it roots itself deep in his consciousness and Trubachevskij, so to speak, gains a thorough mastery over its undecoded meaninglessness. Meanwhile, his timid friendship with Masha is burgeoning into a no less timid youthful romance. And so, in a memorable scene, his high-strung intellectual exertion, his upstirring emotional expérience, his ever-busy intuition all conspire to empower Trubachevskij, in a flash of hard-earned inspiration, to decipher the hitherto enigmatic manuscript of Pushkin.

[Note: in the development of this work of prose fiction the author chooses to ascribe to Trubachevskij the deciphering of what literary scholars believe to be the fragments of the Tenth Chapter of *Evgenij Onegin*. In a footnote, Book 2, p. 4 of the 1936 edition of the novel, Kaverin writes: "Nadejus', chto chitateli (v osobennosti chitateli-pushkinisty) ne rasserdjatsja na menja za to, chto ja pripisal otkrytie fragmentov desjatoj glavy 'Evgenija Onegina,' sdelannoe P.O. Morozovym, moemu Trubachevskomu. Ja mog by, razumeetsja, vospol'zovat'sja kakim-nibud' drugim istoriko-literaturnym otkrytiem, no fakticheskoe verojatie ot ètogo ne vyigralo by, a literaturnoe — proigralo by!"]

Trubachevskij is invited to read a paper about his discovery to an academic audience. Newspapers announce it to the general public. A publisher offers him to have his discovery printed in a book exhibiting his portrait. Trubachevskij cannot resist this offer, against Bauer's better judgment. Thus through Bauer's archives Trubachevskij gains a celebrity which somewhat overwhelms him. His budding romance with Bauer's daughter Masha brings his success to a height too idyllic and radiant for him to foresee any adversities.

However, the same archives deal him a blow from which he barely recovers. Nevorozhin, the evil genius of Bauer's son Dmitri, has schemed to rob Bauer of his rare archival documents whose marketable value, especially abroad, he well understands. Both Dmitri and Trubachevskij become easy or unwitting tools for Nevorozhin to carry out his fraudulent schemes: feeble-willed Dmitri as a natural heir to his father's valuable possessions at a point when the latter suffers from terminal cancer; Trubachevskij as one enjoying Bauer's complete trust and having free access to the latter's archives. Nevorozhin would use both victims to plunder Bauer's archives without incriminating himself. Then he would sell off the manuscripts, rid himself of his unenthusiastic accomplices and appropriate the proceeds of the fraudulent transaction for himself.

The crux of the drama represented in the novel consists in the struggle at whose outcome Trubachevskij both entraps himself and is entrapped in Nevorozhin's conspiracy, because it is as much a matter of Trubachevskij's own "frailty" as it is that of Nevorozhin's cunning. Trubachevskij is unquestionably an honest young man who would never employ impeachable means either to gratify his intellectual curiosity or to attain celebrity. However, his desire for celebrity coupled with his intellectual curiosity conceal a menace of which he is not aware. Trubachevskij very much equates his celebrity with social success and admiration of beautiful women. For a while, in his youthful inexperience, he believes he finds both in the "swinging" milieu of a beautiful loose woman Varvara toward whom he experiences an overwhelming sexual attraction. She happens to be Nevorozhin's intimate. It is after one of her parties that a Pushkin manuscript has accidentally fallen into Trubachevskij's hands. He has every reason to believe that it is one that Nevorozhin has stolen from Bauer's archives. At that juncture, the excitement of discovery and desire for glory somewhat blunt Trubachevskij's sense of ends and means. He delves over head and ears into the study of an unpublished manuscript, with the vision of his second, much talked-about, book glimmering before his eyes. He forgets that the manuscript is unlawfully in his possession. Trubachevskij experiences some fleeting moments of hesitation as his glorious and glamorous end makes him forget the dubious nature of the means. In his mind, he overcomes the temptation. However, the few fleeting moments of hesitation open a crack in his moral integrity, a minute crack, to be sure, but sufficient to prevent him from doing the only right thing that moral integrity commands: to notify Bauer at once of the theft and the possible conspiracy. Nevorozhin understands Trubachevskij's merits and weaknesses and manipulates them for his fraudulent purposes. In order to whet Trubachevskij's literary ambitions, he addresses to him insinuating flatteries interspersed with pertinent observations on his literary discovery. The subtle poison of Nevorozhin's message has sunk deeper in Trubachevskij's mind than the latter realizes, and attains its effect. The vision of glorious and glamorous possibilities that Nevorozhin conjures up in Trubachevskij's imagination undermines his workaday scholastic discipline. He starts floating along in the facile world of superficial social success. He subjects himself to Varvara whom Nevorozhin now plants for this purpose in the student's way. Trubachevskij drifts away from his sober scholastic occupations and starts neglecting his duties, namely, his duties toward professor Bauer. He spends more than he can reasonably afford.

And then the catastrophe strikes. Bauer, his days already numbered, finds out that some of his most valuable documents have vanished from his archives. He summons Trubachevskij and tells him about the theft: the perpetrator must have been familiarized well with the holdings. Trubachevskij must be aware that because of his position in Bauer's archives and his inept comments about the value of the documents, he has laid himself open to suspicion. But he has no chance to explain: an attack of disease strikes Bauer and interrupts the painful interview. Trubachevskij rushes out of Bauer's place to seek out Nevorozhin and to compel him immediately to restitute all the documents stolen from Bauer's archives, under the threat of disclosing the theft to the police. He finds Nevorozhin at the latter's apartment. On confronting him, however, Trubachevskij proves to be no match to Nevorozhin's intelligently foul play. He recovers some of the documents which Nevorozhin happens to have in his apartment and obligingly surrenders to Trubachevskij and which the latter without forethought stuffs into his briefcase. Trubachevskij allows Nevorozhin an hour's grace to bring back the remaining stolen items from an antiquarian bookseller's store. This delay Nevorozhin uses to operate a brazen-faced reversal of roles: he immediately betakes himself to Bauer's place and there, in the presence of the latter's family, denounces Trubachevskij as the villain who has plundered Bauer's archives and tried to sell off the precious manuscripts to him, Nevorozhin. His protestation of offended innocence and good faith sound all the more plausible because Trubachevskij, after waiting in vain for Nevorozhin bringing back the loot, returns to Bauer's place and here, under the very eyes of Bauer, Nevorozhin searches through Trubachevskij's briefcase and discovers the documents stolen from Bauer's archives. Not without Novorozhin's help is Trubachevskij ejected in disgrace from Bauer's home. Because he is denied access to Bauer's home during the latter's remaining short lifetime, Trubachevskij has no chance to see him and to exculpate himself in a personal interview with him.

Thus, because of his own weaknesses, Nevorozhin's intrigues, untoward circumstances such as professor Bauer's illness and death, Trubachevskij falls from his prime glory to his catastrophic disgrace. It is a costly fall. All his intellectual and spiritual preeminence that he has held from his association with professor Bauer and his name vanishes. The malicious rumor of his stealing documents from Bauer's archives spreads all over university, among his acquaintances and even attracts scandal-peddling newspapermen. Most of his friends show an uneasy guardedness toward him. His editor abruptly cancels the contract on his other work on Pushkin. A devastating review cuts up his first booklet whence his glory was to grow. He practically drops out of university. There is no return to his early sweetheart Masha either; he had turned away from her as soon as his infatuation for Varvara had set in. Now, Varvara too asks him to forget her very existence: she is going to marry Dmitri. But the worst grief is that professor Bauer, a great scholar and a good man, may have been bitterly disappointed in him, Trubachevskij, and he will never have an opportunity to redeem himself in Bauer's eyes, now that Bauer is dead. No wonder that so much grief that has so suddenly overwhelmed him has drained his vitality to the point of death wish.

Kartashixin is a son of medical doctors. Both his parents joined the Bolsheviks at the outbreak of the Revolution. During the most agonizing period of the Civil War Kartashixin the father displayed a remarkable military leadership and led the Bolshevik troops to decisive victories over counterrevolutionary forces. Both parents fought gallantly for their cause and died in battle while the young Kartashixin was still a child.

Kartashixin is in some respect Trubachevskij's opposite: he is rather introvert; to his friend's impulsiveness and erratic behavior he opposes his deliberateness and his gift of purposeful observation; not so much animated with spontaneous exuberance as Trubachevskij, Kartashixin is superior to him in willpower. For this reason, undoubtedly, Kartashixin's career is spared any catastrophic reversals.

An orphan from his earliest childhood, Kartashixin has grown under the devoted care of his foster father, an old Bolshevik and companion of his both parents, and an old taciturn lighthouse keeper. At the beginning of the story, while Trubachevskij believes himself to be well advanced in humanities, Kartashixin is still only an irresolute medical school freshman somewhat at a loss what career to pursue. However, he matures very soon. He adjusts himself promptly to his fellow students and their way of life: its hard work, fun and government of student affairs.

After witnessing how the janitor of their house has died and observing those doomed to early death, Kartashixin decides to dedicate himself to the task of lengthening or supporting life by means of the artificial circulation of the blood. Henceforth, he will devote all his scientific efforts, patience, imagination and even health to this purpose. And he succeeds in his endeavor. As his medical studies develop and deepen he is invited by a leading research institute to start work on his project. A fargoing perspective of fruitful scientific activity is opening before Kartashixin.

Willpower is one of the main virtues of Kartashixin. Whereas Trubachevskij succumbs to the lures of an "evil" woman, Varvara, lets himself go and gives up the good girl, Masha, Kartashixin, confronting the same temptation, exerts an immense effort of agonizing self-control. He overcomes the sexual attraction of Varvara. Luck would have it that he meets Masha in his turn. Unlike Trubachevskij, he does not trifle with his good fortune when he sees it coming. He wins Masha for good, thus in a sense superseding his friend Trubachevskij in that respect too.

Finally, Kartashixin, although younger than Trubachevskij, turns out to be something of a big brother to the latter. Rather instinctively than from the clear understanding of the reasons, Kartashixin disapproves of Trubachevskij's dissipations and self-centered daydreams of glory and glamor. And when Trubachevskij is involved in the despoliation of professor Bauer's archives, Kartashixin still comes to his rescue. He bolsters Trubachevskij's crushed spirit. He prevails upon the student government, for lack of immediate rehabilitation, to turn the case over to the impartial inquiry of the public procurator. And this is the beginning of Trubachevskij rehabilitation since only rumor can harm him, whereas truth will help him. Thus Kartashixin contributes to untying the knot that Trubachevskij himself has tied up and now does not know how to disentangle himself from. Even the undoing of Nevorozhin may have come from Kartashixin's quarters. His foster-father, Lev Ivanych, identifies Nevorozhin as one involved in a counterrevolutionary conspiracy in the early twenties. The latter may be someone much more dangerous and substantial than a common crook. This motive is only slightly touched upon. Lev Ivanych may, or may not, have a police investigation instituted against Nevorozhin. In any case, the latter thinks that he is being closed in on.

Next to Kartashixin's well-deserved success — intellectual, professional and sentimental, Trubachevskij painfully realizes how much he himself has failed in his own debut in life. He feels that he must build his life over again on new foundations. This is why he sets off for Dneprostroj, in order to "start living," as he says in his parting note to Kartashixin. In the meanwhile, Nevorozhin sells off Bauer's documents at whatever price he can wrangle in his growing anxiety and precipitously departs from Leningrad with a view to illegally leaving the Soviet Union. In his flight to foreign countries Nevorozhin happens to have boarded the same train as

Trubachevskij has on his way to his new apprenticeship at Dneprostroj. The two men meet for the last time as police are taking Nevorozhin, arrested, from the train to custody.

The Epilogue, set at the winter of 1936, tells the reader that Kartashixin is now a distinguished young scientist. Married to Masha, he has a little boy. He has successfully defended his doctoral dissertation on the artificial circulation of the blood. Young as he is, he has become, at the peril of overworking himself, the leading authority in the field. Trubachevskij, after working and teaching at Dneprostroj, has found a new lease on life. In the 1964 version of the novel, Trubachevskij is called to restore late professor Bauer's archives for the dilapidation of which he feels partially responsible. It is the challenge and the debt of his lifetime. He will soon rejoin his friend Kartashixin in Leningrad.

Dva kapitana (Two captains, 1938-1944)

The novel *Two Captains* covers three decades in the lives of its characters: from before 1916 to the summer of 1944. The protagonist, Sanja Grigor'ev, comes from a poor family of a harbor worker and a washerwoman. He becomes an orphan in his tender age. This is probably the most "Dickensian" among Kaverin's novels. The very opening scene of *Two Captains* reminds one of the beginning of *Great Expectations*: an underprivileged little boy, while playing, unexpectedly meets a runaway convict or someone of similar description on a northern waterfront and takes fright of him. This encounter determines the child's subsequent destiny. Nothing is a more typically Dickensian theme than an orphan's or an underprivileged child's thorny rise to manhood amidst the wickedness of many and the kindness of few. Underprivileged the little Sanja Grigor'ev certainly is. His early childhood is marred by his inability to speak. This defect becomes particularly agonizing when the boy realizes his indirect responsibility for the arrest of his father whose innocence he cannot afterward explain because of his speech deficiency. The subsequent death of Sanja's father, his mother's unhappy remarriage, his miserable treatment at the hand of his vain brute of a step-father who, not unlike Mr. Murdstone, applies "firmness" to educate Sanja, his mother's death and finally even his flight to Moscow bear recognizable similarity to the motives marking the development of a Dickensian child.

From before he can even read he hears, of evenings, his aunt Dasha read aloud some letters. Snatching them away from their intended destination, flood-water stranded them, inside a mailbag, onto their yard some past spring. Ever since, the reading of these damaged missives has become a sort of family recreation, both suspenseful and edifying. The little Sanja does not quite comprehend the contents of those letters but from hearing them read frequently he memorizes some, almost like prayers. They happen to be the letters written by the participants of the polar expedition of Captain Tatarinov, a bold explorer who vanished with his crew and ship somewhere in the Artic Ocean while on an exploratory voyage shortly before the First World War. Some of these letters are written by Captain Tatarinov himself. Flood-water has washed out the addresses. Sanja's family has no means to know that the letters were all addressed to Captain Tatarinov's wife and family who happen to live in the same city. Thus, from his early childhood, even without his own knowledge, Sanja's destiny comes in touch with that of the long dead Captain Tatarinov. Ever since, Sanja has not ceased being attracted to the destiny of the polar explorer.

Shortly after the outbreak of the Revolution, Sanja and his little friend run away, Turkestan-bound, from their native city and land up in Moscow. There, it falls to Sanja's lot to become a school-boy. He goes to a school of which Nikolaj Antonovich, a cousin of the Captain, happens to be the director. An ill feeling sets in and grows between the director and his pupil. As a school-boy also, Sanja becomes a friend of Captain Tatarinov's daughter — Nikolaj Antonovich's niece twice removed. Their adolescence friendship grows into a more mature attachment as they approach their adulthood. However, circumstances threaten to quell their nascent love. Captain Tatarinov's surviving family — his wife Mar'ja Vasil'evna, his mother-in-law and his daughter Katja — have come to believe that Nikolaj Antonovich helped the Captain a great deal in the past and now that Captain Tatarinov is gone, has become their own benefactor and protector. They believe so because Nikolaj Antonovich himself keeps at every turn protesting to this effect in front of the three intimidated females. Out of gratitude toward Nikolaj Antonovich, which he does not deem below his dignity deceitfully to exact, but even more from despair and demoralization, Mar'ja Vasil'evna becomes his wife. It is an unhappy family life. At that juncture the main dramatic knot of the novel comes to be tied up. Sanja's ill feeling toward Nikolaj Antonovich, outgrowing personal grievances, turns into well-justified enmity. When he thinks now of Captain Tatarinov's ancient letter most of whose content his extraordinary visual memory keeps literally intact, Sanja realizes that the villain to whom in his last letter Captain Tatarinov imputed the castrostrophic development of his polar expedition is none other than Nikolaj Antonovich, the Captain's cousin. By supplying the ship and crew with faulty equipment and impaired provisions he had beforehand condemned the ship and crew to death in the wild solitude of the Arctic Ocean. And since Sanja also knows Nikolaj Antonovich's baseness and hyprocrisy, he thinks that in his own selfish interests Nikolaj Antonovich may well have been able to hatch up a criminal conspiracy under his sanctimonious appearances. This accusation is more than the Tatarinov family can possibly take. However, one excerpt from Captain Tatarinov's letter that Sanja recites from memory proves, in Mar'ja Vasil'evna's judgment, the validity of the accusation leveled against Nikolaj Antonovich. She has reluctantly accepted to become the wife of the latter out of gratitude, in the first place, for the help that he allegedly kept providing to her beloved husband. And now she learns that it has all been a lie, that she has been duped into a hateful marriage by a man who not only did not help her beloved husband but rather murdered him. The realization is beyond endurance. She commits suicide. It has turned out to be Sanja's unanticipated office to have provided the last straw. And if it were but for this reason, he is responsible for Mar'ja Vasil'evna's death. This death opens a gulf between Sanja and Katja. Things turn even worse for Sanja when Nikolaj Antonovich plausibly demonstrates that the villain Captain Tatarinov referred to in his letter was another man, Nikolaj Antonovich's namesake. The countercharge is damning if true: Sanja has irreparably slandered an innocent man, has caused the death of Mar'ja Vasil'evna out of personal ill feeling toward Nikolaj Antonovich, has irretrievably wrecked the Tatarinov family. Moreover, he has lost the girl who has meant everything to him. So, this is the challenge Sanja is facing. It will take him a lifetime, the whole span of the novel that is, to contend successfully with the challenge, to prove that he has been right.

Meanwhile, life goes on. Sanja's professional dream, after long schooling and training, comes to be fulfilled. He becomes an arctic aviator. This arduous vocation more than any other occupation in life gratifies his sense of self-fulfillment. In the course of his polar pilot's career Sanja comes across some vestiges of Captain Tatarinov's expedition. He discovers and deciphers the diary of the sole survivor of the expedition. Later, while on flight in northern Siberia, in an Eskimo settlement he discovers a boat-hook with the imprint "Santa Maria," the very schooner aboard which Captain Tatarinov undertook his ill-fated exploratory voyage. Thus, Sanja is able to piece together an ever more accurate picture of the Captain's life and last journey. Himself already an experienced arctic aviator at home in the immense polar regions, Sanja at this point of maturity fully realizes Captain Tatarinov's far-seeing vision, his courage and unselfish dedication. This spiritual kinship with the latter comes to gain additional strength in personal relationship. It takes Katja a long time to heal from the wound inflicted by her mother's suicide. Nikolaj Antonovich has shared this loss since he did love Mar'ja Vasil'evna too. Their common pain has somewhat brought them together, at least enough for her to tolerate his presence. However, Katja can see through his duplicity, selfishness and baseness. And when a few years later she again meets Sanja, her choice is clear. The years elapsed have matured and deepened their love. Katja becomes Sanja's wife. The marriage to Captain Tatarinov's daughter further strengthens Sanja's commitment to what the name of Katja father stands for. More than ever, and now with Katja's support, he dedicates himself to redressing the wrong done to the name of this great man and explorer. Sanja succeeds in persuiding the Government to fit out a special expedition in search of what may have remained of Captain Tatarinov's expedition. However, on the eve of its departure, the expedition is abruptly cancelled and Sanja is re-assigned to agricultural employment: spraying crops with pesticide. Many other re-assignments follow, quite alien to Sanja's cherished ambitions. At the time of the Spanish Civil War Sanja is sent on a secret combat mission to Spain. He returns unharmed. During all these years Sanja's Arctic dreams have faded. It is as if fate kept repelling him from returning to the Arctic, from finding the remains of Captain Tatarinov's expedition. In the meantime, Nikolaj Antonovich captializes on the public's suddenly awakened interest in Captain Tatarinov's biography, interest that Sanja's pioneering work has stimulated. He writes articles on Tatarinov for different periodicals and publications. Leaning to his own advantage on the moral and scientific prestige of the Captain, Nikolaj Antonovich, an intellectual impostor, enters the academic world and becomes a recognized scientific authority on Captain Tatarinov's expedition, and even something of an authority on the Arctic. Deep in his heart, Sanja has never given up his commitment to the Arctic and Captain Tatarinov. He has been only waiting for an opportunity. And the tragic developments of the Second World War offer him one.

The war separates Sanja and Katja again. The point comes when Sanja, shot down in combat, is presumed dead and the news of his heroic death appears in the Air Force newspaper. Katja learns about her husband's death from Romashka, Sanja's old enemy from school-boy days and a contender for Katja's hand. Romashka claims that, both wounded, they were in a hospital train in southern Russia. German tanks attacked the train and shortly afterward Sanja disappeared. Crushed by the news, Katja continues working in a Leningrad hospital, sharing all the hardships of the inhabitants of the besieged city until, her health undermined, she is flown out of Leningrad. From that point on, Sanja and Katja seem lost forever for each other. However, Sanja survives. Betrayed by Romashka (who has given a false report to Katja about Snaja's dissappearance), he crawls away from the massacre and, after harrowing trials, lands in a hospital far away from the war zone. Severely wounded in his legs, he remains incapacitated for months. He is rejected from active service. And to make matters worse, he cannot find any trace of Katja anywhere. At this dead-end, a rescue comes from quite an unexpected party: an old acquaintance of Sanja, an arctic specialist, offers him to return to the North, as Sanja has always dreamt. In connection with war events a frantic activity is going on along the Arctic coast and Sanja, as an experienced arctic aviator, can help. Sanja leaves Moscow without still knowing anything about Katja, but not without settling his old accounts with Romashka. Circumstances have moved ahead of Sanja: by the time he comes to Arxangel'sk as he has been ordered, to join the arctic specialist, the latter has already been gone to a distant point of the Arctic and the authorities do not let Sanja follow him. This time, Sanja energetically works himself through the quandary. Overcoming the medical expertise to the contrary, he forces his way into the Arctic Air Force and again comes to the fore as a gallant Air Force Captain, stationed on active duty in one of the arctic bases. This is where Katja comes to join him as soon as she learns where he lives. So, Katja and Sanja are reunited after many agonizing trials. At long last, with military victory over Germany already in sight, good fortune smiles on Sanja. He unlocks the mystery that has haunted him from very early in his life. While on a special combat mission, Sanja discovers the remnants of Captain Tatarinov's polar expedition as well as the remains of Captain Tatarinov himself. This discovery furnishes tangible clues for Sanja to explain the circumstances under which the expedition perished in the Northern Siberia several decades before and to expose the falsehood of Nikojaj Antonovich. But more important than his triumph over his ancient enemy is Sanja's contribution to the Russian arctic science, and his rise from his enormously difficult childhood to his present station of a dedicated and widely respected Soviet citizen.

BIBLIOGRAPHY

PART ONE

KAVERIN'S WORKS

A. FICTION

———, "Xronika goroda Lejpciga za 18. god." *Serapionovy Brat'ja. Al'manax Pervyj*. Peterburg 1922

———, "Xronika goroda Lejpciga za 18.. god." *Serapionovy Brat'ja. Zagranichnyj Al'manax*. Berlin 1922

———, *Mastera i podmaster'ja. Rasskazy*. Moskva-P-burg, Izd. "Krug," 1923
    Contents: Stoljary; Shchity (i svechi); Inzhener Shvarc; Xronika goroda Lejpciga za 18 .. god; Purpurnyj polimpsest; Pjatyj strannik.

———, ———
    [the same edition as the preceding, reprinted photomechanically]
    University Microfilms, Ann Arbor 1965

———, "Pjatyj strannik. Povest'." *Al'manax Krug*, kn. 1-aja, 1923, pp. 157-198

———, "Bochka," *Russkij sovremennik*, kn. 2-aja. L.-M. 1924, pp. 100-126

———, "Kar'era." Rasskaz. *Leningrad*, No. 21(36), November 20, 1924.

———, "Bol'shaja igra," *Literaturnaja Mysl'*. Al'manax III. Leningrad 1925

———, "Devjat' desjatyx sud'by. Povest'." *Kovsh*, No. 3. L. 1925, pp. 73-120; *Kovsh*, No. 4. M.-L. 1926, pp. 139-205

———, "Konec xazy. Roman." *Kovsh*, No. 1. L. 1925, pp. 161-236

———, "Kutumskie chasovshchiki." (Glava iz rasskaza), *Leningrad*, No. 25(64), July 11, 1925

———, "*Rasskazy*. Izd. "krug," M. 1925
    Contents: Stoljary; Shchity, and others.

———, *Konec xazy. Povesti*. "Zhizn' iskusstva," L. 1926
    Contents: Konec xazy; Bol'shaja igra

———, *Noch' na 26-e oktjabrja. Rasskaz*. "Priboj," L. 1926

———, *Osada dvorca. Povest'*. (Dlja detej i junoshestva) M.-L. 1926

———, "Revizor." *Zvezda*, No. 4, 1926, pp. 5-33

———, *Vperedi vsex*. (Dlja detej i junoshestva) M.-L. 1926

———, *Devjat' desjatyx sud'by*. M.-L. 1927

———, *Bol'shaja igra. Rasskazy*. Izd. "Ogonek," M. 1927

———, *Bubnovaja mast'*. Izd. "Knizhnye novinki," L. 1927
    Contents: Kutumskie chasovshchiki; Segodnja utrom; Shchity (i svechi); Bochka; Skorost' sveta; Goluboe solnce.

———, *Revizor*. "Petropolis," Berlin 1927

———, *Vorob'inaja noch'. Rasskazy*. "Krug," M. 1927
    Contents: Revizor: Segodnja utrom; Bol'shaja igra; Drug Mikado.

——, Skandalist, ili Vechera na Vasil'evskom ostrove." Roman. *Zvezda*, No. No. 2-7, 1928

——, *Vperedi vsex*. "Gos. izd-vo," M.-L. 1928

——, *Osada dvorca*. "Gos. izd-vo," 1928

——, *Skandalist, ili Vechera na Vasil'evskom ostrove*. "Priboj," L. 1929

——, *Devjat' desjatyx sud'by*. Roman. M.-L. 1929

——, *Osada dvorca*. "Gos. izd-vo," M.-L. 1929

——, *Vperedi vsex*. "Gos. izd-vo," M.-L. 1929

——, *Konec xazy*. *Povest'*. *Bol'shaja igra*. *Fantasticheskie rasskazy*. "Priboj," L. 1930
     Added title-page: V. Kaverin, Sochinenija, I.
     Contents: Konec xazy. Povest'; Fantasticheskie rasskazy: Drug Mikado, Segodnja
     utrom, Goluboe solnce, Pjatyj strannik, Shchity i svechi, Bochka, Revizor,
     Vorob'inaja noch'.

——, *Devjat' desjatyx sud'by*. *Roman*. Vol. 2 of *Sobranie sochinenij*. "Priboj," L. 1930

——, *Skandalist, ili Vechera na Vasil'evskom ostrove*. Vol. 3 of *Sobranie sochinenij* "Priboj," L. 1930

——, *Osada dvorca*. "Gos. izd-vo," 1930

——, *Skandalist, ili Vechera na Vasil'evskom ostrove. Roman*. 3rd edition, "Izd-vo pisatelej v Leningrade," L. 1931

——, *Chernovik cheloveka*. L. 1931

——, ——
     [the same edition as the preceding, reprinted photomechanically]
     University Microfilms, Ann Arbor 1971

——, "Xudozhnik neizvesten." *Zvezda*, No. 8, M.-L. pp. 5-82

——, *Xudozhnik neizvesten*. "Izd-vo pisatelej v Leningrade," L. 1931

——, ——
     [the same edition as the preceding, reprinted photomechanically]
     University Microfilms, Ann Arbor 1972

——, *Straus Foma* [rasskaz dlja detej] "Mol. Gvardija," M.-L. 1931

——, *Osada dvorca*. "Mol. Gvardija," M.-L. 1931

——, *Devjat' desjatyx sud'by*. Roman. "Izd-vo pisatelej v Leningrade," L. 1932

——, *Ukroshchenie Mistera Robinzona, ili Poterjannyj raj*. Komedija v 5-ti dejstvijax "Vsekdram," M. 1933

——, *Osada dvorca*. "Mol. gvardija," L.-M. 1933

——, *Ukroshchenie Robinzona, ili Poterjannyj raj*. komedija v pjati aktax i shesti kartinax. L. 1934

——, *Ukroshchenie Mistera Robinzona ili Poterjannyj raj*. Komedija v 5-ti d. M. 1935

——, "Ispolnenie zhelanij." *Literaturnyj sovremennik*. No.No. 1-4, 6-8, 11, 1934
     Subtitle: "Chast' pervaja. Trubachevskij.'

——, *Ispolnenie zhelanij*. Book One. L. 1935

——, *Izbrannye povesti i rasskazy*. L. 1935

——, "Ispolnenie zhelanij." *Literaturnyj sovremennik*, No.No. 1-4, 6, 7, 1936
     Subtitle: "Kniga vtoraja." *Ispolnenie zhelanij*

——, *Ispolnenie zhelanij*. Book Two. L. 1936

——, "Lichnye schety." Komedija v 4 aktax i 12 kartinax. *Literaturnyj sovremennik*, No. 12, Leningrad 1936, pp. 127-159

——, *Ispolnenie zhelanij*. "Goslitizdat," 1937

——, *Ispolnenie zhelanij*. "Xudozh. lit.," L. 1937 (2-oe stereotipnoe izd.)

——, "Aktery." P'esa v chetyrex aktax. *Literaturnyj sovremennik*, No. 12, 1937 pp. 100-140, L. 1937

——, *Aktery* (P'esa v 4-x dejstvijax). Izd. "Iskusstvo," L. 1938

——, Volzhenin V., *Tret'ja nit'* (Dram. èpizod v 3-x kart.). "Iskusstvo," L.-M. 1939
     This book contains: V. Kaverin, "Odna noch'." P'esa v 1-om d.

——, "Dva kapitana." Book One. *Koster*, No.No. 8-12, 1938; No.No. 1,2, 4-6, 9-12, 1939

——, "Dva kapitana." Book One. *Literaturnyj sovremennik*, No.No. 1-3, 5-9, L. 1939

——, *Skazka o Mit'ke i Mashe, o veselom trubochiste i mastere zolotye ruki* "Detgiz," M. 1939

——, *Dva kapitana*. Book One. "Detgiz," M.-L. 1940

——, "Dva kapitana." Book One. *Koster*, N.No. 2-4, 1940

——, *Dva kapitana*. "Goslitizdat," L. 1941
——, *Orlinyj zalet*. M. 1942
——, *Rasskazy*. M. 1942 ("Frontovaja biblioteka krasnoflotca")
——, ——
    [the same edition as the preceding, reprinted photomechanically]
    University Microfilms, Ann Arbor 1965
——, *Dom na xolme*. P'esa v 4-x d. M.-L. "Iskusstvo," 1942
——, *Domik na xolme*. Rasskazy. M. "Voenizdat," 1942 ("Biblioteka krasnoarmejca")
——, *Domik na xolme*. Rasskazy. Baku 1942 ("Biblioteka krasnoarmejca")
——, *Bol'shie nadezhdy*. P'esa v trex aktax. M. 1942
——, *My stali drugimi* [Rasskazy]. "Sov. pisatel'," M. 1943
——, "Dva kapitana." Book Two. *Oktjabr'*, No.No. 1,2,7,8,11,12. M. 1944
——, *Dva kapitana*. Book One and Two. "Detgiz," M.-L. 1945
——, *Domik na xolme*. M. 1945
——, *Russkij mal'chik*. *Rasskazy*. L. 1946
    Contents: Russkij mal'chik; Knopka; Junost'; Belaja jaxta; Sil'nee smerti;
    Proshchal'nyj saljut; Muistro; Starinnaja kljatva; Tician; Kukol'nyj master; Orlinyj
    zalet; Pojas.
——, *Dva kapitana*. Roman. "Leninizdat," L. 1946 ("Biblioteka shkol'nika")
——, *Dva kapitana*. "Voenizdat," M. 1946
——, *Dva kapitana*. Roman v dvux tomax. M.-L., "Goslitizdat," 1946
——, *Dva kapitana*. Roman v 2-x tomax. Izd. "Sovetskaja Kolyma," Magadan 1946
——, "Du'el'" [Otryvok iz nezakonchen. romana]. *Leningrad*, No. 6, 1946, pp. 1-5
——, "Otkrytaja kniga" [Glavy iz romana], *Ogonek*, No. 49, 1947, pp. 19-21
——, *Dva kapitana*. "Molodaja Gvardija," M. 1947
——, *Dva kapitana*. Roman. "Detgiz," M.-L. 1947 ("Shkol'naja biblioteka")
——, *Dva kapitana*. Roman. "Sov. pisatel'", M. 1947 ("Biblioteka izbr. proizvedenij sov. lit-y
    1917-1947")
——, *Dva kapitana*. Molotov, "Molotovgiz," 1948
——, *P'esy*. "Iskusstvo," L.-M. 1948
    [Among other plays]: Kaverin V.A. & Judkevich Z.L., *Dva kapitana*
——, *Dva kapitana*. Roman. "Latgosizdat," Riga 1948
——, *Dva kapitana*. Roman v 2-x t. "Dal'nevost. gos. izd.," Xabarovsk 1948
——, *Dva kapitana*. Roman v 2-x t. "Detgiz," M.-L. 1948
——, Otkrytaja kniga." Otryvok iz romana. *Sov. zhenshchina*, No. 2, 1948, pp. 44-46
——, "Noch' na Pustyn'ke." [Glava iz romana *Otkrytaja kniga*]. *Ogonek*, No. 15, 1948 pp.
    13-14
——, "Sestra." Rasskaz. In the collection *Medsestry Krasnogo Kresta*. Moskva 1948, pp. 41-44.
——, *Dva kapitana*. Roman v 2-x t. Kujbyshev 1949
——, *Dva kapitana*. Roman. "Gos. izd. Karelofin. SSR," Petrozavodsk 1949
——, "Junost'." Subtitle: "Otkrytaja kniga." *Novyj Mir*, No.No. 9,10. Moskva 1949
    [the original Part I of *Otkrytaja kniga*]
——, *Shkola muzhestva*. *Rasskazy*. "Detgiz," M.-L. 1949 ("Shkol'naja biblioteka")
——, *Knopka*. M.-L. 1949
——, *Sovetskaja dramaturgija*. Repertuar teatra junogo zritelja. "Iskusstvo," M.-L. 1950. 2 vol.
    Vol. 2: V. Kaverin, *Dva kapitana*
——, *Shkola muzhestva*. Voronezh 1950
——, *Dva kapitana*. Roman. V 2-x t. Gor'kij 1950
——, Grigor'eva L. [ed], *Teatr v shkole*. *Sbornik p'es dlja samodejatel'nosti*. Novosibirsk 1950
    [Among other plays]: V. Kolesaev, *Dva kapitana*. Sokrashch. variant po p'ese V.
    Kaverina
——, *Dva kapitana*. "Goslitizdat," M. 1950 ("Biblioteka sov. romana")
——, *Detskij teatr v klube*. *Sbornik p'es dlja det. xudezh. samodejatel'nosti* M. 1950
    [Among other plays]: V. Kaverin *Dva kapitana*
——, "Doktor Vlasenkova." Subtitle: "Poiski." *Novyj Mir*, No.No. 2-4, 1952
    [the original Part II of *Otkrytaja kniga*]
——, *Otkrytaja kniga*. Roman. "Molodaja Gvardija," M. 1953
    1. Junost'.-2. Doktor Vlasenkova

——, *Dva kapitana*. Roman. "Sov. pisatel'," M. 1953
——, *Dva kapitana*. P'esa v 3-x dejstv., 7-mi kart., s prologom i epilogom "Detgiz," M.-L. 1953 ("Shkol'naja biblioteka")
——, *Dva kapitana*. Roman. Xabarovsk 1954
——, "Trevozhnaja junost'." P'esa v 6-ti d. i 7-mi kart. *God tridcat' sed'moj*. Al'manax 17. M. 1954, pp. 15-50
——, "Poedinok." Glava iz 3-j chasti romana *Otkrytaja kniga*. *Ogonek*, No. 52, 1954, pp. 10-14
——, "Brat'ja." Glava iz 3-j chasti romana *Otkrytaja kniga Ogonek*, No. 46, 1955, pp. 10-14
——, *Junost' Tani*. "Detgiz," M. 1955
——, *Dochka*. Komedija v 3-x d., 6-ti kart. M. 1955
——, "Poiski i nadezhdy." *Literaturnaja Moskva*. Book Two. Moskva 1956 [the original Part III of *Otkrytaja kniga*]
——, *Otkrytaja kniga*. Triologija. M. 1956
    Vol. I: Part I. Junost'
    Part II: Doktor Vlasenkova
    Vol. II: Part III: Poiski i nadezhdy
——, *Ispolnenie zhelanij*. Roman. "Sov. pisatel'," M. 1956
——, *Dva kapitana*. Roman. "Detgiz," M. 1957
——, "Neizvestnyj drug." *Oktjabr'*, No. 10, 1959
——, *P'esy*. M. 1959
    Contents: Ukroshchenie Mistera Robinzona; Aktery; Skazka o Mite i Mashe; Utro dnej.
——, *Otkrytaja kniga*. Trilogija. "Molodaja Gvardija," M. 1959
——, *Neizvestnyj drug*. Povest'. M. 1960
——, "Kusok stekla." *Novyj Mir*, No. 8, 1960
——, *Tri skazki*. "Detgiz," M. 1960
——, *Avtobiograficheskie rasskazy*. M. 1961
——, *Iz raznyx knig*. M. 1961
    Contents: Kak pishutsja knigi; Neizvestnyj drug; My stali drugimi; Prolog; Iz knigi skazok.
——, *Rasskazy 1960 goda*. [Collection of stories] "Sov. pisatel'," M. 1961 [Among other stories: V. Kaverin, "Kusok stekla."]
——, *Dva kapitana*. Cheljabinsk 1961
——, "Sem' par nechistyx. Povest'." *Novyj Mir*, No. 2, 1962
——, "Kosoj dozhd'. Povest'." *Novyj Mir*, No. 10, 1962
——, *Izbrannoe*. "Moskovskij rabochij," M. 1963
    Contents: Ispolnenie zhelanij. Roman.- Iz knig: Prolog; My stali drugimi; Neizvestnyj drug.- Iz knigi skazok.- Sem' par nechistyx. Povest'.
——, *Kosoj dozhd'. Povesti*. M. 1963
    Contents: Kosoj dozhd'; Sem' par nechistyx; Kusok stekla; Neizvestnyj drug.
——, *Tri skazki i eshche odna*. "Detgiz," M. 1963
    Contents: Pesochnye chasy; Mnogo xoroshix ljudej i odin zavistnik; O Mite i Mashe, o veselom trubochiste i mastere zolotye ruki; Legkie shagi.
——, *Sobranie sochinenij v shesti tomax*. "GIXL," M. 1963
    Vol. I (1963): Ocherk raboty; Pjatyj strannik; Bol'shaja igra; Bochka; Konec xazy; Devjat' desiatyx; Drug Mikado; Goluboe solnce; Skandalist, ili vechera na Vasil'evskom ostrove. Roman.
    Vol. II (1964): Prolog; Xudozhnik neizvesten; Ukroshchenie Mistera Robinzona; Ispolnenie zhelanij. Roman.
    Vol. III (1964): Dva kapitana. Roman
    Vol. IV (1965): Otkrytaja kniga. 1. Junost'. 2. Poiski
    Vol. V (1965): Otkrytaja kniga. 3. Nadezhdy; Utro dnej. P'esa; Neizvestnyj drug. Povest ; Skazki: Pesochnye chasy, Mnogo xoroshix ljudej i odin Zavistnik, Legkie shagi.
    Vol. VI (1966): Kusok stekla; Sem' par nechistyx; Kosoj dozhd'; Dvojnoj portret. Roman; O.I. Senkovskij (Baron Brambeus); O literature i iskusstve; Aleksandr Fadeev; Zabolockij; Majakovskij; Arkadij Gajdar; Jurij Tynjanov; Vsevolod Ivanov; Bulgakov; Bessrochnyj dogovor; Gor'kij i molodye; Volshebnaja palochka; Neotkrytye dorogi; Chitaja Xemingueja; Dikkens i teatr; Evgeniju Shvarcu.

———, *Otkrytaja kniga.* Roman. "Sov. Russoija," M. 1965
———, *Dva kapitana.* Roman. "Det. lit.," M. 1965
———, *Junost' Tani.* M. 1966
———, *Odna noch'.* – K. Paustovskij. Talye vody. "Iskusstvo," M. 1966
———, "Dvojnoj portret." Roman. *Prostor*, No. 2, pp. 24-52; No. 3, pp. 18-63, 1966
———, *Dva kapitana.* Roman. "Mol. Gvardija," M. 1966 ("Tebe v dorogu, romantik")
———, *Dvojnoj portret.* M. 1967
———, "Snegurochka" Fantasticheskij rasskaz. *Nauka i zhizn'* No. 5, pp. 78-82, 1967
———, "Shkol'nyj spektakl'." Povest'. *Novyj Mir*, No. 12, 1968, pp. 3-28
———, *Letajushchij mal'chik.* Skazka. "Det. lit.," M. 1969
———, *Rodnomu Groznomu.* Sbornik stixov. [Ed. by G. Jablokov]. "Checheno-ingush. kn. izd.," Groznyj 1970 [Among other authors: V. Kaverin]
———, *Dva kapitana.* Roman. "Lumina," Kishinev 1971
———, *Dva kapitana .* Roman v 2-x knigax. "Xud. lit.," M. 1971
———, *Dva kapitana.* Roman. "Det. lit.," M. 1972 ("Shkol'naja biblioteka")
———, "Pered zerkalom." Roman v pis'max. *Zvezda*, No. 1, 1971, pp. 93-156; *Zvezda*, No. 2, 1971, pp. 9-109
———, *Pered zerkalom.* Roman v pis'max. M. 1972
———, *Izbrannoe.* M. 1973
        Contents: Predislovie; Skandalist, ili Vechera na Vasil'evskom ostrove. Roman; Ispolnenie zhelanij. Roman; Pered zerkalom. Roman v pis'max.
———, *Dva kapitana.* Roman. "Dal'nevost. kn. izd-vo," Vladivostok 1973
———, *Dva kapitana.* Roman. "Lumina," Kishinev 1973
———, *Dva kapitana.* "Pravda," M. 1973

ENGLISH TRANSLATIONS

———, *The Larger View*
        Translated from the Russian by E. Leda Swan. London 1938 [original Russian title: *Ispolnenie zhelanij*]
———, *The Larger View*
        Translated from the Russian by E. Leda Swan. New York 1938
———, *Two Captains*
        Translated from the Russian by E. Leda Swan, New York 1942 [Book One of the novel]
———, *The House on the Hill*: a Play in Four Acts
        Translated by Alexander L. Meyendorff n.p., 1943 [this translation, in the form of a typescript, is owned by Harvard College Library]
———, *The Unknown Artist*
        IN:
        Olesha, Iurii Karlovich, *Envy. The Unknown Artist*
        With an Introduction by Gleb Struve
        Translated by P. Ross London 1947
———, *The Unknown Artist*
        [the same edition as the preceding, reprinted photomechanically] University Microfilms, Ann Arbor, 1959
———, *Open Book*
        Translated by Brian Pearce
        London 1955
———, *Open Book*
        Translated by Brian Pearce
        Moscow 1956
———, *Two Captains*
        Translated by Brian Pearce
        London 1957

194 BIBLIOGRAPHY

——, *Two Captains*
Translated from the Russian by Bernard Isaacs
Moscow 1972
——, *"Shields and Candles"*
Translated by Gary Kern. *Russian Literature Triquaterly*, No. 2, Winter 1972, pp.
125-132
[original Russian title: Shchity i svechi]
——, *The Unknown Artist*
Translated by P. Ross
Westport, Conn., 1973

OTHER TRANSLATIONS INTO WESTERN LANGUAGES

FRENCH

——, *Peintre Inconnu*
Translated by Claude Frioux
Paris 1964
——, *Devant Le Mirroir*. Roman
Translated by Irène Sokologorski
Paris 1973

GERMAN

——, *Zwei Kapitäne*. Roman
Translated by Hilde Angarowa
Berlin 1946. Verlag der Sowjetischen Militärverwaltung in Deutschland
——, *Zwei Kapitäne*. Roman
Translated by Hilde Angarowa
Wien, 1948
——, *Glückliche Jahre*. Roman einer Jugend
Translated by Veronika Enssler
Berlin, 1955. Verlag Kultur und Fortschritt
——, *Unbekannter Meister*
Translated by Gisela Drohla
Frankfurt a.M., 1961
——, *Das Doppelte Portrat*. Roman
Aus dem Russischen und mit einem Nachwort von W. Kazak
Frankfurt a.M., 1973

ITALIAN

——, *Il Pittore È Ignoro*
Translated by Alberto Pescetto
Torino, 1966

B. CRITICAL AND OTHER WORKS

——, A paper on contemporary prose at the Institute of the History of the Arts. The paper in
question and the following discussion are summarized in "Diskussii o sovremennoj
literature," *Russkij sovremennik*, No. 2, pp. 273-278, L.-M. 1924
——, An autobiography in the collection *Pisateli. Avtobiografii i portrety sovremennyx russkix
prozaikov*. Ed. by V. Lidin. M. 1926, pp. 133-134
——, V. Zil'ber [Kaverin's original family name], "Senkovskij (Baron Brambeus)," in *Russkaja
proza*. Sbornik statej pod red. B. Eixenbauma i Ju. Tynjanova. "Academia," L. 1926
——, "Pisateli o sebe," *Na Literaturnom Postu*, No.No. 17-18, 1927

——, *Baron Brambeus. Istorija Osipa Senkovskogo, zhurnalista, redaktora "Biblioteki dlja chtenija."* L. 1929
——, "Protiv raboty naugad," *Rezec*, No. 26, p. 8, 1929
——, An article in the collection *Kak my pishem*, pp. 59-74, L. 1930 *Prolog. Putevye rasskazy.* M.-L. 1931
——, *Lenin o pechati;* populjarnyj ocherk. M. 1932
——, "Kak ja napisal roman *Dva kapitana.*" *Koster*, No. 7, 1946, p. 14
——, "Gor'kij i molodye," *Znamja*, No. 11, 1954, pp. 158-167
——, "Poiski i reshenija," *Novyj Mir*, No. 11, 1954
——, *Literaturnaja Moskva.* 2 vols, M. 1956. Kaverin was one of the editors of this publication.
——, "Zametki o dramaturgii Bulgakova," *Teatr*, No. 10, 1956
——, An autobiography. *Sovetskie pisateli.* Avtobiografii v dvux tomax. Vol. 1, pp. 496-510. M. 1959
——, "Ocherk raboty." *Voprosy literatury*, No. 9, 1960
——, "Neotkrytye dorogi." *Formuly i obrazy*, pp. 68-78, M. 1961
——, Bulgakov M., *Zhizn' gospodina de Mol'era.* "Mol. Gvardija," M. 1962 ("Zhizn' zamechatel'nyx ljudej") Posleslovie V. Kaverina
——, Pirson, Xesket [Pearson, Hesketh], *Dikkens.* "Mol. Gvardija," M. 1963 Per. s angl. M. Kan. Posleslovie V. Kaverina ("Zhizn' zamechatel' nyx ljudej")
——, "Ocherk raboty," *Sobranie sochinenij.* Vol. I, pp. 5-24. M. 1963
——, *Ocherk raboty.* "Sovetskaja Rossija," M. 1964
——, Shchedrost' talanta [Dejateli literatury i iskusstva o tvorchestve xudozhnika L. Gudiashvili. Kaverin is one of the commentators]
    Lit. Gruzija, No. 1, pp. 60-65
——, "Jurij Tynjanov." K 70-letiju s dnja rozhdenija. *Novyj Mir.* No. 10, 1964, pp. 232-247
——, "K istorii voprosa." *Voprosy literatury*, No. 8, 1964, pp. 38-47
——, "O tvorchestve M. Bulgakova," *Literaturnaja Rossija*, April 2, 1965
——, "Kak pojavilsja baron Brambeus." *Nauka i zhizn'*, No. 4, April 1965, pp. 127-131
——, "Za rabochim stolom," *Novyj Mir*, No. 9, 1965, pp. 151-168
——, *Zdravstvuj, brat. Pisat' ochen' trudno.* Portrety. Pis'ma o literature. Vospominanija. M. 1965
——, "Malinovyj zvon." Putevye zapiski. *Novyj Mir*, No. 3. 1966, pp. 105-140
——, "Desjatiklassniki." [O rabote nad romanom o desjatiklassnikax]
    Smena, No. 15, 1966, p. 14
——, *Jurij Tynjanov.* Pisatel' i uchenyj. Vospominanija. Razmyshlenija. Vstrechi. "Mol. gvardija," M. 1966 ("Zhizn' zamechatelnyx ljudej") P. 8: V. Kaverin, "Proizvedenija Ju. N. Tynjanova" and bibliography about Tynjanov pp. 216-220
——, Preface of Ju. Tynjanov, "Iz zapisnyz knizhek," *Novyj Mir*, No. 8, August 1966, pp. 120-121
——, "Neskol'ko let," *Novyj Mir*, No. 11, November 1966, pp. 132-158
——, *Baron Brambeus* (M., 1966)
——, "Poèzija prozy," [K 75-letiju so dnja rozhdenija K.G. Paustovsʰogo]
    Vokrug sveta, No. 6, 1967, p. 42
——, "Glashataj novoj èpoxi." K 100-letiju so dnja rozhdenija A.M. Gor'kogo [Otvety pisatelej na anketu red. zhurn. "Vopr. literatury." Kaverin is one of the commentators].
    Voprosy Literatury, No. 3, 1968
——, "Teatr dlja sebja" (O detskom chtenii; avtobiogr. zametki)
    Det. literatura, No. 1, 1968, pp. 66-69
——, "Zagadka detstva" [O stixax N.A. Zabolockogo dlja detej]
    Prostor, No. 10, 1969, pp. 108-109
——, Ju.N. Tynjanov, *Pushkin i ego sovremenniki*
    Moskva 1969
    Kaverin is one of the editors of this book
——, "Sobesednik. Zametki o chtenii," *Novoyj Mir*, No. 1, 1969, pp. 155-169
——, "Ideja prizvanija," (Besedu vel L. Antopol'skij) in *Voprosy Literatury*, No. 6, June 1969, pp. 124-131
——, "Vozvrashchenie k Ispanii." [Vospominanija o lit. kritike i perevodchike O. Saviche. Iz knigi *V starom dome*]
    Avrora, No. 12, 1970, pp. 30-31

196   BIBLIOGRAPHY

——, "Javor" [O tvorchestve pisatelja V.A. Dmitrieva] *Voprosy Literatury*, No. 4, 1971, pp. 153-161
——, "V starom dome," *Zvezda*, No. 9, 1971, pp. 180-200; *Zvezda*, No. 10, 1971, pp. 138-186 [Lit. vospominanija]
——, *Sobesednik*. *Vospominanija i portrety* Moskva 1973

PART TWO

WRITINGS ABOUT KAVERIN AND HIS WORKS

A. CRITICAL WRITINGS

Jurij Tynjanov, Review of *Serapionovy Brat'ja*. *Al'manax Pervyj* in *Kniga i Revoljucija* No. 6, pp. 62-64 (1922)
A.K. Voronskij, Review of *Serapionovy Brat'ja*. *Al'manax Pervyj* in *Krasnaja* Nov. No. 3, pp. 265-68 (May-June 1922)
Evgenij Zamjatin, "Serapionovy Brat'ja," *Literaturnye Zapiski* No. 1, pp. 7-8 (Pb. 25 May 1922)
V. Pereverzev, "Na frontax tekushchej belletristiki," *Pechat' i Revoljucija*, kn. 4, pp. 127-133 (1923)
M. Shaginjan, *Literaturnyj dnevnik*. Stat'i 1921-23. 2nd ed., Izd. "Krug," (M.-L. 1923)
Viktor B. Shklovskij, *Sentimental'noe puteshestvie*. *Vospominanija, 1917-1922*. (Moskva-Berlin, "Gelikon" 1923)
Evgenij Zamjatin, "Novaja russkaja proza," *Russkoe iskusstvo* No. 2-3, pp. 57-67 (1923)
V. Gol'cev, Review of *Devjat' desjatyx sud'by* in *Pechat' i Revoljucija* No. 8 (1926)
E.F. Nikitina, *Russkaja literatura ot simvolizma do nashix dnej*. Literaturnosociologicheskij seminarij (M. 1926)
A.R. Palej, Review of "Vorob'inaja noch'," in *Pravda* 8 February 1928
V. Goffenshefer, Review of *Skandalist* in *Molodaja Gvardija* No. 12, pp. 203-204 (1928)
F. Ivanov, "Skandalist, ili Vechera na Vasil'evskom Ostrove," *Krasnaja Nov'*, No. 5 (1929).
E. Severin, Review of *Devjat' desjatyx sud'by* in *Pechat' i Revoljucija* No. 1, pp. 85-86 (1929)
Viktor B. Shklovskij, *Sentimental'noe puteshestvie* ("Federacija," M. 1929)
M. Grigor'ev, "Literaturnyj gomunkuljus," *Na Literaturnom Postu*, No. 23-24, pp. 35-45 (1930)
[?], Review of *Konec xazy*, *Sochinenija* I, 1930 in *Kniga stroiteljam socializma* No. 1, p. 80 (1931)
V. Tarsis, *Sovremennye russkie pisateli*. Ed. and completed by I.A. Oksenov. (Biography and bibliography)(L. 1930)
V. Sajanov, "Put' Kaverina." Preface of *Sobranie sochinenij*, Vol. I ("Priboj", 1930)
G.L., "Kaverin V.A." A biography and bibliography in *Literaturnaja Ènciklopedija*, vol. 5, col. 12-13 (Izd.-tvo Kommunisticheskoj Akademii 1931)
M. Grigor'ev, "Pod znakom formalizma," (O tvorchestve V. Kaverina), *Literaturnaja Gazeta* No. 4, 19-go janvarja 1931
[?], Review of *Xudozhnik neizvesten* in *Kniga Stroiteljam Socializma*, No. 35, pp. 84-85, December 1931
E. Shnejder, Review of *Xudozhnik neizvesten* in *Leningrad* No. 1, 1932, p. 89
A. Selivanovskij, Review of *Xudozhnik neizvesten* in *Literaturnaja Gazeta* No. 1, 4 January 1932.
R. Miller-Budnickaja, "Èpigon formalizma," *Zvezda* No. 2, pp. 152-156, 1932
N. Korickij, "Medlennoe rasstavanie" (about *Skandalist*) in *Literaturnyj Sovremennik* No. 2-3, 1932.
G. Munblit, "Razmyshlenija o nezakonchennoj knige," (about *Fulfillment of Desires*), *Znamja*, kniga 9, September 1935, pp. 196-201.
Raisa Messer, "Bol'shoj schet," *Literaturnyj sovremennik*, No. 11, pp. 147-156 (1936)
N. Afanas'eva, "O knige V. Kaverina 'Ispolnenie zhelanij'" in *Literaturnyj sovremennik* No. 9, pp. 127-148 (L. 1937).
Ju. Isakov, "Razgovor o literature. Pis'mo iz Leningrad," *Literaturnaja Gazeta*, No. 2, 10 janvarja 1939.
B. Ivanter, "Voennoe vospitanie i detskaja literatura," *Detskaja literatura*, No. 2, 1941.
V. Smirnova, "Dva kapitana menjajut kurs," *Znamja* No. 8, 1945
B. Solov'ev, "Romantika muzhestva," *Novyj Mir* No. 8, pp. 103-109, 1945 [about *Dva kapitana*].
E.F. Usievich, "Sanja Grigor'ev pered pedagogicheskim sudom," *Oktjabr'* No. 11-12 (1945)

Gromov, P., "Roman o geroe nashix dnej" [recenzija na kn. V.A. Kaverina *Dva kapitana*, M.-L., "Detgiz," 1945] *Zvezda*, No. 4, 1946, pp. 144-146

Nikolaj Maslin, "Veniamin Kaverin," *Novyj Mir*, No. 4, pp. 272-290, 1948

Usievich, E. *Knigi i zhizn'*. Sbornik statej. "Sov. pisatel'," M. 1949
    Contents: among other articles: "Sanja Grigor'ev" [the protagonist of Kaverin's novel *Dva kapitana*]

"Geroi ne nashego vremeni," *Literaturnaja Gazeta*, 4 January 1950 [a letter written by a group of students apropos of *Otkrytaja kniga*]

Z. Papernyj, "Kniga, kotoraja nichego ne otkryvaet," *Znamja*, kniga 1-aja, pp. 179-183 (1950).

B. Galanov, "Tema i ee voploshchenie," *Znamja*, kniga 11-aja, November 1952, pp. 175-179 [review of *Otkrytaja kniga*]

Biography of Kaverin in *Bol'shaja Sovetskaja Enciklopedija*, vol. 19, p. 245, 2nd edition, 1953 (short bibliography added)

B. Kosteljanec, "Zhivoe edinstvo," *Zvezda*, No. 11, November 1954, pp. 159-162

L. Levickij, "Okrytaja Kniga," *Zvezda*, No. 6, pp. 173-175, (1954)

Biography of Kaverin in *Pisateli-laureaty Stalinskoj Premii. Kratkie biografii*, pp. 44-49 (M. 1954)

Petr Ershov, "O romane V. Kaverina "Otkrytaja kniga"", *Novyj zhurnal*, Kn. XL, pp. 290-293 (New York 1955)

Evgenij Zamjatin, "Novaja russkaja proza," in his collection of articles *Lica*, pp. 191-210, (Chekhov Publishing House, New York 1955)

A. Elkin, "Dva kapitana ostajutsja na kurse," *Komsomol'skaja pravda*, No. 76, 30 March 1957.

Inostrannaja literatura, February 1958 (Critical comments about Kaverin)

Ark. El'jashevich, "Zamysel i ego voploshchenie," *Neva*, No. 4, pp. 211-217, April 1958 (review of *Otkrytaja kniga*)

Ark. El'jashevich, "Geroi istinnye i mnimye," *Zvezda* No. 2, February 1958, pp. 189-209.

E. Usievich, "Sanja Grigor'ev," *Puti xudozhestvennoj pravdy*, pp. 134-164 (M. 1958)

Kaverin's autobiography in *Sovetskie pisateli*. Avtobiografii v dvux tomax Vol. I, pp. 496-510 (M. 1959)

Kaverin's correspondence with Gorky about Senkovskij: Iz perepiski M. Gor'kogo s K. Fedinym, M. Prishvinym, A. Vinogradovym, V. Kaverinym, A. Lunacharskim, *Voprosy literatury*, No. 3, pp. 24-26 (M. 1959)

G. Trefilova, Posleslovie k "Dvum kapitanam," (M. 1961)

Besedy o knigax V.P. Kataeva, L.A. Kassilja, V.A. Kaverina Dlja uchashchixsja VII-VIII klassov. M. 1961

G. Gor, "Pisatel' i nauka," *Russkaja literatura* No. 3, 1962

Gor'kij i sovetskie pisateli, neizdannaja perepiska in *Literaturnoe nasledstvo*, vol. 70 (Izd-tvo Akademii Nauk, M. 1963)

Russkie sovetskie pisateli-prozaiki. Biobibliograficheskij ukazatel' Vol. 2 (L. 1964)

Eganjan, Ju.M., "Roman Dva kapitana v tvorchestve V.A. Kaverina." Sb. Statej (Erevanskij un-t), t. 1, Serija obshchestv. nauk, vyp. 1, 1965, pp. 101-109

Kaverin's biography in *Kratkaja Literaturnaja Enciklopedija*, vol. 3, col. 285-286; a bibliography added (M. 1966)

Hongor Oulanoff, *The Serapion Brothers*, pp. 146 ff., (Mouton, The Hague 1966)

——— "Kaverin's *Xudozhnik neizvesten*: Structure and Motivation," *The Slavic and East European Journal*, Winter 1966, vol. X, No. 4, pp. 389-399.

V. Ivanov, "Stanovlenie idejno-esteticheskix principov sovetskoj literatury," *Kommunist*, No. 4, 1967

T. Xmel'nickaja, "Avtobiograficheskaja proza Kaverina (V. Kaverin. "Zdravstvuj, brat. Pisat' ochen' trudno ...")" in *Novyj Mir* No. 1, January 1967, pp. 253-256

E. Volkova, "Celeustremlennost' poiskov," *Novyj Mir*, No. 9, September 1967, pp. 231-238.

G.A. Zajceva, "Sjuzhet kak sredstvo raskrytija xaraktera geroja v tvorchestve V.A. Kaverina," *Uchenye zapiski*, No. 225, pp. 167-181 (1966) [this information is taken from *Letopis' zhurnal'nyx statej* (1968), vol. 17, p. 173]

Hongor Oulanoff, "V. Kaverin's Novels of Development and Adventure," *Canadian Slavic Studies*, II, No. 4, (Winter 1968), 464-486

M. Sinel'nikov, "S nevernyx pozicij: polemicheskie zametki v svjazi s nekotorymi vyskazyvanijami i nekotorymi proizvedenijami V. Kaverina," *Literaturnaja gazeta*, No. 32, 6 August 1969, p. 4

Krasnov-Levitin, "Neohumanism." [quoted from "The Third Year of the "Chronicle of Current Events," by D. Pospielovsky, *Radio Liberty Dispatch*, New York, June 10, 1970]

D.G.B. Piper, V.A. Kaverin. *A Soviet Writer's Response to the Problem of Commitment* (The Relationship of *Skandalist* and *Khudozhnik Neïzvesten* to the Development of Soviet Literature in the Late Nineteen-Twenties), Duquesne University Press 1970

Zas'ma, R.L., "Vstrecha s sovremennost'ju. V poiskax geroja." (V.A. Kaverin, sb. *Prolog*) *Uchen. Zap. Vladimir. Ped. In-ta*, t. 30, 1971, pp. 61-91

Zhores A. Medvedev and Roy A. Medvedev, "A Question of Madness," in *The New York Times Magazine*, November 7, 1971

Hongor Oulanoff, "Kaverin's Early Prose: *Masters and Apprentices*," *Russian Literary Triquaterly*, No. 2, Winter 1972, pp. 261-277

Gary Kern, "The Serapion Brothers: A Dialectics of Fellow Traveling," *Russian Literary Triquaterly*, No. 2, Winter 1972, pp. 223-247.

B. BIBLIOGRAPHIES

Sovetskoe literaturovedenie i kritika. Knigi i stat'i 1917-1962 godov. ("Nauka," M. 1966)
Sovetskoe literaturovedenie i kritika. Knigi i stat'i 1963-1967 godov (M. 1970)

PART THREE

BACKGROUND READING

M. Aldanov, "Mikrofon," *Kovcheg. Sbornik russkoj zarubezhnoj literatury* (New York 1942)
Aristotle's Theory of Poetry and Fine Art (New York 1951)
Arthur E. Adams, *Stalin and His Times* (New York 1972)
N. Aseev, "Kljuch sjuzheta," in A.I. Beleckij, *Novejshaja russkaja literatura* (Ivanovo-Voznesensk 1927)
V. Azhaev, *Daleko ot Moskvy* (Groznyj 1949)
Gaston Baty & René Chavance, *Histoire des Marionnettes* (Paris 1959)
A.I. Beleckij; N.L. Brodskij; L.P. Grossman; I.N. Kubikov; V.L. L'vov-Rogachevskij, *Novejshaja russkaja literatura*. Kritika. Teatr. Metodologija. Temy. Bibliografija (Ivanov-Voznesensk 1927)
Miguel de Cervantes Saavedra, *The Ingenious Gentleman Don Quixote de la Mancha* New York 1958
I. Erenburg, *Den' vtoroj* in Il'ja Erenburg, *Sobranie sochinenij*. Vol. 3 (Moskva 1964)
——— "Ljudi, gody, zhizn'." Book 3. *Novyj Mir* No. 11, November 1961
Herman Ermolaev, *Soviet Literary Theories 1917-1934. The Genesis of Socialist Realism*. University of California Publications in Modern Philology, vol. 69 (Berkeley & Los Angeles 1963)
M. Gershenzon, "Mocart i Sal'eri," in *Mudrost' Pushkina* (Moskva 1919)
J.W. von Goethe, *Wilhelm Meister's Apprenticeship* (In 2 vols, Boston 1901)
G. Greene, *Travels with My Aunt* (New York 1970)
Rainer Vadim Grenewitz, *V.. Kaverin's Mastera i podmaster'ya* (M.A. Thesis, Cornell University, 1965)
E.T.A. Hoffmann, *The Best Tales of Hoffmann* (New York 1967)
Susanne Howe, *Wilhelm Meister and his English Kinsmen. Apprentices to Life* (New York 1930)
Johan Huizinga, *Homo Ludens. A Study of the Play Element in Culture* (Boston 1960)
Walter Kaufmann, *Tragedy and Philosophy* (New York 1969)
Gottfried Keller, *Green Henry* (New York 1960)
Walter Kerr, *Tragedy and Comedy* (New York 1967)
Robert Kiely, *Robert Louis Stevenson and the Fiction of Adventure* (Harvard University Press, Cambridge 1964)
Arthur Koestler, "Character and Plot," *Science and Literature* ed. by Edward M. Jennings, (New York 1970)
M. Kuznecov, *Sovetskij roman. Ocherki* (Moskva 1963)
L. Leonov, *Russkij les* in Leonid Leonov, *Sobranie sochinenij*, vol. 9 (Moskva 1962)

D.S. Lixachev, *Chelovek v literature drevnej Rusi* (Moskva 1958)

Lewis Mumford, *The Myth of the Machine. The Pentagon of Power* (New York 1970)

Robert J. Nelson, *Play Within a Play* (New Haven 1958)

I.M. Nusinov, "Mocart i Sal'eri," in I.M. Nusinov, *Istorija literaturnogo geroja* (Moskva 1958)

Yuri Olesha, *Envy and Other Works* (New York 1967)

Jérôme-Antoine Rony, *Les Passions* (Paris 1967)

V. Shklovskij, *Povesti o proze* (2 vols, Moskva 1966)

A. Slonimskij, "V poiskax sjuzheta," in A.I. Beleckij, *Novejshaja russkaja literatura*, (Ivanovo-Voznesensk 1927)

Aleksandr Solzhenicyn, *Sobranie sochinenij* (6 vols, "Posev" 1969)

Gleb Struve, *Soviet Russian Literature 1917-50* (Norman 1951)

Abram Tertz, *The Trial Begins and On Socialist Realism* (New York 1960)

Louis Vax, *L'Art et la Littérature Fantastiques* (Paris 1963)

Xronika tekushchix sobytij No.No. 1-24 in *Sobranie dokumentov Samizdata* vol. 10 (Radio Liberty Committee, New York 1972)

INDEX

OTHER BOOKS FROM SLAVICA PUBLISHERS

Bulgarian Folk Dances, by Raina Katzarova-Kukudova & Kiril Djenev, 174 p., numerous illustrations, 2nd printing, 1976 (first printing, Sofia, 1958).

A Synchronic Study of Verbal Aspect in English and Serbo-Croatian, by Midhat Ridjanovic, ix + 147 p., 1976.

Introduction to Old Church Slavic, by William R. Schmalstieg, 290 p., 1976

Vampires of the Slavs (a collection of readings) ed. by Jan L. Perkowski, 294 p., 1976.

Bulgarian Phonology by Ernest Scatton, xii + 224 p., 1976.

Common Slavic Progress and Problems in Its Reconstruction, by Henrik Birnbaum, xi + 436 p., 1975.

Russian Word-Formation, corrected reprint, by Charles E. Townsend, xviii + 272 p., 1975.

On the Syntax of Be-Sentences in Russian, by Catherine V. Chvany, viii + 311 p., 1975.

Balkanistica: Occasional Papers in Southeast European Studies, ed. by Kenneth E. Naylor, I (1974), 189 p., 1975; II (1975), 153 p., 1976.

A Russian Course, by Alexander Lipson.

Introductory Workbook in Historical Phonology, by Frederick Columbus, 39 p., 1974.

Topics in Slavic Phonology, ed. by Demetrius J. Koubourlis, viii + 270 p., 1974.

Elementary Russian Syntax, by Michael K. Launer, ix + 140 p., 1974.

Tolkovyj slovar' russkogo jazyka, ed. by D.N. Ushakov, original edition in 4 volumes, Moscow, 1934-1940; reprint (slightly reduced, corrections indicated, 4 volumes bound in 3), 1974.

Medieval Slavic Texts, Vol. 1, Old and Middle Russian Texts, by Charles E. Gribble, 320 p., 1973.

Russian Root List with a Sketch of Russian Word Formation, by Charles E. Gribble, 56 p., 1973.

Papers of the Yugoslav-American Seminar on Music, ed. by Malcolm H. Brown, 208 p., 1970.

Hungarian Morphological Irregularities, by Lester A. Rice, 80 p., 1970.

Aspects of Russian Morphology, A Semiotic Investigation, by Michael Shapiro, 62 p., 1969.

Studies Presented to Professor Roman Jakobson by His Students, ed. by Charles E. Gribble, 333 p., 1968.

Yugoslav Literature in English: A Bibliography of Translations and Criticism (1821-1975), ed. by Vasa D. Mihailovich and Mateja Matejic, ix + 328 p., 1976.

Agreement in Contemporary Standard Russian, by Dina B. Crockett, iv + 456 p., 1976.

Papers from the First International Conference Banff '74, 5 volumes covering history, literature, and linguistics, 1976.

The Grammatical Categories of the Macedonian Indicative, by Victor Friedman, 1977.

Lithuanian Reverse Dictionary, by David F. Robinson.

The Memoirs of Princess Natal'ja Borisovna Dolgorukaja: Original Text, Annotated, with Facing English Translation and Historical and Linguistic Commentary, by Charles E. Townsend.

Slovarik russkogo jazyka 18-go veka/A Glossary of 18th-century Russian, ed. by Charles E. Gribble, 1976.

Hospodine Pomiluj Ny, A Study of the Language , Verse, and Origin of an Old Slavic Hymn, by F.V. Mares, 1977.

A Comprehensive Russian Grammar by A.A. Barsov, ed. by Lawrence W. Newman.

Russian Declension and Conjugation: A Structural Description with Workbook, by Maurice I. Levin, 1977.

Reading Contemporary Russian, by Jules F. Levin, Peter D. Haikalis, and Anatole Forostenko, 1977.